Miss Major Pauline Cushman

Yours Truly

Maj Pauline Cushman

Miss Major Pauline Cushman

The Exploits of an Extraordinary Union Scout
and Spy During the American Civil War

F. L. Sarmiento

With a Short Biography of
Miss Major Pauline Cushman
by Frank Moore

LEONAUR

Miss Major Pauline Cushman
The Exploits of an Extraordinary Union Scout and Spy During the American Civil War
by F. L. Sarmiento
With a Short Biography of Miss Major Pauline Cushman
by Frank Moore

FIRST EDITION IN THIS FORM

First published under the titles
Life of Pauline Cushman
and
An Extract from *Women of the War*

Leonaur is an imprint of Oakpast Ltd
Copyright in this form © 2023 Oakpast Ltd

ISBN: 978-1-916535-28-2 (hardcover)
ISBN: 978-1-916535-29-9 (softcover)

http://www.leonaur.com

Contents

DEDICATION

TO THE MOTHERS, WIVES AND SWEETHEARTS
OF THE BRAVE MEN
ON WHOSE BEHALF THESE ADVENTURES WERE UNDERTAKEN
AND THROUGH WHOSE GLORIOUS INSTRUMENTALITY
THEY WERE HAPPILY CONSUMMATED;
TO THOSE WHO HAVE HAD THE EARLY EDUCATION
THE MATURER GUIDANCE,
THE LOVE AND CONFIDENCE OF THE NOBLE MEN
COMPOSING THE ARMY OF THE SOUTHWEST,
THIS RECITAL OF ADVENTURES,
SHARED PARTLY WITH THEM.
IS RESPECTFULLY DEDICATED.

Preface

The great Rebellion, which has now, (1865), for nearly four years been waged with such unwavering ferocity against the legitimate government of the United States, amid its wonderful display of gigantic enterprise and power, has been prolific of incidents for the historian, the poet, and the dramatist. A contest, carried on in such stupendous proportions, and over so vast a field, arraying all the most adventurous and intrepid spirits of both North and South, in armed hostility, and absorbing in the vortex of war so many fearless and energetic subjects of other nations, has enriched the pages of history with new and startling annals.

The wildest and most dashing legends of the past have been wellnigh eclipsed by the realities transpiring in our own midst and almost before our very gaze; and in a future and more peaceful age, the chronicler will revert with wonder to the every-day record of the times in which we live Among all that these shall offer to the coming years, few will be more striking, or more picturesque, than the simple narrative of plain truth presented to the reader in this work.

Previous to the arrest of Miss Cushman, vague rumours were circulated among the insurgents, that information was conveyed to General Rosecrans of all the movements of the Confederates; that now it was a boy, then a dashing officer, and again a simple countrywoman; but all agreed that whatever passed in the rebel camp was safely reported to the enemy, and that many of their schemes were thus rendered entirely abortive. They also more than suspected that this spy had mastered all their fortifications in Middle Tennessee, and so great was their exultation at the capture of our heroine, that, but for her fortunate rescue by the Union Army, nothing could have saved her from the most fearful of deaths.

All the officials and soldiers of the Army of the Southwest are enthusiastically fond of the "Scout of the Cumberland"—their "dear

Major Cushman"—as they delight in calling her. She is emphatically "the Daughter of the Regiment," and no knight in the days of chivalry ever believed more firmly in the charms of the lady whose colours he wore, and in whose honour he was ready to shiver a thousand lances, than the rank and file of that army, in the courage, the heroism, and devotion to the old flag, of her whose history we now relate.

The details are given, as they were gathered, from her memoranda, and from the lips of the subject herself; and while in some minor matters the author has gleaned his information from other sources, the main facts of the narrative are solemn truths, as received from her, and which Miss Cushman avers she at least can never forget. If the public are as deeply interested in its perusal, as has been the author in its preparation he feels that his labours will not have been in vain.

Introduction

The career of the subject of this work, the beautiful and accomplished Miss Pauline Cushman, or "Major" Cushman, as she is entitled to be called, and most generally is called, is one so varied by patriotic incident and stirring adventure, that the ear of young or old can never become satiated by its recital. Since the days of the Maid of Saragossa, no woman has ever lived who has so completely come up to the ideal of a heroine, as Miss Pauline Cushman. Dashing, charming, fearless, yet lady-like, she combines in herself all the daring of the soldier with the tenderness and modesty of the woman. Not one of the milk-and-water women of the day, whose only thought is of dress and amusement, but one of the women of old, whose soul was in their country's good, and whose fearless, yet womanly, because *noble*, actions, shall live forever.

Pauline Cushman is such a woman as a soldier could worship! And such a one as our "ladies" aforesaid might take example by, for she has brought to those deeds of daring which it is our happy province to relate, with the true dignity of her sex, all the patriotic fervour and courage of the immortal heroines of history. Yes, the deeds of the "Scout of the Cumberland," beautiful and fearless as she is, will live as long as American hearts beat, and be related by the future historians of our land as the most romantic and most remarkable episode of this fearful rebellion.

It is, then, with sincere pleasure, that we have undertaken their recital; and, to be enabled to do so correctly, no pains have been spared. Many of the incidents we have heard from the lips of the heroine herself; while others, again, have been sifted from official documents, or the verbal description of friends who either knew her in her youth, when a simple child of the prairies, or had learned to love and respect her in her later and more momentous and stirring role of the Scout of the Army of the Southwest.

In these researches, it is but justice to Miss Cushman to add, we have been struck not less by the charming modesty of the lady than by the heroic qualities of which she is the happy possessor, while her patriotism in sacrificing her all to the country which had shielded her youth is a trait that should endear her to every loyal heart, and make her name a "household word" throughout the land.

Another feature that has struck us, in sifting out the materials of this work, is the deep feeling of respect, the almost devotion, with which those who have known her best speak of her. With the soldiers and officers of the Army of the Southwest, her name is a talisman; while more than one veteran of that noble army, which she has by her self-devotion more than once saved, has spoken of her in trembling tones while the tears of gratitude ran down his bronzed face. The deeds of their dear "Major" live in those thousands of hearts of that army of freemen. She is their heroine—the Heroine of the People— the beautiful romance of this dread rebellion.

Crossing the rebel lines, alone and almost unarmed at a critical moment when every ford, bridge, and path was jealously guarded, daily and nightly, by the exasperated insurgents, she made her way to their camps and fortifications in Upper Tennessee, and managed to render herself familiar with their plans and projects, which she communicated to the United States authorities at Nashville, whence they were made at once available to Gen. Rosecrans. Upon this expedition she met with many rebel officers, among whom was the famous partisan leader, John Morgan, and so thoroughly ingratiated herself with them that she was enabled to render the most essential aid to the cause of her country.

On her attempted return from her last expedition, she was arrested by rebel scouts, conveyed to the headquarters of Gen. Forrest, and by his orders to Gen. Bragg, by whom she was personally interrogated, and threatened with summary execution. A few days later she was found guilty by a rebel court-martial held at Shelbyville, and condemned to death, by hanging, as a spy. Her subsequent rescue, and adventures in the cause of her country, shall here be detailed at length, with not one word to extenuate, nor one word to heighten the dramatic simplicity of their truth.

One word, however, must be added before we close this introductory chapter. We have said that Miss Cushman has given all to her country. We have spoken literally the truth.

The flag she had so gallantly served restored her to safety, but not to the health she had lost by fatigue and exposure in its service; and, although, wherever she has gone, since her return to the North, she has received a generous welcome from our people, her own means of subsistence have been well-nigh wrecked in the disabilities entailed upon her by her illness.

This book is intended to throw some light upon a career that has become so interesting and precious to the nation, and, at the same time, to illustrate the secret history of the recent struggle on the borders of Kentucky and Tennessee. It remains for loyal men to say whether or not they will be grateful.

Chapter 1: Her Earlier Life

In writing the adventures of the beautiful and patriotic woman, the true portrayal of whose stirring deeds is the object of this volume, it might at first sight be conceived that the early incidents of her life played but a small part in the interest of the romantic yet o'er true tale. This, however, is not the case. The life of Miss Pauline Cushman has been a romance from her cradle. Nay, more: the strange interest which surrounds her commenced, one may say, even before her birth, and has continued down to the present time, when her history and glorious achievements resound from every tongue. Yes, the "Major," as Miss Cushman is entitled officially to be called, was *born* a heroine; nor can anyone who has beheld her entrancing form and flashing eye doubt but that the original element has grown apace with her fair self.

It may not, therefore, be inappropriate to give some interesting details of her earliest recollections, and some short account of her parentage; for, as an Irish wit has said, "There is no place, after all, so appropriate to commence a thing as at the beginning."

Miss Major Pauline Cushman was born in the city of New Orleans, on the 10th day of June, 1833. Her father was a Spaniard, a native of Madrid, who came to the United States some years before the birth of Pauline, and established himself in the great trading city of Louisiana as a dry-goods merchant, in which business he rapidly rose to consideration and influence. Her mother was a French lady of excellent social position and attainments, the daughter of a highly respectable wine grower, whose vineyards lay in the neighbourhood of Bordeaux.

There were some circumstances of romance connected with the union of her parents that, no doubt, gave a bias and a tinge to the mind of Pauline. The father, the son of an old soldier in the Armies of Napoleon, and afterward identified with the political troubles of Spain in 1820, had fled to the south of France as a refugee, and it was during this period of exile that he became acquainted with the mother, whose attachment to the fugitive stranger was so bitterly opposed by her relatives for reasons of commercial prudence, that the couple determined to elope, making America the haven of their flight. They married, but did not succeed in leaving France for some months later.

At the period of their arrival on our shores, the city of New Orleans was in the very height and glow of the sudden and rapid prosperity attendant upon the development of the cotton trade, and the traffic of the great western rivers, whose treasures all were lavished in her lap. Pauline's father soon found an advantageous opening, and for several years was fully successful in business. At length, however, an unlucky speculation gave the first blow to his good fortune and his losses followed one upon the other in quick succession. Unable to stay the tide, after a long and unavailing struggle, he abandoned his enterprises in the Queen City of the South, and removed to Grand Rapids, in the State of Michigan, when Pauline was about ten years of age. He there opened an establishment for purposes of trade with the Indians, as Grand Rapids was still little more than a frontier settlement, and soon again found himself in active and successful business.

Meanwhile, Pauline was growing in beauty and intelligence. She was the only girl in a family of eight children, the eldest of whom had died on shipboard, during the passage of her parents to America. The other six brothers, some of whom were born in Louisiana and some in Michigan, were all bright, gifted boys, and all looked upon Pauline as the star of the family. Still, notwithstanding the caresses at times lavished upon her, there were circumstances surrounding the domestic life of the young girl that clouded the joy of her earliest years. Her father, with many excellent traits of character, was not a person calculated to make the domestic circle tranquil and happy, and the mother, a tall, slender, delicate French woman, chafed under the many inconveniences of American life, contrasting so unpleasantly with the gentler customs and the luxuries of her native land.

But this lady was mild and kind, and bestowed upon her daughter the most unbounded affection. She was a strict Catholic, too, and carefully trained Pauline, in the closest observance of all the services and ceremonies of her church. Miss Cushman even now speaks with an emotion bordering upon superstitious reverence of that tall, white figure with the pale Madonna like countenance, gliding to her bedside, at the hour of twilight, or in the earliest dawn, to kneel there, in silent supplication to the Virgin, for her sake.

The modest, unassuming, and retiring character of this pious lady marked another and still stronger contrast between her outward character and that of her Spanish husband, who was a man of strong masculine aspect and demeanour. While she courted the seclusion of the domestic circle at home, he was best pleased with the din and rush

16

of the outside world, the hubbub of the throng, and the busy tumult of affairs. An enthusiastic and very faithful Freemason, he was, by no means, delinquent in the duties of life but the peculiar softness of his wife's temperament was frequently jarred by the natural rigidity of his own, and thus the youthful Pauline was often called upon to witness scenes that made home far less desirable than to the young it should ever be.

Pauline, however, fought against the evil and annoying influences of this domestic dissension, and as her inclinations led her mostly to indulge in outdoor sports, she was enabled, in a great measure, to disperse in the sunshine of forgetfulness the noxious gloom which ever and *anon* brooded over their little household. Her refuge was the plains and wild companions that surrounded her new home, and in these scenes of romantic freshness and fantastic daring was laid the foundation of that courageous spirit which has since enveloped her every action.

Chapter 2: Pauline; or, "The Laughing Breeze"

The new life to which the youthful Pauline was now introduced at Grand Rapids was by no means calculated to prepare a young girl for what is termed "society," for Grand Rapids was at that time little more than an Indian trading station; but it endowed her with what is much better, health, beauty, and strong nerves. During the day the young Indian girls or youths were her constant companions—the first teaching her to braid the many little objects which they sell, and the latter instructing her in the various accomplishments which are the preparatory school of the youthful warrior.

At her father's store the little Pauline met many of the most noted "braves" of the Indian tribes of that neighbourhood, and with all of them was a favourite, for often, when the poor Indian hungered or was thirsty, the little "Laughing Breeze," as they poetically called her, was ever at hand to relieve their wants. These acts of the innocent little child soon became known, and the *wigwam* of the red man was ever open to welcome her.

These scenes of peaceful interest, however, were often varied by others of the most terrific nature. Grand Rapids, as we have said, was a frontier trading post, to which the various Indian tribes of the neighbourhood came to exchange furs, skins, etc., for the commodities of civilized life. Among these last essentials, "fire-water," as the redskins denominate that curse of men—whiskey—played, of course, a prominent part. Degraded by its influences, their sole thought was to obtain it. When drinking deeply of the maddening "fire-water," the most fearful scenes would follow.

At such moments the white settlers were often in imminent peril, for the savage nature of the wild inhabitant of the prairies would at such, time return in all its force, and their yells and gleaming fires could be seen and heard for miles around. But around the little Pauline a halo of sacredness was thrown that was respected even by the savage. With them she was ever safe—going and coming as one of their own.

Nor did the little white maiden cease her benefactions in return for these ovations. Often, in the gloom of stormy nights, when cold and tempest reigned outside, dusky faces would be seen peering in at the window of her father's modest but comfortable tenement. These were poor Indians seeking food and shelter at the hands of the white man, and little Pauline was ever ready to open the door and offer them a cordial welcome The strength of feeling that the American aborigine hides beneath his usually grave and taciturn exterior is proverbial, and the tiny benefactress of these poor wanderers soon found that her name had sped over a far wider range than even her charity; and the return came back not only to her father's till, but in a thousand grateful·acts to her.

Presents of *moccasins* richly wrought with beads and lined with fur; utensils of curious and elegant form carved in birch wood; models of canoes and *wigwams* dexterously wrought in the bark of the same tree; rustic stools and chairs of twisted branches; mats, cushions, gloves and hoods of beaver and otter skins; and, in the appropriate season, green wicker baskets filled with the wild wood flowers and berries, sent in by her red friends, attested the affection and the taste of these children of the wilderness. Along with these gifts of a lighter nature came baskets of game, venison, wild turkeys, prairie hens, bears' meat, and "buffalo hump" from the forest and plain, and delicious salmon and trout from the neighbouring lakelets and streams. In fine, Pauline became, among the *wigwams* around the village where she lived, a veritable queen.

Time passed, and the little Pauline grew up as straight as an arrow and as beautiful as one of their prairie roses. None could shoot the rifle more unerringly than she. She was equally at home on shore or afloat—whether coursing the broad plains mounted on the back of a half-tamed steed, without saddle or bridle, or stemming the fierce current of the mountain streams in her light canoe—while few even among the dusky brethren of the forest could wing an arrow with greater certainty. Is it to be wondered at, then, that she should attract the admiring gaze of those untutored sons of the far West, who shared her sports and who learned in her daring grace to revere her fortitude? Certain it was that one, a noble youth, with the blood of nineteen summers in his veins, haunted the footsteps of the young pale-faced maiden.

The "Leaping Thunder," as his people called him, had listened too long to the voice of the Laughing Breeze. The maidens of his tribe pleased him no more. Their skins were dusky. In them flowed not the same blood that filled the veins of the daughter of the white man. With all the passion of his nature, the Indian loved her—but he was unknown. As yet he had done no act that should entitle him to the favour of a noble, courageous girl like our heroine. True, he was the best shot of his age, among his tribe. Nor was he less distinguished in the various sports and exploits of his people. But no scalps hung, as yet, at his belt. The young warrior had yet to pass through the bloody baptism of his fathers before he could hope for the smiles of even the women of his own tribe.

Long the young "brave" thought over the only means of winning the fair Pauline which, to his untutored breast, suggested itself. Unable to see the vast gulf which separated his people from the pale-faced intruders, his sole thought was, by deeds of heroic daring, to win the beauteous Flower of the Prairies, whose laughing voice had sounded so pleasantly in his ears.

His determination taken, he stole out once more to behold his loved one. It was twilight the long, slanting sunbeams kissed tenderly the flowers and waving grass. The "Laughing Breeze" had wandered out to inhale the evening air; in another moment the youth was by her side. Waiting not to hear her answer, he breathed, in the poetic language of his race, his words of love. Then like a flash he was off— away to win the proud title of "brave" among his people; and gain favour, as he believed, in the eyes of the fair-faced maiden.

A grand buffalo-hunt, in which the brave youth joined, furnished him unexpectedly with the much sought opportunity to distinguish himself. A hostile tribe, envious of their success, seized the chance of superior numbers to assail them. The scene was a narrow mountain-pass, the steep sides of which presented no outlet for escape.

The struggle was long and doubtful. Many of the weaker party had fallen, and there seemed to be no merciful escape for the survivors. The "Leaping Thunder" performed prodigies of valour, and made many of the foe bite the dust beneath his bow and lance; but the opposing band were partly armed with rifles, and his comrades were falling fast, their inferior weapons proving of but little avail, comparatively, against the death-dealing implements invented by the white man. The "Leaping Thunder," among other cuts and scratches, had received a gunshot wound in the right side, which, although not fatal, was exceedingly painful and bled freely.

The battle was almost lost, and, in a few moments more, his own strength would be gone, and he, with the remnant of his band, be mercilessly butchered, or reserved for an infinitely worse fate at the stake. With a sudden, despairing, yet heroic impulse, the young warrior, nerving himself for the task, and murmuring the name of his lady-love, dashed headlong upon the loading chief of the enemy, and fortunately reached him. His opponent was a Goliath of the forest, known in the border annals of the day as the "Buffalo Bull"—one skilled in all the athletic and warlike accomplishments of his kindred, and the stripling who attacked him seemed to rush upon certain death.

But whether taken unawares, or partially exhausted by his previous efforts, the "Buffalo Bull" fell from his horse under the frantic charge and spear-thrust of his youthful antagonist, whose remaining comrades, inspired by the spectacle, rushed with a mad yell of victory on the followers of the fallen chieftain, and succeeded in putting them to flight. The "Leaping Thunder" was at once cared for with all the assiduous skill of forest surgery, and, after a brief period of rest, brought back in triumphal procession to his village near Grand Rapids the scalp of the renowned "Buffalo Bull" dangling at his girdle, with numerous other sanguinary trophies of his first mortal combat and success.

Joyous were the shouts, and many the congratulations and wild sports of his people, but the heart of the young warrior failed him, when he beheld not the loved face of the "Laughing Breeze."

He sought the village through, but she was not there. The maidens of his tribe sought to attract his attention, but their efforts were vain. The old men praised him, and spoke of him as their worthy successor, still all was distasteful to him: the eye of the beauteous pale face beheld not his triumph—Pauline, his loved one was away! and, wandering out he sought involuntarily the path which he had seen her tread so lately.

He is right—she is there. Who else—mortal or fairy—could tread without shaking the dew from the lilies? The "Laughing Breeze" stands before him. and once more does he pour forth the burning eloquence which his heart dictates. In the flowery language of his race, and with all the music of his rich sounding voice, he bids her come be his queen the mistress of his household. But this time he waits for an answer: he is a warrior now and *dare* speak. He is proud, yet his noble head stoops to hear the murmured answer of the maiden. At length she speaks:

"My brother, the 'Laughing Breeze' dare not mingle with the 'Thunder.' To the 'Leaping Thunder' is it left to sound in savage majesty through the clifts and rugged peaks of nature; but the 'Laughing Breeze' is the breath of civilization. The Indian and the 'pale face' cannot mingle!"

In sorrow the brave youth departs: his face is downcast, his heart beats wildly. As he goes he turns to look back: the last rays of the setting sun light up his noble frame, while the murmuring winds bear to the weeping maiden his last words.

"Thou hast said truly. The Indian and the 'pale face' dare not mingle!"

Chapter 3: Behind the Scenes

Soon after the adventures related in our last chapter, our heroine determined to start for New York, and of the reasons that led to this determination we will give a brief synopsis.

Grand Rapids, the scene of her earlier youth, had, in common with the frontier towns of the far West, become populated with a new and advanced element. New faces were seen in the usually tenantless streets; new buildings were spoken of as about to be erected; improvements everywhere. In the meantime the dusky face of the Indian became scarcer and scarcer. "Westward the star of empire takes its course," and in its channels lay the little town of Grand Rapids.

Every day some new emigrants arrived, and, with this influx of new population, came new ideas and longings. Luxuries that were unheard of in the "good old times" soon became as plentiful as the wild birds and timid deer had been before.

These newcomers, too, brought with them their tales of the wonders of the great cities of the eastern seaboard. Their talk was of the great and curious sights so common in the famous cities of New York, Boston, Philadelphia, Baltimore, and Washington.

Added to this were the reminiscences of such of their own townsmen as had ventured on business or pleasure toward the Atlantic seaboard; making them dream of the delights of those fabled cities, as the staunch Mussulman dreams of the "Paradise" of his Prophet. Detroit and Cincinnati were something wonderful, but the Yankee and Quaker capitals, not to speak of that great centre of delights, New York, were quite beyond the scope of their most fertile imaginations.

In short, Grand Rapids, so long given up to savage, or at best semi-civilized thoughts and desires, was fired with that unconquerable love of luxury and show which had for so long a time ruled the greater men and women of our seaboard towns; and for an article to have been made in New York or Philadelphia was a recommendation at once.

Flaring "New York Stores," "Quaker City Saloons," and "Empire Restaurants," became the order of the day; which is not to be wondered at when we see even now, in our great eastern marts, common or very indifferent goods sold quite readily when stamped with the golden lies of "Paris" or "London."

It is not our desire then to scoff at the excellent inhabitants of the wild frontier town: we are too open to the same reproach. We wish merely to note its effect upon the volatile and susceptible nature of our heroine, the fair Pauline.

That she had been a ready listener to all the wonderful tales of that mysterious and unknown life which belonged alone, so it was said, to the great cities of the Atlantic coast, can easily be imagined by anyone conversant with the peculiar gifts of the young girl.

Warm, impulsive, endowed with an imagination that lent bright rainbow-hues to even the most ordinary circumstances of life, the glowing descriptions of the fascinations to be found there fastened upon her with peculiar force. She thought of their thousand delights from morn till night. They were her waking and her sleeping dream! Pauline's education, too, had been of that varied nature that suggests change and adventure. Through frequently hearing her parents speak in the French and Spanish tongues she had acquired a certain proficiency in both those languages, while her reading had been more varied than extensive; just tempting her to wander to new fields, where she might *live* the romance of which she had heard and read.

Add to these elements, an exquisite though uncultivated voice, the soft, winning notes of which were as free and unrestrained as one of her prairie birds, and we have the scope of her preparation to battle with that great world, all knowledge of which had been confined heretofore to mere hearsay or to some few books. To anyone else it would scarce have been a very extensive capital to start upon, but to one endowed with the grace, beauty, and, above all, *tact* of Miss Cushman it was found all sufficient.

We find her, therefore, soon after these changes were wrought in the little town of Grand Rapids, in New York, waiting, like Micawber, for something to "turn up." This came about much sooner even than she had expected, for, whilst in this expectant mood, she met Mr. Thomas Placide, Manager of the New Orleans "Varieties."

Struck by her handsome face and figure, he at once proposed that she should enter into an engagement with him, and appear at his theatre. This proposition was not received without some hesitation, but to one so full of the love of adventure there could be but one response.

Life behind the scenes is at all times a *terra incognito* to the young and romantic, and to the highly imaginative a source of delight and curiosity that is not easily satisfied. One can hardly see the beautiful *ballet girls* in their snowy dresses and charming little slippers, glittering with gems and eating golden fruit with fairies for waiting-maids, without believing, to a certain extent, in their reality. We know that the jewels are not real; that the fruit is as hollow as the apples of Sodom; that the beautiful fairies wear cotton gowns when at home, and that the charming and fascinating *mademoiselle* this, that, or the other, dresses scarcely any better. Yet the enchantment is such that we believe, in spite of ourselves, that there must be *some* foundation for all this loveliness, independent of the gaslights and music.

And, indeed, there is a romance, not always soft and beautiful, but much more frequently stern and fearful, in stage-life, that is to be found under no other circumstances.

Pauline determined to test this novel experience: she accepted Mr. Placide's proposition, and in due time made her appearance at his theatre.

To say that she was admired is to express too tamely the feeling which she soon inspired in the hearts of the impressible people of New Orleans, for at this time she was overflowing, one may say, with all the charms of a most wondrous beauty. And here we may be pardoned if we divert the course of our recital for one brief moment, while we give an extract from a New York paper, describing Miss Major Pauline Cushman, as she appears even at the present time, after facing death by the bullet and disease, and living adventures that would break down a man, much less a woman.

But to the extract:

This famous Federal scout and spy, Major Pauling Cushman, is now in New York, attracting much attention. Few, if any, of our American women have rendered the Federal cause such inestimable service as this bold and beautiful lady. These services have been appreciated by government and by generals in the field, and their letters, testimonials, and personal acknowledgments prove their love and esteem for this truly loyal lady. In appearance Miss Cushman is lavishly endowed with the wealth of nature. Her form is perfect—so perfect that the sculptor's imagination would fail to add a single point, or banish a single blemish. Her arm is equally beautiful, resembling in mould, the marble efforts seen in the great art-galleries of Europe.

The outlines of her face are of exceeding beauty, and the perfect features are set off to the best possible advantage by a pair of large, flashing black eyes, which look out with a keen, brilliant expression Miss Cushman's hair is black as night; but those who have seen her at the front would hardly recognise her. Then she was obliged to assume numerous disguises—at times figuring as a private soldier, again acting the clerk, now on a scout, and often as a temporary officer upon some general's staff. With all of this stern experience and hardships of actual campaigning—entered into from a pure love of liberty—Miss Cushman is still (at time of first publication), the full possessor of all those accomplishments that characterize her sex. With the purest motives and ardent devotion to country, she has seen war in all its phases, without being dazzled by its glitter or contaminated by its corrupting influences.

Such a woman was Pauline Cushman. Beautiful of strong mind, extraordinary good sense, and a power of fascination almost unexampled, is it a wonder that the happy possessor of all these qualities so seldom combined in the one person—should enslave the hearts of young and old, male and female?

The young girl had, however, to contend with many fearful and many very disagreeable things in this life behind the scenes. A love for the pure and good was, unfortunately, not always found among the motley denizens of that unknown land, where "shams" of all kinds, in canvas and cloth, paint and pearl-ash, abound, and it was only by a show of that daring and resolute spirit for which our heroine was so remarkable, that she was able to escape the fearful vortex of these most corrupting influences. A little incident which occurred about this time will illustrate this spirit, and that too, in a characteristic manner, showing at once the daring nature of her indignation when aroused, and the true depth of feeling of her woman heart.

Among the visitors behind the scenes at the theatre was a young Frenchman—a man of fashion and immense wealth, and acknowledged to possess all the accomplishments and fine appearance that are considered necessary for a man of the world, together with all the nobler traits that should actuate a true man. Indeed, none but admired his good looks and gentle manners.

On beholding Pauline, however, he seemed to lose all restraint over himself. Love consumed him with such an intensity that it burned out all other feelings. He had married some time before, and a dear little boy, whose infant face bore all the traces of that singular beauty which formed the charm of its father's, had blessed his union. Yet, in spite of all this, the wretched man was enamoured of the fascinating *peri* who had become the talk of the town, on account of her accomplishments and beauty. Rich presents were sent to her. Diamond bracelets, and, what she loved better, beauteous flowers, were scattered at her feet. But she returned them all, though unaware of the circumstance that her impassioned lover was already a married man.

In the course of time, however, the circumstance came to her knowledge. Returning home one day she found a lady awaiting her.

"*Madame!*" she cried "I come to implore you to arrest the fatal passion which is consuming my husband!" And then, gazing upon the extreme beauty of the young girl, she continued: "But no! it is impossible! He *cannot* resist such fascination—he could not hate you, even were you to command him to do so. Alas! alas! he is lost to me forever!"

It was the miserable and almost heart-broken wife of the wretched man who had so long persecuted our heroine with his attentions.

For three long hours those two women sat together: Pauline reassuring and comforting the weeping wife, and the wife, in turn, clinging to her and blessing her—the saviour of her husband's love. At last, kissing away her tears, Pauline bade her depart, assuring her that all should yet be well.

That night the theatre was, as usual, crowded with men of fashion—among them, Pauline's lover, who besought, in earnest tones, a few moments' conversation with our heroine. This was accorded, and in the burning language of passion he urged her to fly with him. His wealth, his life, everything he possessed in the world, he said, should be hers. At the first word the hot blood of indignation boiled in the cheeks of the young girl, and, as she has since expressed it, she felt like dragging him by the nose on to the stage, and there, right in the full sight of the audience, boxing his ears soundly.

One thought alone restrained her—the thought of the weeping and disgraced wife, and the infant child who would live to inherit its father's shame. Affecting, therefore, to listen to him, she appointed an hour to meet him at her lodgings, after the performances should be over, and despatching a note to his wife, awaited the *denouement*. It soon came. Flushed with delight and anticipated triumph, the guilty man hastened to the rendezvous. Springing lightly up the steps he met the indignant and withering glance of the young girl so much his superior. By her side, with one arm thrown protectingly about her, knelt the injured wife, while at her breast nestled the innocent child, happily unconscious of the fearful meaning of the scene.

What followed we will not attempt to relate. It is never well to draw the veil of domestic troubles. The eye of the stranger should not pry within its sacred folds. Suffice, then, to say, that in the course of an hour after the scene of which we have attempted to give a brief outline, husband and wife left the house, rejoicing in a renewal of those bonds of love and confidence which should ever form the ties of married life; while their loved child clung to its mother's breast, saved forever from the disgrace which had but so lately hung over it.

In conclusion, we may say that, humbled and repentant, the young husband, who was at heart a really good man, never forgot the lesson thus taught him; thus did both husband and wife bless the beauteous being who had, at the same time, reunited and saved them. Saved them! The one from a life of remorse, and the other from that life of aching void which is the miserable fate of a woman whose "liege lord" and husband has ceased to love her.

At no house was Miss Cushman more welcome than at that of the young couple, ever after. And the kindness and sisterly affection shown her by the grateful wife has been treasured by her as among the most delightful reminiscences of her stay in the Queen City of the South.

Now, the whole family have passed away. The husband, with all the heated ambition of his native clime, joined the traitor bands that were striving to destroy our glorious land, and fell, fighting gallantly but wrongly. He must sleep, as many a noble fellow must sleep, in the future of our country...

Unhonoured and unsung!

... for, to the loyal man, the curse of treason blights every worth. In *its* cause, bravery is crime. Verily, after this war we shall not know where the bones of traitors lie; nor does it behove us to care!

As for the young wife, unaccustomed to privation and trouble, for their wealth was swept away by the dread whirlwind of rebellion, she sunk beneath this last blow—her husband's death—and was soon laid in the beautiful cemetery of New Orleans, her little child in her arms.

Chapter 4: South Carolina and Uncle Sam

Stage-life, however, has its amusing incidents as veil as tragic: in fact, it is a kaleidoscope, ever changing—a medal with two sides, of which the public see but one at a time.

It is to be supposed, then, that actors are not always what they appear to be to those who sit in front of the footlights. Indeed, they are, in nine cases out of ten quite the reverse.

The comic actor, who makes the whole theatre resound with the laughter caused alone by the expression of his face, may be in the green-room a sober cynical old fellow; while the heavy villain of the piece be just as gay and good-hearted as the other *seems*—until his time arrives to "go on" once more, when, of course, he must be black and lowering again.

Everyone has heard of the melancholy gentleman who went to a celebrated French physician, to be cured of the deep despondency which had seized him.

"Sir," he said, "I am dying—dying from melancholy," and upon examination it was found to be actually the case.

"Dying of melancholy!" exclaimed the physician. "Well, my friend, there is nothing easier than to effect a cure. You have only to go to the Theatre Port St. Martin, and see this great comedian who has set all Paris in a roar."

"Alas, sir," responded the unhappy man, "I am that actor!"

It was the truth. He, whose appearance alone was sufficient to convulse any audience before whom he might appear, was dying of sadness, and, we believe, did actually, while under one of these fits of melancholy, put an end to his existence, by committing suicide.

There are two sides, therefore, to stage-life, as in every other life, and having given one experience of our heroine in the sadder one, we will now relate another in a more merry vein, and one which shows equally the idiosyncrasies of her character.

Miss Cushman had ever held the opinion that actors should act for the public and not for each other, and by doing so had so gained the sympathy of the public that there seemed a direct communication between her fair self and the audience.

Whatever she did, therefore, the charming and fascinating girl had the public with her, a fact that was not very palatable to some of the other *attachés* of the theatre.

One time, John E. McDonough, the well-known purveyor of the *Seven Sisters*, was performing the part of Uncle Sam in that portion of the entertainment entitled *Uncle Sam's Magic Lantern*.

This was at Louisville, and as Miss Cushman had to assume the double character of rebel sympathiser as well as the character of the play, an appropriate part had, it was deemed, been selected for her. In this scene, *i.e., Uncle Sam's Magic Lantern*, thirty-four young ladies were to appear, representing the various States which go to compose our glorious Union, and carrying in their hands shields bearing their relative names.

The part of South Carolina had been set aside especially for Miss Cushman, and, as it suited her purpose, she accepted it.

The scene commenced. At the back of the stage a large canvas was rolled up, exhibiting the glorious old frigate *Constitution*.

Miss Cushman declares that at sight of the noble effigy she had difficulty to keep from throwing down the banner bearing the hated name of South Carolina, and giving three cheers for the brave old *Constitution*. But she had her part to play, and dare not reveal her true feelings. When, then, Uncle Sam, pointing to the effigy, made his usual speech, she retorted in the saucy language of the play.

The same happened again, when Columbia brings to mind the fact that the poor negro is suffering; for on board the frigate *Constitution* is represented all the prominent politicians of the day, some of whom are striking a poor negro on the head, using it as a wedge wherewith to break the *Constitution*.

"See," says Columbia, "see how they beat his head—why, they'll break it!"

28

"They don't care, so they break my *Constitution*," responds Uncle Sam.

"What say you, Carolina?"

"I say that the only respectable figure in the whole batch is the almighty negro!" said Carolina.

This, in spite of the objectionable sentiment, and owing alone to Miss Cushman's popularity, was warmly applauded, which seemed to annoy the worthy John.

The next scene is a slave auction, showing the fearful and disgraceful nature of that scandalous traffic. This is followed, by way of contrast, by a "happy family" —a negro *pater familias* surrounded by his sable little ones, all enjoying the hoe cake, and playing on the fiddle.

Columbia, turning to South Carolina, demands again, "What think you now, Carolina?"

To which the truant State replies in the doggerel verse of the play:

There are greater sins at the door of this nation,
Than the fiddle and hoe on a cotton plantation.

This too was applauded, be it remembered, from the mere fact that Miss Cushman spoke it.

Deeply annoyed, Mr. McDonough. turned to our fair heroine, and, forgetting time and place, exclaimed aloud, and so that everyone in the house heard it:

"Miss Cushman, you will speak to me and not to the audience!"

"Indeed!" retorted the lady, thus attacked, "indeed, Mr. McDonough, I think, on the contrary, that it is to *them* that I have to look for support. If I didn't attract *your* recommendation would certainly not secure me even a walking part."

By this time the audience had entered fully into the "squabble," if we may call it so, and, highly amused, warmly supported the lady. High words followed; while throughout the house resounded such phrases, as "That yhere girl's got spirit, lean tell you!" "I reckon she has!" etc.

It was some time before quiet was restored, and all the parties reconciled. This was done at last, however, and ever after, we believe, Mr. McDonough entertained a high opinion of her.

This feeling he evinced afterwards, when Miss Cushman was arrested, in accordance with the deeply-laid plans of the government. Believing it to be all real, poor man, he ran all over Nashville, the great drops of perspiration rolling off him, trying to get her released. Not a general but was appealed—to not an officer but was cajoled, all in vain; the government was inexorable; and after a good day's run, and almost melted, poor Mr. McDonough came to our heroine with the sad news that all his "heated" efforts had been vain.

How Miss Cushman, or rather, how the mischievous girl, kept from laughing at this announcement, knowing, as she did, that the fearful arrest was but a sham, no one but herself can tell. Mr. McDonough, by-the-by, did not like the joke excessively, and afterwards declared that he had known at the time that the arrest was only a "sham." But we are in advance.

On entering on the life of an actress, the beautiful girl had thought to find that vent for her imagination which her previous life, wild and romantic as it had been, had hitherto refused her. She thought, too, that pecuniary success might attend the effort. Here, she would at once come before the world, and be recognised as one of those favoured beings whose claim to our applause and our greenbacks no one who has any respect for himself or the "opinions of mankind" can dare to ignore. She would be hailed with rapture the moment she appeared behind the footlights, by houses crowded to repletion; bouquets and *billet doux* would be showered upon her from the stage-boxes by beautiful ladies, attired like angels; and the handsomest of men, in killing whiskers and cravats, would besiege the green-room doors to offer her hearts and hands innumerable.

And then, the stage itself, both before and behind the curtain! what a fairy world it was! All play and no work! no care, no anxiety, no contact with anything low or mean! Nothing but scenes in lordly halls and palaces, mermaid grottos and sylvan bowers, exquisitely painted, and bespangled, and illuminated at all hours, with no end of gas. All the attendants ever blooming and beautiful to behold; submissive and enthusiastic in their service, and constantly arrayed in satin velvet and silk stockings. No dust, no lamp-black, no messenger boys no irksome prompter's bell.

In front, a never-ceasing throng in ecstasies of rapturous applause; critics devoting their whole time to the laudation of this wonderful newly-risen star; flowers, pearl bracelets, and packages of *bon-bons* on the stage, and a drawer full of invitations to rides, drives, rural breakfasts, dinner parties, *soirees* and balls with the most distinguished personages of the land; managers on their knees, daily and nightly, offering fresh engagements, at any price demanded, and imploring their acceptance; delicious serenades each pleasant evening, and nosegays at the chamber door, accompanied with scented love-letters, every breakfast time. Then, at no remote period in the future, the desires of life crowned with a golden harvest, to be shared with some chosen one, whose true devotion would be worth more than all the rest beside; the wide world and all its teeming pleasures open, to be roamed through at will, and a name written at the pinnacle of the glittering lists that deck the temple of fame.

All this the impassioned girl believed; she saw, although never allowed fully the opportunities for which her heart yearned, the most of her stage dreams realised; and yet there was a something behind all this—a vacant place in her soul that they filled not The fact was, Pauline Cushman was born an actress—but with the world for her stage—with the bloody drama of war as the piece, and her part that of a heroine whom future generations should look up to with wonder. No stage of a mere theatre was sufficiently large for her; her mind, her heart, her spirit, needed a greater field.

When a child yet, she had often clung to the knee of her respected grandfather, who, with his good wife, had forgiven the truant spirit of his child, and followed her to America. When a mere child yet, we say, had Pauline crouched at her grandfather's knee to listen to his memories of the times long gone. He had been a soldier under the great Napoleon, and, like most old veterans, loved to fight his battles over again by his fireside.

At such moments, the most enthusiastic listener was ever the little Pauline, in spite of the fact that she had several brothers present, whom one would naturally suppose more likely to become interested in such recitals than a girl. Such, however, was not the case; the little Pauline it was who always begged her aged grandsire to tell her all about the wondrous battles fought in the days of his youth; and soon the little girl was as enthusiastic over "*L'Empereur*" as himself. At his tales of prowess and daring, her big eyes would brighten and flash with a kindred feeling; while they would re-echo back his own look of proud devotion, whenever he mentioned the name of his revered chief—that wonder and terror of the world—Napoleon!

Then the old man would clasp her to his breast, and exclaim, "*Ah! quel dommage!* what a pity, little one, that thou art not a lad! What a brave little soldier thou wouldst make!"

In narrating these circumstances, we are simply endeavouring to trace the gradual growth of a mind which has played no trivial part in the history of the war for the Union in the Southwest, and which may, yet, still more strikingly illustrate the annals of this memorable struggle. While we do so, the reader may notice how, piece by piece, the mental character and the career of Miss Cushman emerge into a fixed place and settled form, and how the results now known to the world have followed from their source in natural order.

It shows how wonderful are the decrees of fate—or more, the ways of Providence! All of these various experiences were necessary to mould the beautiful and daring girl for the part that her country and her destiny demanded of her, and, one after the other, they came, in their just order, and with a connecting link that astonishes and awes the reader. Have we not said truly that Pauline was born a heroine? Having pleasurably, we trust, then, traced the path of her glorious future from the very fountain-head, we will now proceed to relate her adventures as the Scout of the Cumberland—prefacing it with the remark, that strange and varied as had been her former career, its romance paled before the startling adventure and fearful reality of her after-life. This, however, needs a new chapter wherein to relate it.

Chapter 5: In the Provost-Marshal's Office

In the meantime, the *tocsin* of war had sounded its dread summons throughout the land, calling on all, men and women, to the rescue of our glorious and beloved Union. Our fields, so long unfurrowed, save by the peaceful plough, were to be riven and scarred by the iron hoof of the charger. The wheat, garnered usually with such care, was to become sodden and damped with the blood of its owners. The fiend Rebellion was abroad, and in its monster tracks all the furies of misery and desolation.

Slowly the long period of bloodshed and devastation dragged its length along—leaving, especially on the face of the Southwest, its cursed trail of ruin—until, in March of the year 1863, we find our heroine performing at the Mozart Hall, or Wood's Theatre, as it is generally called, in Louisville.

This beautiful and delightful city was, and fortunately, at that time the headquarters of the rebel sympathisers of the Southwest, and every day the government was set at naught by their machinations. At last, they got so bold, from long-continued success, that they dared to boast openly of their achievements in behalf of the rebel cause, and to scoff at the weakness of the government that was powerless to restrain them.

The provost officers of Louisville were in despair, for these crafty sympathisers were as tricky as foxes, and as deceitful as the evil one himself. It was at this stage of affairs that our heroine arrived.

The house at which she boarded being kept by rebel sympathisers, Miss Cushman was unavoidably thrown into company with people of even decided disloyalty.

Annoyed at this, she was frequently upon the point of leaving the house, never more to return; but just at this moment an event occurred that decided her to remain, believing that she could aid her country thereby.

The circumstance was this: Among Miss Cushman's acquaintance she numbered two paroled rebel officers, Colonel Spear and Captain J. H. Blincoe, whom she had, apart from all political considerations admitted to a certain degree of friendship. At that time. Mr. McDonough and his inevitable *Seven Sisters*—of whom we may wish, as they say in the East, that they "may live forever!"—was in town, and Miss Cushman was acting the part of Plutella in this celebrated piece. Now everyone that has ever seen this widely popular play will remember that Plutella has to assume, during the course of the piece, many characters. At one time she is a dashing officer of *Zouaves*; at another, a fine gentleman of fashion, and in this last character is supposed to drink wine with a friend.

One afternoon, then, she was visited by her two rebel friends, Colonel Spear and Captain J. H. Blincoe, who, whilst talking over the play, suddenly exclaimed, "Miss Cushman, suppose you drink a Southern toast this evening, and see what effect it will have upon the audience."

"But good gracious, gentlemen!" returned our heroine, with a laugh. "I should be locked up in jail if I were to attempt anything of that kind."

"Never fear that," they continued, now in earnest, for they had spoken before as though in jest. "Never fear that. They would certainly never lock up so charming a lady in a prison. Besides, we will give you three hundred dollars in greenbacks if you will do it."

"Why certainly you are not in earnest, gentlemen?" demanded Pauline, her eyes beginning to flash with indignation.

"We most assuredly are, fair lady, and were never more so in our lives."

Pauline thought for a moment; then, pretending to assent, she said: "Who will prepare the toast?"

"We will see to all that," they responded. "Only consent, and we will make the rest all right."

"Let me have time to think it over," she pleaded and with that the subject was dismissed for the time being.

They had no sooner left the house, than, with eyes flashing and cheeks burning, the young girl flew rather than walked to the office of the provost-marshal, Colonel Moore. She had been introduced to that gentleman a few days before, by Mr. Edward Bowers, the treasurer of the theatre, and having found him gentlemanly and kind, determined now to tell him of this intended outrage upon the feelings of the loyal people of Louisville, and, as she deemed it, direct insult to herself.

On entering his office, Miss Cushman found the provost-marshal as kind and courteous as ever. Slim, with a spare face, and small, beautifully-shaped hand and foot, the colonel possessed a countenance which inspired one at once with confidence A peculiar smile, too, which extended all over his face, giving its good-humour to every feature, lent a new assurance to our heroine that neither she nor her errand would be misunderstood. Besides, she had a gentleman and a soldier to deal with; for this Colonel Moore it was, who performed that gallant exploit at Milliken's Bend; where, with but one hundred men, he repulsed near thirty thousand of the rebels under General John Morgan.

To such a man Miss Cushman did not hesitate to state her case; nor was the reception of her confidence calculated to create any misgivings as to the prudence of her course. Colonel Moore was all kindness and gentleness; and after interrogating her, and becoming assured of her earnest loyalty and patriotic purpose spoke thus:

"Miss Cushman, you have assured me of your love for the Union, and your earnest wish to do nothing but what is loyal and just, nor have I any doubt of your patriotism; but I must remark one thing, and that is, that we are often compelled, in the furtherance of our loved cause, to do things which are repulsive to us."

"Well, sir?" interrupted the young girl, half guessing his meaning.

"Well, I advise that you drink this rebel toast, as is proposed."

"Drink to Jeff. Davis and the Southern Confederacy?" exclaimed Pauline, scarce believing her ears "Oh, colonel, you surely cannot mean this!"

"Miss Cushman, you love the Union and our country, do you not?" asked the colonel, gravely

"More than I do life itself!"

"Then do my bidding. If you were not perfectly loyal I should at once arrest you, at even the bare mention of such a thing; as it is, I request you, in the name of that country which you love so dearly, to drink this toast. Moreover, I promise you that I will be present at the theatre when the event comes off."

Amazement had so fastened upon the young girl, that, for a few moments, she stood like a statue; her beautiful eyes cast down, and her little foot beating the floor in silent wonderment. The words of the tind officer, however, reassured her.

"Fear nothing," he said; "it is for a deeper reason than you think for that I beg of you to do this thing. Good may come of it, to your country, that you know not of."

"Enough! I will do it then!" was the determined answer of our heroine.

With many thanks the colonel now bid her farewell, and, but half satisfied, Miss Cushman took her way back to her lodgings, to prepare for the new role which she was to act, and to get ready for the momentous affair of the evening.

Chapter 6: The Rebel Toast

With fleeting steps our heroine hied to her home, the words of the kind Provost-marshal floating through her brain. What he had meant by advising her to act so treasonable a part she could but instinctively guess. It was enough for her to know, however, that good to her country was to flow from it, and that some design of which she knew as yet nought certain was hidden beneath it.

The fact, though, that she was about to take apparently so treasonable a step, would at times appal her, throughout the whole afternoon, until the remembrance of the kind manner and gentle words of Colonel Moore reassured her.

If the obnoxious act had to be done, she thought it were well to do it quickly. She determined then to drink the rebel toast that evening.

But there were a number of things to be done first. The rebel officers had to be informed of her willingness to carry out their plot; while, to give greater *éclat* to the whole thing, sundry rebel sympathisers (old women) were privately informed, under most fearful vows of secrecy, that something rich was about to come off that evening at the theatre. Of course, this was equal to publishing it, for, as *Punch* says, Women *can* keep a secret, but it *takes a great many of them to do it*. One old lady, indeed, an inmate of the same boarding-house with Miss Cushman, nearly wore her poor old limbs off, spreading the news.

This old lady, by-the-by, was quite a character—frequently amusing the household by speaking of "a pair of bedsteads," and "a few of them molas"—and yet this refined Southern woman would have scorned to speak to a Northern school-master, or a Yankee school-marm. She was one of the descendants of the F. F. Vs., and of course could not mingle with the Yankee mud-sills, even though they might be her superiors in education and manners. Ah, what a thing is blood!

Let us leave the old lady, however, and return to our subject.

In due time all the preparations were made, and, although it had seemed to our heroine that the afternoon never would pass away, at last the slanting rays of the sun denoted the approach of that evening which was to be so fraught with adventure. Then, as though to make up for their former tardiness the hours fairly began to fly, and the heart of the young girl beat fast at the thought that the momentous time was approaching. At last, the hour arrived for her to set out to the theatre. She had no sooner stepped inside the building than she found that her patent telegraph had worked to some purpose. The house was literally packed. Not even standing-room was to be had for love or money. Every rebel sympathiser in the place had heard of it, and those who could possibly get their noses in were there.

How Mr. McDonough must have chuckled, as, unconscious of the true cause, he perhaps dwelt upon the consoling idea that he had made a hit at last, and was to draw crowded houses ever after. He was soon to be enlightened, however. The time approached for the play to begin. The men in the orchestra began screwing up their big fiddles, and then unscrewing them, in their usual mysterious manner. Ushers began to call out the numbers of seats, and to slam the doors in their wonted style. The "call-boy" flew here and there, and at last, in obedience to the prompter's bell, the curtain began to rise, discovering Mr Pluto at breakfast, within the shades of Hades. There was, however, a veritable Pluto to burst upon them soon that they wot not of. This was coming.

In the meantime, the jokes and mirth of the *Seven Sisters* were more than ordinarily relished. It may have been that those in the secret were so delighted at the prospect of seeing the Federal authorities thus wantonly insulted that they greeted everything with rapture, and that this became contagious among the good Union people of the house, who, of course, were ignorant of the plot. Be that as it may, the audience was assuredly in a most excelled, humour, and not a joke or look of the actors, no matter how miserable, but brought forth storms of applause.

At length the momentous hour arrived, and, advancing in her the-atrical costume to the foot-lights, our heroine, goblet in hand, gave, in a clear, ringing voice, the following toast:

"Here's to Jeff. Davis and the Southern Confederacy. May the South always maintain her honour and her rights!"

The young girl had prepared herself for a fearful outbreak of popular opinion, but for a moment even the hearts of the audience seemed to stop beating.

Then, however, it burst forth, and such a scene followed as beggars description. The good Union portion of the audience had sat at first spell-bound and horrified by the fearful treason thus outspoken, while even the "*secesh*" were frozen with the audacity of the act, though conscious that it was to occur. But then came the mingled storm of applause and condemnation. Fierce and tumultuous it raged, until it seemed as though it would never stop. Nor was the excitement behind the scenes less intense. Mr. McDonough, rushing up to our heroine, demanded in his most tragic tone "what she meant by such conduct;" while the rest of the professional gentlemen and ladies avoided her as though she had suddenly been stricken with some fearfully contagious disease.

The brave girl, however, had her cue, and boldly avowed that she "wasn't afraid of the whole Yankee crew, and would do it again!"

In short, our heroine carried out her part so well that not one there doubted for a moment but that she was a most virulent secessionist.

An ancient artist was once rendered famous through painting a curtain so naturally, that he deceived a brother artist by it—making him actually believe that it was a *bona fide* drapery.

"What think you of my painting?" asked the first.

"Draw aside the curtain which covers it, that I may judge," was the response, thus showing that the artist was misled even by his own art.

If this little incident may be taken as a criterion, Miss Cushman must certainly be a famous actress for through her acting she even deceived her fellow actors.

Miss Lottie Huff, who was playing the part of "Tartarine," and who was at the same time a spy of the government, was particularly bitter against our heroine; and had not words enough in her vocabulary to express her disgust that such a rank traitor should live. Miss Cushman kept her own council, however, and nerved herself to the work. As she has since expressed it in her own forcible language:

"Let the spirit which burned in the breasts of Joan of Arc and the

Maid of Saragossa be mine and, living or dying, let me be one of the chosen witnesses that heaven has raised up amid these gloomy days to bear testimony to the valour of our American hearts the devotion we can offer in the cause of Republican freedom, and the undying faith which we will ever maintain in the liberty and union of our beloved land. Still then, troubled heart! Onward in the cause of right. Now, and hereafter, let every throb, and if needs be, every drop of your life's blood be given only to your country!"

Alone, and without guidance, with a beauty unsurpassed, and a most difficult role to play, the position in which our heroine found herself was anything but agreeable. With every confidence in Colonel Moore, she was still in the dark as to his object; beside, it cut her to the quick to have her old stage companions turn coldly from her, and she would have given the world to have been able to throw her arms about their necks and undeceive them as to her traitorous proclivities. But she dare not: she must bear it all—bear it for her country's sake.

"Let each throb, and, if needs be, each drop of her life's blood be given for it!"

To heighten the "situation," as a dramatist would say, Miss Cushman had not yet left the theatre when the guards arrived to arrest her. These, however, were deterred from putting their errand into immediate execution through respect for Mr. Wood, the proprietor of the theatre; and at last, it was arranged that she was to report at headquarters the next morning at ten o'clock.

On doing so she was greeted warmly by the excellent colonel, and even General Boyle relaxed from his accustomed rigor.

"By Jove! it was capitally done!" exclaimed the first, in his feminine but pleasant voice.

"You acquitted yourself famously, Miss Cushman. You deserve our thanks, and the thanks of the government, and rest assured you shall receive them. There are, however, many things to be done yet. You have sowed the seed: you must now prepare to reap the harvest. You must enter the secret service, this will be the more easy, from the fact that you will probably find your discharge from the theatre awaiting you when you return. Please therefore, hold yourself at my order, as I have General Boyle's consent to this arrangement, and let me, as a word of advice, and as the apparently fitting consequence of your arrest, advise you not to talk quite so *secesh*, but to moderate yourself in this respect, *especially in public*, as though you had received a severe reprimand from General Boyle and myself.

"In private, you can, of course, abuse the government, and say all the harm you can about it; by these means you will inspire confidence in the disaffected, and be of incalculable use to your country and ourselves. Expect to hear from me soon in relation to this, and till then, *adieu*."

Promising to carry out his suggestions to the letter, the young girl left the office. On arriving at her boarding-house, she found a note awaiting her. The colonel was right in his surmises, for the note read thus:

Miss Cushman:
By order of the management, I am requested to inform you, that your services are no longer required in this establishment, it being inferred that you will be unable to continue your present role for some time to come.
Regetting that it is my unpleasant duty,
        For the Management,
                                        H. B. Phillips,
                        Stage Manager for Mr. George Wood
                            Proprietor of Wood's Theatre.

Pauline was discharged, but Mr. Wood, fearing that the young girl would find herself without money, or otherwise distressed, was thoughtful enough to send her a half-week's salary a kindness which she never forgot.

Chapter 7: Mysteries of the Secret Service

Thrown afresh, as it were, upon the great world, the young girl was, to say the least, placed in a most awkward position. Shunned by her former friends as bearing the brand of disloyalty—slighted by this one—jeered at by that had she not possessed that little yet all powerful inner voice, which tells us when we are right, she must have sunk beneath it.

The thought, however, that she had sacrificed her feelings for her country's good, bore her up, and she held her head erect through it all.

Upon the plot succeeding she had received the sincere congratulations of both Colonel Moore and General Boyle; moreover, she had now the entire confidence of the disloyal portion of the population, who sympathised with her very much, and made numberless professions of their friendship. This state of affairs was, it may be supposed, immediately turned to account. Miss Cushman's wits were too sharp to allow even half an opportunity to escape her. As Colonel Moore had said, she had sowed the soil: she must now begin to reap the harvest which it had produced. And indeed, it was a harvest, and a rich one, that now opened before the courageous young girl.

Louisville was undermined, one may say, by disloyal sentiment and treasonable plots.

Like a swarm of mosquitos, the base crew of "sympathisers," too cowardly to fight, and too dishonourable to be true to the government—which was even then shielding them—would first be here and then there; annoying, yet seldom, if ever, to be caught.

The extent to which this had reached will be better understood when we detail some of the contrivances which the government officers had to sift out and prepare against. All that human, or, rather, *fiendish* subtlety could devise to annoy and harass the loyal and Union people of that section, was conceived and carried into immediate execution by these cowardly wretches. Information was given to their friends across the "lines;" letters sent and received; demonstrations against the Union and Union officers arranged; while disloyal badges and songs were a matter of hourly notice.

Some of these petty, yet most annoying—aye, sometimes even dangerous plots—were conducted by wealthy and well-known citizens of Louisville; among whom none were more persevering than a person who kept a large military furnishing store near Wood's Theatre, which our soldiers and officers will doubt less remember from the good prices charged there All these plots Miss Cushman was the means of bringing to light, and their fitting punishment; and to do so, had to assume numberless disguises, and act many parts.

Her most usual places of resort were the small saloons on Market Street, Louisville, where she would notice very respectably-dressed men, whom she knew to be men of position, talking with shabbily-clothed countrymen, or other suspicious looking characters. These, of course, were easily marked, and frequently they would act quite regardless of the rough, clumsy, country boy, lolling by their side; disclosing, unwittingly, their secrets, and only finding out their mistake when summoned to the provost-marshal's office, to account for their treasonable speeches and actions.

At other times, she would be sprucely dressed as a young Southern gentleman of means, and play billiards at one of the fashionable billiard-saloons of the place; thus picking up much information of the rebels, their hopes and plans.

Her most dangerous work, however, was scouting in search of guerillas; discovering their whereabouts; tracking down their haunts, etc.
And as the desperate character of these vagrants is well known, we
need not dwell upon the degree of courageous daring and wonderful
perception needed to prevent discovery, and, at the same time, obtain
the desired information. Still, in these dangerous ventures, as in all
other undertakings of the same nature, a special providence seemed
to have a guard over our heroine. And full many the night has her
heartfelt thanksgiving been offered up to that God who allows not a
sparrow to fall without his knowledge, and who had so wonderfully
preserved her in her midnight excursions in the cause of her country.

To accomplish these objects, Miss Cushman was compelled, not
only to don male attire, but frequently to be in the saddle all night; and
varied and strange were her experiences; for she had a wary foe to deal
with, and a thousand dangers beneath her every footstep, liable to be
sprung upon her at any moment. These adventures, however, were not
without their amusing side—for instance, it was interesting to watch
the different plans hit upon by the sympathisers to send and receive
communications through the lines. To accomplish it, the most singular
contrivances were in vogue.

One means of getting letters through was to fold, them up length-
wise and stuff them in the craw of a chicken. This passed muster for a
long time, until at last it was discovered. Another means of transport-
ing important letters and despatches through the lines was, to mix
them up through a bag of flour, and retail them out to customers
known to be O. K. One would scarce notice the slip of paper hidden
in the flour. This, too, was discovered by our heroine. As for false soles
in shoes, hollowed-out heels, in which were despatches and drawings
of fortifications, etc., they were of common occurrence.

The greatest service, however, that our heroine rendered her country whilst in Louisville, and the one, especially, for which all who have
the well-being of our brave soldiers at heart, should owe her eternal
gratitude, was the saving the lives of a number of poor wounded soldiers, who had been assigned to the merciless care of the boarding-
house keeper with whom Miss Cushman at one time lived. This fiend
of a woman, for she could have been no less, believing our heroine to
be one of her own miserable party, took her entirely into her confidence.

For some time before, Miss Cushman had noticed that the woman
appeared to have something on her mind, and noting her conversing

41

aside with a suspicious-looking character that visited the house, determined to sift the matter to the end. It was, indeed, a blessing that she did so, as the sequel will show. One night, then, after all in the house were supposed to have retired, Miss Cushman was surprised to see a light in the room of the woman who kept the house. Upon watching her, it was found that she was engaged mixing some white powder with some ground coffee, which she had in her room.

Without knowing exactly what was intended by this midnight operation, Miss Cushman, affecting to be ill, knocked gently at the door, which was stealthily opened; though not before the powdered coffee had been hastily put out of sight When the door was opened at length, the woman at first affected to have been fast asleep. Seeing, however, that it was only our heroine, she became more composed.

"Oh, it is only you, is it?" she asked, apparently relieved.

"That is all," returned Miss Cushman. "I came down to get some cologne, for I feel quite ill. But what has kept you up so late? and what mysterious brewing were you at when I knocked first—that you kept me waiting before you opened the door? Something wicked, I'll be bound!"

"Nothing of the sort, my dear; without you call killin' off a few Yankees wicked; and I reckon yer too good a Confederate for that," answered the woman.

"Killing off a few Yankees?" asked the fair girl, in surprise.

"Yes, only a few, unfortunately. Drat me if I wouldn't like to kill off the hul lot," responded the fiend of a woman.

"But how are you going to accomplish it without being detected?"

"Oh, easy enough. You see, them tarnal Federals will insist on quarterin' some sick and wounded soldiers here, and I jist reckon they ain't a goin' away soon agin; or if they do, it'll be in their coffins; for I'll give 'em each a dose of this regularly," (holding up a package of the same powder which Miss Cushman had seen the woman-fiend mixing with the coffee.) "I'll jist give 'em a slow dose of this, an' I reckon they won't do the Federals much good afterwards."

"A slow dose of this?" gasped the young girl, incredulous, for she couldn't believe that any one in human form should harbour such infernal thoughts. "A slow dose of this?"

"I reckon! And that's jist the thing'll do them, too. I 'spect you'll say so too, if yer look at the paper."

Slowly our heroine took the proffered paper, and read the label upon it. As she did so, a sudden faintness came over her. Sick and wounded soldier! Great God! the paper contained the most deadly *poison*!

The idea was so horrible that, for a few moments, the young girl stood paralyzed. To think of any one being so perfectly fiendish as to murder poor sick and wounded soldiers! The very thought transfixed her, as though the poison had entered her veins. Noticing this, the woman turned hastily towards her.

"You ain't gettin' squeamish, I reckon, are yer? for if yer are, I can tell yer these yere quarters'll be gittin' too hot for yer," remarked the woman, threateningly.

"Squeamish? Oh, no! But you have forgotten that I felt faint, and that I came down for the cologne," responded the quick-witted girl, endeavouring to master her feelings.

"Well, now, so I did," said the woman. "I declare if I didn't forget all about yer gettin' sick, and actually did believe for a minute there, that yer had turned a darn'd Yankee. Ha! ha! ha! That's a good joke, that is! But it wouldn't a been a joke if it had been true, I can tell yer; for you would a died and I would a swung for it, I 'spect —that is, if the 'Yanks' could a caught me afore I got across the 'lines.'"

Joining in the merriment of the wretch of a woman as well as she was able, Miss Cushman tottered from the room, and, without un-dressing, waited until the fearful woman had really gone to bed—we will not say to *sleep*, for such a wretch could not certainly sleep. Our heroine then flew, rather than walked, to the provost-marshal's office, where she disclosed the whole horrible plot.

For prudential reasons—the averting any blame from Miss Cush-man being one—this woman was not arrested at the time. The poor sick and wounded soldiers, however, did not fall within her clutches; and as soon as Miss Cushman was out of the way of harm from her, the wicked wretch, met with her just punishment.

Chapter 8: More Traitors Exposed

Prominent among those thronging the headquarters of the briga-dier-general, in the city of Louisville, about this time, might have been noticed a bright, handsome woman, who seemed exceedingly anxious for the success of some suit in which she was engaged. Her dress and manner indicated that she belonged to the higher walks of life, but otherwise there was nothing in her conduct or appearance by which a careless observer would distinguish her from the hundreds of others who daily gather at the office of a commanding general, seeking favours as numerous and diverse as the applicants themselves.

The practised eye, however, could easily discern certain suspicious circumstances attaching to her and suggestive of the idea that beneath all this pleasant exterior there might be an undercurrent of deceit and treachery. But her story was plausible, her manners winning, her conversation sprightly and interesting. The impression made by her upon all with whom she came in contact was in the highest degree favourable, and it seemed both ungallant and unjust to harbour the shadow of a suspicion that she was otherwise than a high-minded, honourable woman, who would scorn any of the petty meannesses of such frequent occurrence within our lines.

It subsequently transpired that her name was Ford, that her husband was a Baptist clergyman a man of ability and reputation, formerly editor of a religious paper in that city, and now representative in the Confederate Congress from that district of Kentucky. She herself belonged to one of the first families of the city, and moved in the highest circles of an aristocratic society. To a naturally brilliant mind, strengthened and polished by a thorough education, were added the ease and grace of an accomplished Southern woman. In the palmy days of peace, she had been the centre of a bright galaxy of wit and beauty, dispensing to her admirers a bounteous hospitality, as genial as it was welcome. Now all was changed. These social gatherings had long been discontinued, the family circle was broken and scattered her husband was a fugitive from his home, and she was seeking from the Federal authorities permission to pass southward beyond their lines and join him in his exile.

Lounging about the same headquarters, on the same morning, with seemingly no particular business or present occupation save to watch the movements of others, was a quiet-looking man, who now and then cast sharp, quick, and stealthy glances at this Mrs. Ford, apparently regarding her with much interest. Presently, seeing her somewhat apart from the crowd, he approached, and, in a respectful, diffident manner, engaged her in conversation, which continued for some time, and, from the animated character it gradually assumed, was evidently upon some subject in which both parties were deeply interested. That it was of a confidential and private nature was easily inferred from the caution maintained during its continuance.

It seems that, after some commonplace talk, the stranger informed her that he was not what he then seemed, but in reality, Captain Den-

44

ver, of the Confederate Army, visiting Louisville as a spy upon the movements of the Federal Army. Highly gratified at this intelligence, the lady became very friendly, and at once invited the captain to visit her house. The invitation so warmly given could not be declined without apparent rudeness, and so was accepted, but with, as the lady thought, a rather unnecessary and suspicious hesitation.

Whatever unwillingness the captain may have outwardly exhibited in accepting the proffered invitation, he was not slow in availing himself of its present privileges and prospective pleasures. Calling soon afterwards at the residence indicated, he was cordially received by the family, whom he found strong in their sympathy with the South. Conversation naturally turned upon the war, and by a warm espousal of the Confederate cause he soon succeeded in ingratiating himself into their confidence, and, by way of showing *his* confidence in them, revealed his intention of presently escaping through the Federal lines to the nearest Confederate command, taking with him as large an amount of quinine, morphine and other medicines as he could safely carry.

Confidence thus implicitly reposed in the acquaintance of but a few hours could not be otherwise than pleasing to the fair hostess; and surely a reciprocal confidence would be little enough expression of gratitude in return. It was not safe; it was not wise; but "there can be no harm in trusting so true and firm a Southerner as Captain Denver," thought Mrs. Ford.

It was her purpose, too, she said, to smuggle through the line's large quantities of medicines, and at the same time carry to the Confederate authorities valuable information of Federal movements and plans. Her husband was in the South, and she apprehended no difficulty in procuring a pass allowing her to go to him, so soon as the circumstances of her case could be brought to the personal notice of General Boyle.

The enterprise in which both were about to engage now became the exclusive topic of a lengthy conversation, in the course of which the captain remarked that he had not sufficient money to make as extensive purchases as he wished, and was desirous of assistance from the friends of the cause in Louisville. Mrs, Ford thought this need not trouble him. She could arrange it to his satisfaction, and appointed an interview for the next morning, at which she hoped to report the complete success of her efforts. The evening passed rapidly, and the captain took his departure, leaving his entertainers highly pleased with him as a valuable acquaintance and co-labourer in the cause of the South.

The same evening the captain chanced to meet in the office of the Galt House an old friend, Dr. Rogers, surgeon on the staff of General Sterling Price, a paroled prisoner, and now, by order of General Rosecrans, on his way to Cairo to report to General Tuttle for transportation by the first boat to Vicksburg. According to the terms of the cartel agreed upon by the Federal and Confederate authorities, surgeons were held as non-combatants and not subject to exchange; but the doctors, with others, found in the hospital at Iuka, had been detained by General Rosecrans, in retaliation for the arrest and imprisonment by General Price of certain Union soldiers in Mississippi, and as hostages for their return. Their release had been followed by his; and he was now, as stated, *en route* for Cairo.

At their meeting the next morning, Captain Denver mentioned the doctor to Mrs. Ford as his friend, and an intelligent and accomplished gentleman, with whom she would no doubt be highly pleased, at the same time remarking that he was on his way South, and it would be greatly to their advantage to go thither under his protection. To this she readily assented, and desired the captain to procure her an interview with the doctor. This not very difficult task was speedily accomplished, and the doctor called upon her that evening.

Sometime having passed in conversational pleasantry, the doctor adverted to the carrying of contraband goods, and spoke discouragingly of its policy, saying that anything of the kind would be a violation of his parole, and might lead to his arrest and imprisonment. With apparent sincerity, Mrs. Ford promptly replied that, though an enemy of the Federal Government, she was an honourable enemy, and would engage in no enterprise to which the military authorities would refuse their sanction.

The doctor seemed satisfied, and did not revert to the subject, but, instead, imparted to her, in strict confidence, a secret of the utmost importance. It will be remembered that some months previous to this George N. Sanders had successfully escaped from the rebel States, and made his way to England for the purpose of negotiating a Confederate loan. High hopes of success, on his part, were entertained, and his return was anxiously looked for by the rebels. Mrs. Ford, with her whole heart and soul in the cause, was more sanguine even than her most sanguine friends; and imagination can scarcely conceive the bright colours with which she painted the future of the embryo Confederacy.

Who, then, shall describe her surprise and joy when told by the doctor that their friend, Captain Denver, was no other than this same George N. Sanders, who had eluded the guard at the Suspension Bridge, and was now on his return to the Confederate capital? She was also informed that his mission had been completely successful—that the loan had been taken by the Rothschilds, and that Sanders had in possession the evidence and documents connected therewith, all written in cypher. She was cautioned against hinting a word of it to anybody, or even intimating to Sanders that she knew him in any other character than as Captain Denver. He would accompany them to Vicksburg in his present disguise, and, until that point was reached, safety required that it should be penetrated by no one, however friendly to the South. The interests at stake were too vast to be hazarded by exposure to a mischance, which a single careless word might bring upon them. In case, however, he should be suspected, it would be their business to assist him in the secretion of his papers.

The arrangements for the journey were discussed, and the suggestion of the doctor warmly espoused by Mrs. Ford. Her eyes sparkled with delight as she asked a thousand questions about Sanders: how he had managed to escape the vigilance of the Federals; by what means he had accomplished his mission; what was the state of feeling in Europe, the prospects of recognition, and so on. The doctor answered as best he could, and at length took his leave to make final preparations to start the next evening. Passes were obtained, tickets bought, trunks checked, berths secured in the sleeping-car. Everything bade fair for the successful termination of the enterprise.

The night was passed comfortably in sleep, from which they were awakened, on arriving at Cairo, to find themselves under arrest. Denver and Rogers were indignant, but Mrs. Ford trembled like an aspen leaf, and had the earth opened under her feet, revealing a bottomless chasm in which she must inevitably be buried alive, she could not have been more astonished and horrified. She could find neither tongue nor heart to utter a word in defence, and was led away in silence. A personal examination brought to light a number of letters and a large quantity of quinine concealed about her clothes. The trunks were found to contain similar contraband goods, and much information of value to the rebels.

Grieving will not restore lost opportunities, nor bring to the surface sunken treasures: else had not the hopes of Mrs. Ford been thus ruthlessly dashed to the ground, her letters and goods fallen into the hands of her enemies, and the riches of the Confederate loan taken to themselves wings and flown away.

After a protracted investigation, Mrs. Ford was sent South; since which time she has engaged in the business of publishing a book, giving an account of her experience and treatment under Federal rule. Captain Denver, *alias* George N. Sanders, *alias* Conklin, it is needless to say, was simply our famous spy and scout, while Dr. Rogers, of Price's staff, was a member of the detective police of the Army of the Cumberland.

Chapter 9: All About a Ghost

Although most useful to her country and the local government at Louisville, our heroine was not destined to remain long there. A larger field was thrown open to her, and with her usual ambition and dashing courage the beautiful woman determined to espouse the opportunity to serve her beloved land in a more exalted sphere.

In saying this, however, we do not wish to imply that her services at Louisville were not both exalted and most valuable, and her efficiency wonderful in scenting out the guerillas and counteracting the plots of the many rebel sympathisers who were harboured in that locality.

Her midnight rides and attendant adventures we have not attempted to narrate, from the simple fact that they would demand too much of our available space. It has been our desire, also, to arrive as quickly as possible at the more interesting episodes of Miss Cushman's life as a government spy; and we are not willing, though often tempted, to linger on the way. However, we cannot pass over another of the incidents that befell our fair heroine here without mentioning, if it were only for the sake of its amusing character.

If we could give, in its recital, but one-half the amusing *vim* that the lady herself throws into it, we might hope to have the reader enjoy it as much as we did ourselves, on first hearing it. However, to our story.

It happened one night, when Miss Cushman was out scouting, that she found herself in quite a deserted region, away from every house and, apparently, every human being. That morning early, she had set apart for watching the Kentucky farmers come into market. These last were of course men who had taken the oath of allegiance to the government, and solemnly sworn to support the Union and the laws. What these oaths were worth we will see when we have to deal with their neighbours, the Tennessee farmers. As it was, they had already been detected conveying contraband news in all imaginable ways, some even hiding letters in the handles of butter-kettles, etc.

Finding it to be rather too early as yet for these gentry, our heroine determined to snatch a moment's repose; so, fastening her horse to a small sapling near at hand, she laid her down in the high grass, a large stone her only pillow.

In spite of these obstacles to balmy sleep our heroine found herself soon so completely tired out that she slept soundly—how long she knew not.

At last, however, she was awakened by the sound of voices singing. Their thick, guttural pronunciation soon showed them to be poor ne-groes, who had assembled secretly to worship that God before whom all good men are equal. Their quaint but often touchingly simple hymns showed this; and with devotional ear the lone girl drank in the sweet sounds. By the light of the blazing fire which they had made, and around which they were clustered, she discovered that she was upon a small bluff, elevated above them, and overlooking their place of resort, though hidden from them. She could therefore look on without fear of discovery, though it is true that she had little to fear from those poor children of bondage; for never, in the whole course of her adventures, was she betrayed by a negro.

Raising herself, then, she viewed in reverential awe the little gath-ering beneath her. About them arose the wild rocks and hanging ferns; above them, gemmed with many a star, hung the blue vault of heaven. Their only church was the free fields which the God of nature had endowed them with; their pastor, one of themselves, with nothing to guide him but that innate sense of right which even the roughest of us feel. It was a scene to bring tears of sympathy to the eyes, and deep, burning thoughts to the mind.

All sadness, however, was to have a sudden end. The singing had ceased, and one of the humble congregations had arisen to pray:

O "Lord! bress all dese poor negros!" he mumured. "Bress dem all, Lord, and help dem to fight de debbil and all dem wot keeps dem from der rights. Grant dat de day of jubulum come right soon, and, as young massa wot's dead used to say, all dese poor child'en of bondage be liberated forever more, grant dat his spirit rest ober us, for he wur a good young man! Grant, den, Lord, dat it be wid us dis night!"

Just at this juncture, unfortunately for the seriousness of the party, the branch of the tree against which our heroine was leaning gave way, precipitating her into the midst of those clustered beneath. With a yell of terror that would have struck awe into a hyena the whole congregation arose, and, uttering cries of "Young massa!" "Young massa come to life again!" scattered in all directions. In vain our heroine called to them to stop: the more she protested that she was not, as they supposed, a ghost the faster they ran; until at last, seeing the utter impossibility of staying their flight, the amused girl gave herself up to a hearty fit of laughter, which, no doubt, sounded fearfully weird in the ears of the absconding "darks."

We can imagine the wonderful tales that these poor, ignorant people will relate, probably for all time to come, of how "young massa's" ghost appeared; and only hope that this explanation will reach some of the parties concerned in the "big scare."

★★★★★★★★★★★★★★★★★

To return to our heroine, however. It happened just about this time that Mr. J. R Allen, proprietor of the New Nashville Theatre, arrived in Louisville. He had been to Cincinnati to secure a good company of actors, and, meeting Mr. Wood, of the Louisville Theatre, was recommended to secure Miss Cushman. "She is a good-looking woman and an accomplished actress," said Mr. Wood; "but she will talk '*secesh*.' If you can only keep her out of the provost-marshal's hands you will make a good thing, for she will be popular at once." It is thus shown how perfectly Miss Cushman played her part as a sympathiser with Secessia.

So, it was proposed to Miss Cushman that she should become one of the "bright, particular stars" of Allen's New Theatre, Nashville, Tenn., pretty close on to rebeldom, and then the active field of operations for the army of the Southwest.

Upon consulting with Colonel Moore, the engagement was approved of, inasmuch as it did not necessarily interfere with her duties as a member of the army police. Armed, therefore, with letters of introduction to Colonel Truesdail, the head of the provost-marshal's bureau in that city, Pauline set out for Nashville.

We say *set out*, but it was not such a simple thing as those words would imply. First of all, to go to Nashville one had to have a "pass." To maintain her assumed part the authorities had of course to refuse to grant her one. Nothing remained but to "run the blockade," as it was called.

Proceeding, therefore, to the cars, she got a "*secesh*" gentleman going to Nashville to take charge of her trunk; then, going to one of the guards stationed at the door of each car, she requested leave to speak with a friend inside, "only for one minute."

The guard looked at her, but her pleasing face triumphed, and, drawing aside his musket, he allowed her to pass. Of course, once she got in, she was not in a hurry to get out again, and she remained there until the officer of the guard came to inspect the passes. To escape his supervision was more difficult, and she had to manufacture a story for the purpose, showing at the same time her order from Mr. Allen to report immediately, at his theatre.

Although not altogether satisfactory, no officer could have the heart to send her back. If he had even thought of doing so, she had a few tears ready for an emergency, and what disarms a man as soon as a beautiful woman in tears. Our heroine was therefore soon on her way to her new field of operations, the base, at that time, of that glorious old Army of the Southwest, whose deeds shall live as long as men have tongues to relate and ears wherewith to listen. Of her adventures there we will speak in another chapter.

Chapter 10: Nashville and the Rebellion

In order to a better understanding of our heroine's adventures, we deem it important to digress for a moment from the thread of her story to give a picture of the once proud city she was now entering, and which place, to speak in army phrase, forms the base for her future operations.

Previous to 1861, Nashville was one of the most beautiful, gay, and prosperous cities of the Union. Her inhabitants numbered thirty thousand, and were rapidly increasing. She was the wealthiest place of her class in the country. Her public buildings and private edifices were of the grandest and most costly character. The State Capitol rose from a rock one hundred and seventy-five feet above the Cumberland River—is said to be the finest structure of its kind in America, and cost over a million of dollars. Church-edifices reared their tall spires upon every hand. An extensive State penitentiary, a medical college with three hundred students, and a university, styled the "Western Military Institute" and boasting of three hundred scholars, were here located.

At one period twelve newspapers were published in this city—five of them being dailies. She possessed a large banking capital. Her suspension bridge, spanning the Cumberland River, was a glory in architecture and popular estimation. Her public water and gas works were ample, and built at great expense; and she boasted of eight elegant stone turnpikes, leading to the interior in various directions and to adjoining States. At her feet was poured the traffic from three extensive railroad-thoroughfares, which extended hundreds of miles to Alabama, to Georgia and East Tennessee, and through Kentucky to Louisville. She lay at the head of navigation of the Cumberland River a fine boating-stream during two-thirds of the year and navigable for small craft the year round.

Her merchants controlled a vast cotton and tobacco trade, and supplied the Southern interior, hundreds of miles in extent, with dry-goods, hardware, and the thousand articles of American and foreign manufacture. Her business streets were lined with monster mercantile concerns, and her suburbs were resplendent with beautiful cottages and almost palatial mansions and delightful groves of aged forest-trees. A visitor to this fair city previous to the rebellion, when viewing all that we have just described, and witnessing in addition the fleet of steamers at the levee, the rush of business upon the streets, and the sweeping-by of dashing carriages and gayly-arrayed riding-parties mounted on blooded horses, might safely conclude that Nashville was one of the favoured cities of the world.

The boom of the cannon that first opened upon Sumter proved the funeral knell of all this peace and happiness. Intoxicated with prosperity, its votaries abandoned the principles of government which alone had created and secured it. Spoiled by a pernicious social system, they launched forth upon an ocean of false doctrines which were repudiated by all civilized nations. The story of the political storms in Tennessee—of the persistent efforts of the Nashville secession leaders—of the several votes forced upon the people before secession could be invested with legal semblance—of the distrust and reluctance of the masses—we need not pause to relate: it is history.

Once fully committed to the rebellion, the rebel leaders at Richmond deigned to throw some sops to their Western "metropolis," and extensive military-depots were created, shops and foundries were set in motion, cannon were cast, gunboats were put in process of construction, percussion-caps and soldiers' clothing were manufactured by the million, and thousands of hogs were packed for the use of the Confederate Armies. Verily, it was asserted that Nashville would speedily eclipse Louisville, Cincinnati, and St. Louis—that her prospects were excellent for becoming, in fact, the capital of the great Southern Confederation.

Thus, for a season, affairs went, on swimmingly in Nashville, and until the fall of Fort Donelson occurred. Up to that period, almost, there had existed a strong Union element in the city; but the secessionists had taken measures to root it out effectually, the prominent Union men being driven from their homes to the North. A "vigilance committee" had been formed, its avowed object being to "spot" every adherent to the old government, and to notify him to take the oath of allegiance to rebellion, to enter its ranks as a soldier, or contribute visibly and liberally to its support, or to choose the alternative—banishment from the place.

Such a notice was served upon the venerable patriot, Judge Catron, of the Supreme Court of the United States, who was a resident of that city. He scornfully cast the dust of the rebellious city from his feet, and left his home and property to their fate. Upon the evening of the day preceding the surrender of Fort Donelson, the rebel citizens of Nashville held high carnival. They met in a public place, indulged in wild, vociferous speechification and shouts, and improvised a torchlight procession, carrying secession flags, emblems, and transparencies, bearing aloft huge, rough iron pikes—which latter invention signified utter demolition of the invading Yankees. The orgies were under the management of little Dick Cheatham, the mayor of the city. Speeches were made of an extravagant character—a liberal portion of them being devoted to denunciation of the Unionists of that city and State.

"Yes," quoth Cheatham, "drive 'em out from among us. Let me deal with these traitors, and I will hang 'em first and try 'em afterwards!"

But there was a fate in store for the rebels of Nashville of which they little dreamed. Up to the time above mentioned, all had gone well at Donelson. Hourly reports came up that the Federal Army was kept at bay and their gunboats repulsed. Steamers were plying busily between the city and the fort, forwarding supplies and reinforcements. The weather was extremely inclement, the late snows and rainstorms of winter being at hand, and the men of both armies were suffering almost incredible hardships, standing ankle-deep in the frozen slush and mud of the trenches.

During the week previous, the ladies of Nashville, with a devotion worthy of a better cause, had loaded a steamboat with carpets taken from their floors, and spare bedding and warm clothing of all kinds, for their suffering soldiers. Upon the surrender these carpets were found cut into strips, with a hole in the centre, hanging over the shoulders of the half-frozen rebel soldiers.

The Sabbath of February 16, 1862, is an epoch in the history of Nashville and of Tennessee. Until ten o'clock that morning all was well with the rebellion. The last boat up from Donelson, arriving several hours previous, reported still stronger evidence of the defeat of the Federals. At the usual hour the church-bells of the city called its people forth to public worship. It was a beautiful Sabbath morning, bright sunshine succeeding many days of winter darkness and storm, and there was a general attendance. The clergy of Nashville had offered their prayers for the rebellion—for they were wild secessionists to a man—and had taken their texts, when, lo! a hum of excitement and commotion began to be manifest in the streets.

Some notices were handed in at the doors and were carried to the sacred desks. The ministers paused, and clutched eagerly at what they supposed was welcome intelligence. They read it aloud with ashen cheek and faltering tongue. Donelson had surrendered!—the Confederate Army was captured!—the Federal gunboats were now on their way up the river to destroy the city!

The people rushed from the churches to find confusion and dismay visible in the streets upon every hand. There was now a gathering-up of valuables and a pressing of teams of every description. Wagons, carts, drays, and every animal that could be found were at once put in requisition. The city authorities were palsied. The rebel army stores were opened, and the citizens urged to aid in removing the vast amounts of pork, sugar, etc., to the railroad depot and to the interior. But the people had their personal safety nearest at heart, and the invitation was disregarded.

A crowd of the poorer classes swarmed around the commissary and quartermaster depots, and began an indiscriminate appropriation of hams, shoulders, sugar, clothing, and goods of every description. The wholesale stores, and even dry-goods and silk houses, were burst open, or purposely thrown open, and whole bolts of cloth, entire pieces of costly fabrics, armfuls of boots and shoes, and rolls of new carpeting, were thrown pell-mell into the street, or lay loose upon the floors and walks, awaiting the disposal of the mob.

Squads of soldiers assailed the beautiful suspension bridge with axes, saws, and cold chisels, and, after hours of cursing and exertion, succeeded in utterly destroying it. The elegant railroad bridge was given to the flames. At the State House were seen gangs of excited men in shirtsleeves, rushing out with the archives and other valuable public property, and tossing them loosely into wagons, to be carried to the Chattanooga depot for instant shipment to the South. Ere long the *hegira* of Nashville secessionism was under full headway.

Families were hurried off in every possible manner, the turnpikes leading southward being lined with the fugitives. By sunset all had gone who could go; and these kept going all night, many of them not stopping until they reached Shelbyville, Fayetteville, and even Huntsville, Alabama.

This frantic evacuation was in character with the preceding features of the rebellion—as wild and as causeless. Vast amounts of property were needlessly destroyed, and the boastful secessionists who had so valiantly carried the pikes in procession the night previous, and had cheered at the spectacle, had shown the world that their courage was of words rather than of deeds. No gunboats came up the river; and not until a full week afterwards—the following Sabbath—did the Federal Army arrive opposite Nashville.

After a day or two, the valorous rebel citizens, recovering from their fright, began to realise the value and comforts of home, and commenced their return to the city. During the entire week after the flight, Mayor Cheatham was anxiously casting about for some appearing Federal force, to whom he could perform the farce of a formal surrender of the city. Upon the succeeding Sabbath, the Federal Army appeared across the river, and Cheatham and one or two other city dignitaries crossed in a "dug out," and, in terms and manner very different from the week before, he tendered the submission of the helpless and prostrate city.

The Federal Army met with a chilling reception upon its entering Nashville. The streets were almost deserted; the stores and shops were entirely closed; there was not a hotel open. Where, but a few days before, rebel flags had waved defiantly upon hundreds of house-tops, now not one could be seen to greet the presence of the National forces. If there were a few Unionists present, they were as yet too greatly cowed, and the Federal power was too recently asserted, to permit a demonstration in the midst of such universal hatred.

Matters thus remained during Buell's campaign in the South. Upon his retreat to Kentucky in pursuit of Bragg, the rebel citizens of Nashville were greatly emboldened. And when Bragg again retreated from Kentucky and moved up to Murfreesborough, they were still confident of his victory over the Federal forces; for, up to this time, they had not lost confidence in the ultimate success of the rebel armies and leaders. But when General Rosecrans entered Nashville with his army, matters began to wear a different aspect. Other causes also contributed to this result. New Orleans was conquered and firmly held; the National Government was beginning to put forth its power in earnestness—its vast armies and fleets assailing the rebels upon every quarter; and we had commenced undermining them in their most vital point, by operating against them with their slaves. The vast fortifications now being erected by the Federals around the city assured them that they were conquered, and the influence of all this upon such a people was plainly visible.

Still, they clung feebly to hope, until after the final defeat of Bragg before Murfreesborough. From that day to the present the leading rebels of Nashville and of all Tennessee have despaired, and, as time has rolled away, they have gradually become more disheartened in their own bad cause, and more ready and desirous to make their peace with the Federal Government.

We stated that she was one of the brightest, most wealthy and prosperous cities of the Union. Of all this she is now (1863) the exact reverse. Her finest buildings, such as her colleges, churches, and elegant stores, are used as military hospitals and store-houses. Her streets are dirty, and, where main outlets from the city, they have been cut in two—dug out, as though a canal was being made through them—the dirt thrown up on each side, as barricades against a rebel attack upon the city, when it was invested and threatened last year. Her suburbs are a mournful wreck in many localities—houses deserted, fences gone, fruit-trees gnawed and disfigured; and the pedestrian is only reminded that he is passing over what was once a smiling garden, by his feet catching against some yet struggling and crushed grape-vine or rose-bush.

The groves—the glory of the place—are cut down, and the grounds present the appearance of a new "clearing," a stump-field. St. Cloud Hill, once the fashionable retreat, where children romped amid the lovely shade, and where lovers lisped in cooing numbers, is now a bleak, barren, granite mountain, a frowning fortress rising from its summit, with cannon trained upon and about the devoted city. The old, wealthy merchants—those who yet remain—are prostrate in the dust of bankruptcy, and new traders—men from the North—are daily rising up in their places. The several printing-offices are held by the United States authorities as subject to confiscation, and some of them are leased, and their material is now being used in battling for

56

free government. The extensive Methodist Book Concern (Church South) has long been closed and in the hands of the United States Marshal, its managers and apostles taking to the rebellion, at the very outset, as naturally as the young waterfowl seeks its familiar element.

In short, the city of Nashville is stagnant, prostrate and in the abject position of a subjugated city. She is changing, however; and as the Union is more surely restored, and its future guaranteed, she will revive. New men will enter, and new and better times will ensue. She will be purged from the curse that has afflicted her and dragged her down. Slavery will no longer blight and wither her morals; nor will a haughty, unproductive aristocracy prey upon her vitals. Tennessee, with free labour, has the capability of becoming one of the grandest States of the Union; and Nashville is her crown-jewel. May the old State speedily emerge from the mire in which she has been forced to wallow by the wildness of her spoiled leaders, and may her coronal gem, the "Rock City," shine all the brighter for her momentary eclipse when, no longer a type of devastating rebellion, her name shall stand as a synonym of prosperity, beauty, and progress!

Chapter 11: The Army Police and Its Chief

As described in the previous chapter, such was Nashville, where our fair lady had arrived without further interruption, and where she immediately took up her abode at the City Hotel, kept by a Mr. Wyndham. All "Secessia" of course heard at once of her coming, and numerous were the visits of condolence, or, rather, congratulation at her escape from the Federal power at Louisville—for already had the fact become bruited abroad that she had succeeded in getting away from that city without even getting a "pass," or taking the oath of allegiance. Of course, these visits were received in a manner calculated to strengthen the belief entertained by her sympathising visitors, that she was a staunch rebel.

She arrived on Saturday; on the Monday following the theatre opened with "The Married Rake"—Miss Mary Mitchell, sister, we believe, of the beautiful and accomplished Miss Maggie Mitchell, being leading lady. In compliance with military orders, the overture consisted always of three national airs; at least, they were to be played during the evening—while the performers, if they sang at all, were compelled to select at least one national song. Miss Cushman, of course, had to comply with the regulations, though it was generally believed, by her rebel friends, that she did so under protest.

She was, however, very successful, and equally popular, on account of her sprightliness and beauty, with both Union people and "*secesh*" sympathisers. The soldiers loved her because they could not help admiring so magnificent a specimen of a woman—rebel or not; while the rebels liked her, thinking that she was of their own mongrel party. Her stay at the theatre, nevertheless, was a short one; for one day, on returning home after rehearsal, she found a note awaiting her from the chief of army police of Nashville.

This worthy individual, who has been a terror to evil-doers in the Southwest, and who figures somewhat prominently in our story, was engaged, with two others, at the outbreak of the rebellion, in the construction of a railroad from New Orleans to Houston, Texas. Upon the fall of Fort Sumter, the secession element in the State became too strong to be endured by Northern men, and early in May, soon after the violent deposition of Governor Houston, Colonel Truesdail left Texas and came to Missouri. Upon General Pope taking command of the army in Northwestern Missouri, he was appointed Military Superintendent of the North Missouri Railroad. Soon after, General Pope was recalled to St. Louis; and the colonel then contracted to supply General Grant's army with beef, and continued the business under General Jefferson C. Davis, and again under General Pope when he re-entered the field.

With him he also had charge of the police and secret service, the scouts and couriers, and the forwarding of mails and despatches; and in these and other labours he performed valuable service in that wild, interior country. Throughout the New Madrid, Island No. 10, and Fort Pillow campaign, in the trip up the Tennessee, and during the operations in front of and beyond Corinth, he remained with General Pope, by whom the worth of his great services was freely and constantly acknowledged. When the latter general was ordered to Virginia, he invited Colonel Truesdail to go with him; but, preferring to remain in the West, where his family reside and his property is, and where he believed he would be more useful, he declined the invitation,

General Rosecrans, upon assuming command of the Army of the Mississippi, retained the colonel in his position. The completely unsettled condition of affairs in Mississippi at that time gave room for the display of his peculiar genius. The army mail and police service were irregular in their workings, and scarcely more than nominal in their existence. A new and complete organisation of each was soon effected.

Military mail-agents were placed on the boats and trains, and offices opened all along the route between Cairo and Corinth. A police system was put into operation that began at once to be felt throughout the army and all the country within our lines.

The first arrest made under it was that of a high official in General Grant's employ, who was convicted of the fraudulent appropriation of several thousand dollars, and sentenced by that general to two years imprisonment. Colonel Truesdail continued in this department until the assignment of General Rosecrans to the command of the Department of the Cumberland, when he was induced to accompany the general to his new field of operations—although, personally, he was disinclined to longer service, having now been actively and constantly engaged since the beginning of the war, absent all the while from his home and family.

At Bowling Green the army mail system was organised; and policemen were put at work, not only there, but in the larger towns along the line of the Louisville and Nashville Railroad, and a surprising amount of knavery, smuggling, and guerillaism was discovered. Upon reaching Nashville, the police business at once assumed vast proportions. The city was full of violent and confessed rebels, most of whom were both smugglers and spies, as opportunity offered. The army had drawn thither its usual corrupt and festering element of camp-followers. The entire community was rotten, morally and socially.

Murder, robbery drunkenness, and all the nameless vices of rebeldom and war, were openly and shamelessly rampant. The government was victimized at every turn. Horses and mules, stolen from neighbouring farms and stables, were hawked about the streets for purchasers, at prices ranging from ten to fifty dollars per head. Arms were pilfered and sold for a trifle. Boots, shoes, uniforms, camp-equipage, ammunition, and supplies of every kind, serviceable to the rebel army, were daily sent beyond our lines in every possible way that the ingenuity of bad men and women could devise.

In a short time, the influence of the army police was felt in every part of the city and army. His patrols were upon every road leading from the city, arresting and searching rebel emissaries, and at times confiscating considerable amounts of contraband goods. His detectives were in every hotel, and upon every car and steamer. Assuming the role of rebel sympathisers, they were introduced into the proudest and wealthiest secession families. Passing themselves of in many cases, as spies of Wheeler, Bragg, and Morgan, they acquainted themselves with the secrets, the hopes, and the intentions of that entire people. Men were also busy among our own camps, detecting army vice and fraud. Their searching eyes were on the several army departments, hospitals, theatres, houses of ill-fame, and every centre of public interest; and a minute report of all these investigations and their results would thrill the land.

Many offenders thus detected were vigorously dealt with; and yet the police records of the department reveal instances of young men made wiser and better by the kindness shown and the advice given them. Humane, benevolent, and far-seeing, yet prompt to visit with merited punishment the hardened offender, none were more ready than our Chief of Police to temper justice with mercy. The many instances of charity to the destitute, of forgiveness to youthful follies of the young men whom he has aided and counselled, of widows and orphans he assisted to fuel and bread during the hard winter at Nashville, of the young women found in male attire whom he and his assistants have decently clothed and sent to their homes and of deserted children for whom he has found asylums, would of themselves fill many pages of this work.

True, errors and wrongs may have been committed; many an arrest may have been made without good reason therefor, and many goods seized that ought to have been untouched; true, many bad men may have wormed themselves into its service; but, where such has been the case, none more ready to make restitution none more severe in punishment of official treachery and knavery, than its justice-loving chief. All in all, he has done well, and has exercised the utmost care in the selection of his subordinates. For be it always remembered that there are but few men fitted for the business of a detective, and a still less number are found who will follow it. In large cities, and with armies, the detective is a necessity; and yet it is a profession whose follower is and must be one continued counterfeit. Bad men can make it detestable; but pure-minded, upright officers, operating secretly and in disguise though they may, *can* perform their duties with marvellous certainty in the detection of crime, with incalculable benefit to the public, and without injury to the innocent.

That the most worthy motives actuate the subject of this sketch in all his official dealings, the author has abundant reason to know. Colonel Truesdail (he is called "colonel" by general consent, though a civilian and quite regardless of titles) is possessed of a handsome private fortune, which thus far has been diminished, rather than increased, by his army labours. Though a Southern man as regards the location of a great portion of his property and by reason of many years' residence in the slave States, he has from the first been an original and uncompromising friend of the Union.

The results of the army police operations have been immense, both in gain to the government and prevention of crime. Hundreds of horses and mules have been seized and turned over to the quartermaster's department. Scores of smugglers and spies have been detected and punished, thus largely curtailing this under-ground trade, alike beneficial to the rebels and detrimental to us. Large amounts of goods and medicines have been confiscated and sold, where the parties implicated were found *flagrante delicto*; and thus, this branch of the army has considerably more than repaid its entire cost to the government. Connected with it also, is the spy department, from which a line of communication has been constantly maintained throughout the rebel States, to the extreme limits of the Southern Confederacy.

As may be readily supposed, such an extensive army organisation ere long attained considerable notoriety. It marshalled its friends and its enemies in almost regimental numbers. Even in the army it has been violently assailed—not only by the vicious in the ranks, but by officers whose evil deeds were not past finding out. If any direct charge was made, however, to General Rosecrans, it was at once and fully investigated; and in no one instance has the charge been maintained, as affecting the good character of its chief or of his principal aids.

Chapter 12: Her Instructions and the Oath

Such was the man before whom our heroine was to appear; and, on entering his office in obedience to his summons, she was politely received by the chief himself, who greeted her at first as a stranger, but, after dismissing his clerks, acknowledged the many excellent reports which he had received from Louisville respecting her services to the government whilst there. He finished by saying, in an earnest, impressive manner,

"But, Miss Cushman, all that you have yet done is as nothing compared with the service which it is now in your power to render your country. I have heard much of your courage, your devotion, and ready expedients; but what I want you to do now will demand a quickness of intellect and a powerful constitution, a ready wit and the courage of a soldier tried in a thousand fields; and I know not, indeed, why I have selected you in preference to everyone else, except it be that I know you to be *true,* and to possess that unusual courage which is needed for this expedition."

"You flatter me, sir, by your kind opinion," remarked Miss Cushman, bowing in return to the high eulogy vouchsafed her by her superior officer. "May I ask what this service is which you demand of me?"

"It is an undertaking of extreme, of unusual, peril, Miss Cushman," answered the colonel, as though to warn her that it was no slight service that was demanded of her.

Miss Cushman looked up into his dark, Spanish-looking face, heavily and forcibly furrowed. It bore an expression more solemn than usual, while an anxious, troubled look was in his coal-black eyes.

"It is an undertaking, Miss Cushman, that may lead to glory or end in death," he continued, still warningly.

"I do not fear the latter," answered the young girl, calmly.

"Aye, but *ignominious death!* death by the bullet or, worse, as a spy, by the *rope!*"

At these words the beautiful girl shrank back, and almost involuntarily clasped her neck with her hands. It may be that she paled slightly, but she answered in a firm tone:

"Colonel Truesdail, hundreds, aye, thousands, of our noble soldiers, each one of greater service to our country than my poor self, have gladly given up their lives in her cause. Should I hesitate to do as much? No; I will do all that a woman *should* do, and all that a *man* dare do, for my country and the glorious Union!"

"Spoken like a brave woman!" exclaimed the colonel in ecstasy, regarding the noble and inspired form of our heroine with a look of admiration. "If you are prepared, then, to undertake the work, I will no longer withhold the secret of its nature. But you are sure——"

A disdainful waving of the young girl's hand interrupted him. It seemed to say, What I have once promised I will perform. There were many of the Indian associations of her youth still clinging to Pauline Cushman, and the action was full of the dignity of the forest and its red-skinned denizens.

The colonel understood it. "I will say no more then, of danger. To a mind like your own the word but spurs you on to new efforts, while I doubt if your heart ever knew the word at all. Your past life assures me of this, and your actions, your every gesture, proclaim it. What the government wants, then, is for you to secretly visit the headquarters of the rebel General Bragg."

"Go to Bragg's headquarters! It is a rough road! one along which more hemp grows than corn," remarked our heroine, lightly.

"It is indeed a rough road; but the benefit to your country, if you accomplish it, will be correspondingly great, for we are particularly anxious now to learn the plans and intentions of General Bragg. The whole fate of the country may depend upon it."

"Never fear, colonel: if within the possibility of man or woman you shall have them."

"It is well. I have selected you for several reasons: first of all, you will have more opportunities, as a woman, of gaining the good favour of the rebel officers with whom you will necessarily come in contact. These you must play upon, making them your tools: you can do it," he added, smiling. "Another reason is that your late role as a '*secesh* sympathiser" is widely spread all over rebeldom, and you will not create suspicion by coming among them. As though to favour your undertaking, too, many rebel women are being sent South, in obedience to General Mitchel's late order to that effect."

"I think, too," interposed Miss Cushman, "that I can add a new reason, which is, that I have a brother, A. A. Cushman. who is a colonel somewhere in the rebel army he and I never having agreed in politics."

"So much the better. You can then make it appear as though you were searching for your brother. This may be of great service to you in enabling you to travel from headquarters to headquarters, for down there their knowledge of the whereabouts of individuals is very obscure, more so than with us in the North, where we have railroads and telegraphs traversing every section of the country. Having come to this determination, then, there remains but two things to be done yet: the first is, to receive your instructions, which I will proceed to give you; the second is, to take the required oath of faithfulness in the performance of your arduous duties.

"As to your instructions, give them your greatest attention. The expedition you have so bravely resolved to undertake will not only be attended by great responsibility but with great personal risk, involving perhaps your life. It behoves you therefore to be careful, ever on your guard and vigilant. With other ladies, you will be, for good reasons, ordered out of the Federal lines, under General Mitchel's order sending rebel sympathisers in Nashville, South. You will be given a printed copy of such order. This you will carry with you, and under no circumstances will you communicate, to the dearest friend you have any idea but that you are a refugee, and a real victim. Others going with you will favour you in this respect.

"In doing so, you must be careful, and cautious against talking and saying too much, merely answering, in a modest and intelligent manner, the many questions that will be put to you. Make your answers according to the instructions I shall give you, and be careful to make the *same answers to all parties*, either officers, soldiers, or civilians, so that you may avoid making inconsistent or contradictory statements. This is of great importance. Your story once framed, never deviate from it. Keep constantly before the minds of all you come in contact with your great anxiety to find your brother, an officer in the Confederate Army.

"Let this, to all appearances, be the all-absorbing object of your thoughts and affections; casually alluding, however, to your ill-treatment by the Federal officers in Nashville, in thrusting you out of the city alone and unprotected, and not allowing you even time to procure your baggage. On reaching the enemy's pickets, show your papers, and request to be taken to the headquarters of the commanding officer. On reaching them, state to the officer your case in a frank and free manner; express great anxiety to find your *brother*, and ask him to give you protection and aid.

"The Confederate Armies are now located at Columbia, Shelbyville, Wartrace, Tullahoma (Bragg's headquarters), and Manchester. I desire you, if possible, to reach all these points, under the *pretence of searching for your brother*. When you reach the first commanding officer, ask him to give you a kind letter to the next commanding general, and so on, till you reach the command in which your brother may be. In visiting various headquarters, you will doubtless be detained some time at each, and questioned closely as to our forces in and around Nashville. Your answers will be in accordance with the instructions I shall give you. Be careful, at all times, to make no inquiries yourself, of officers or others, as to the strength of the Confederate forces, their movements, the amount of artillery, ammunition, etc., as this might create suspicion.

"In consequence of your attractive personal appearance and modest demeanour, you will have many attentions paid you by general and staff officers, and will be invited to ride out through their camps, and visit their fortifications. Accept all these invitations, but with some hesitancy and *seeming caution* as to the *propriety* of such excursions. While riding with them, ask to visit the poor sick and wounded soldiers in the hospitals. When there, you can inquire of the surgeons as to whether they have all necessary medicines and hospital supplies; from what source they receive them; the number of sick and wounded soldiers, etc.

"While passing through the different camps, pay particular attention to the extent of the fortifications; the size and number of pieces of artillery in position the extent of the fortifications on the south side of Shelbyville and Tullahoma, and on the east side of the latter place. Retain in your mind the exact location of all these works, taking the great Huntsville north and south road, near the railroad depot, in Tullahoma, as the centre of the town. From this point you can get a good view of many of their works. Impress upon your mind all important sayings of officers, as to supplies, contemplated movements, etc.

"You cannot, and will not, make any memorandum or tracings of any kind. There is but one kind of memorandum you can keep, and that is, of your expenses. Put down name of house, amount of your bill, and the date. This is the common practice, and will excite no suspicion, and will serve you when you return to refresh your memory of any events that may transpired.

"Be careful to learn the names of men and women who visit the rebel forces from Nashville. They have a large number of men and women employed as spies who visit Nashville and return with goods and information. Ascertain, as far as possible, without making their acquaintance, every particular concerning them."

These instructions given, the colonel advanced with serious mien to our heroine again:

"Miss Cushman," he said, "not for one moment do I doubt your sincerity in our cause. There are, however, some formalities which I dare not dispense with. One of my instructions, then, is to have you repeat the following oath. The lives of many depend on it!"

Slowly and impressively, he then read the following sacred obligation:

United States of America, Department of the Cumberland, Office Chief of Army Police, May 26, 1863.

I, Pauline Cushman, do solemnly swear that I will bear true allegiance and fidelity to the Government of the United States of America, and that I will faithfully serve the same, during the time that I am employed in the service of the Army of the Cumberland, to the best of my knowledge and ability; that I will observe and obey all the instructions which may be given me; that I will, in no manner or form, convey or give any information to the enemies of the Government of the United States, which will be of advantage to them, or injury to the Federal cause So help me God.

Slowly and clearly our heroine repeated the impressive words of the oath, and clasping a small American flag, which stood near, to her breast reverentially kissed its folds, while she echoed the words, "So help me God!"

Chapter 13: Sent Beyond the Lines

The romance of the affair in which our heroine had embarked her fortunes and her hopes had, it is but reasonable to suppose, concealed hitherto the full extent of the dangers to which she would necessarily be exposed. The adventures which she was to live so soon required the stoutest nerve, the coolest self-possession, the most evenly-balanced judgment, the quickest perceptions, and the most exhaustless fertility of resources. A man may, in open day, and in the presence of his comrades, perform feats of valour, and, aided by the drill-room, practice equal exploits of skill. He is one among many who are exposed. He is cheered and sustained by the gaze of his comrades, and he has no isolated responsibility resting upon him, especially where he is merely acting under orders. But the secret agent sent among the disloyal at home, or the enemy beyond the lines, is alone.

He, individually, must bear the vigilant scrutiny of many eyes, keenly alive to danger. He, alone, must possess the tact and the ready ruse to evade the strictness of hostile military rules and the research of acute and suspicious intellects, seeking openly, as well as in the dark, to guard their own designs and penetrate those of their opponents, just as he is doing. He must be book and sword, and counsellor, all in one, to himself, and if he fail, if an unlucky accident, an unforeseen combination of circumstances, a single moment of unwariness, or a too hasty conclusion, betray him amid the meshes he is threading, woe to him! He is a spy, and even by military law he has nothing to expect but instant and ignominious death. A look, a word, the dropping of a paper, the rustle of a leaf may, at any moment, seal his doom at the very height of expected triumph, and then the quick bullet, the steel or the rope is his portion.

Even should he safely perform his task, among the very people he has served he has long to struggle against the obloquy which seems to attach to the very name of "spy." Even the supreme testimony of Washington himself, and the touching eloquence of the pen of Fennimore Cooper have scarcely, at this late day, dispelled the cloud that rested until and after death upon the name of "Harvey Birch."

Moreover, to the moral risks of every kind involved in this service must be added the continual discomforts of scanty fare, and rude exposure on lonely bivouacs; the long, toilsome march on foot, or the dreary ride through an enemy's country; the necessity of pressing onward through mist and rain, and snow, and frost, over rugged mountains; through arid or marshy valleys; wading swamps and rivers; scaling or descending precipices at any hour of the day or night, just as occasion may demand. These, too, forming but a part of all the enormous catalogue of miseries, the faithful scout must regard as matters of course in the life that he has chosen.

Why, the majority of ordinary men would shrink from the very thought of such a struggle in return for such poor compensation as the regulations of the service can allow: and yet, reader, among our true-hearted American women, delicately reared and nurtured as they are, have been found spirits that have not quailed before all these perils and fatigues—noble beings, who, fired by the pure flame of patriotism, have braved the night, the wilderness, hunger, thirst, and the anger of the enemy only that they might benefit their country. Have we not justly claimed a place for one among the galaxy of heroic spirits which our country claims as its own? Is it asking too much that her gallant exploits should be impressed on every loyal heart? But to our story.

Many matters had to be arranged in connection with our heroine's departure, the further to hoodwink the secession sympathisers of Nashville. Considerable stir was then created, all, of course, in an underhand manner, so as to make the matter more impressive.

As might be expected, these cowardly rebels—for they were *rebels* in every respect, except in that of courage to maintain their principles in the field—these cowardly rebels, then, were much exercised upon hearing that our fair heroine was to be sent across the lines, for having uttered treasonable sentiments and given countenance to the rebellion.

The query naturally arose among them—"Who next? If this woman deserves to be sent across the lines, what fate should await myself, who have been furnishing information to my rebel friends, and aiding the Confederate States in every manner possible?" and the answer came: Death—*death* should be the meed of such villains, and the cowardly traitor would sink his bead abashed, for, in spite of our sinfulness, we all know perfectly well when we are doing anything wrong. So, with the traitor to his country and his flag, he is as conscious of guilt as was Cain when he fled from the avenging hand of his God; yet so strong a hold has the devil upon him that he still *persists* in his infernal course, the only end of which, as he well knows, must be dire and certain ruin.

Oh, who can understand the dread infatuation of these men? Who credulous enough to believe, without ocular demonstration, that there are men sinful enough, *mad* enough to assail a government such as ours has been? Future generations must disbelieve it. They cannot be brought to the thought that in the latter part of the nineteenth century, when civilization and progress had attained their highest eminence, that there were men, *Americans*, who would have retarded the wheel of Progress, and sent it retrograding into the ages of darkness and barbarism. Such, however, is the end and aim of this rebellion. Alas! that we should have to record it.

The "secession sympathisers" of Nashville were such benighted, such demented creatures. Without the coinage to seize the spokes of the great wheel, they smoothed the path down which they fondly believed it must pass over; oiling, with their snake-like tongues first this, then that difficult passage, until the slime of their treacherous venom should pave the path for the destruction of their country. What fate should be theirs? Loyal men, we ask you. Should they not burn with shame now, when they read of the heroic actions of that woman—a lone, weak woman—in behalf of that country which they would so meanly have ruined? But they would not. No, there is not a traitor in Nashville at this day—*and there are plenty of them*—that would feel any sensation of shame whatever. They are past blushing.

At the period of which we write, however, they were ready with their accursed sympathy for our noble-minded heroine, because they believed her to be one of their own kind. On the morning, then, on which it had been bruited abroad that she was to take her compulsory departure, there was quite a crowd of these gentry gathered in front of her apartments.

It was a glorious May morning when Miss Cushman was thus called upon to commence her journey, and everything about her wore a joyous air, except the countenances of the secret sympathisers, which were in gloomy keeping with the dark fate which they supposed was to be the bad fortune of our heroine. Major J. B. Stockton, who accompanied her, also wore a fitting solemnity of countenance; though, had he had his way, it is probable that he would have laughed in spite of himself, at the change which must have taken place in the faces of the spectators had they known the real circumstances of the case. It was as much as our heroine could do, to keep a straight face through it all.

At last, she was seated in the close-covered carriage which Major Stockton had brought to convey her, first to the office of the chief of police, and next beyond the limits of the Federal "lines." On arriving at Colonel Truesdail's office, Miss Cushman was received, as usual, most kindly, and many excellent verbal hints and directions were given her. After these were delivered and thankfully listened to, the colonel arose, and, extending his hand to our heroine, spoke as follows:

"You have selected a dangerous role, my fair lady; but I believe you have the courage and perseverance to carry it out. If you do, no name should be inscribed higher upon the scroll of Fame. If you fail, which, alas! I fear, your grave will be among the unhonoured and unsung. This is not consoling language, fair lady," he continued; "but I do not wish to have to acknowledge to myself that I have withheld one atom of truth bearing upon this venture which you are about to undertake. If, therefore, now that you have fully thought it over, and had ample time for reflection, you should hesitate, it is not too late to retract——"

"Retract!" interrupted our heroine, scornfully. "I thought, Colonel Truesdail, that I had already given some proofs of my determination when engaged in a just cause. I am not one to retract when I am once convinced that I am right! No, sir. The worst can come—heaven forbid that it should!—yet, I say it can come, *and find me prepared to meet it without one regret.*"

Regarding the noble woman with the deepest admiration, as one entirely above the ordinary scope of mortals, the colonel extended his hand afresh, and grasping that of the young girl warmly, bade her Godspeed. "May heaven protect you, Pauline Cushman. That you may return safe to us is my earnest prayer!"

"But here," he added, "I have a present for you," and taking a fine "six-shooter," with all the requisites, from the table, he presented it to her. "It may prove that best of all friends—a friend in need."

"Believe me, when it does, I shall not hesitate to call upon it," answered the young girl, merrily. Then thanking the colonel for his handsome present, she bade him a final *adieu*, and re-entering the close carriage, and accompanied as before, took the road leading. . .

Away down South to Dixie.

On arriving at a spot removed from any houses, and three miles distant from Nashville, Miss Cushman and her companion alighted. They found there Colonel Truesdail's own servant, who held by the bridle a magnificent bay horse, fully caparisoned, and winch impatiently pawed the ground. The boy, who was in the secret, on recognising Miss Cushman, at first seemed much agitated, and at last fairly burst into tears, so satisfied was he that Miss Cushman was going never to return alive. In touching accents, he begged of her to stay; for the lady had been kind to him, and he had learned to look upon her as some beautiful star, whose presence had guided him, and who sometimes even deigned to smile upon him.

Our heroine had, however, a duty to perform, and comforting the poor boy as well as she was able, and shaking the hand of her friend, Major Stockton, mounted her horse, and galloped gayly down the Hardin pike, followed by the good wishes of the major, and the prayers and invocations of his humbler but no less honest companion.

Chapter 14: Milam, the Smuggler

Our heroine was now fairly launched out for herself, and began to experience all the varied sensations of hope and anticipations of good and evil which her situation and lonely position might reasonably inspire. Not a *fear*, however, blanched her cheek for even an instant—she was too much of the soldier for that; but she weighed all the probabilities, and, while not shrinking from even the worst, dared to look it boldly in the face.

She left those behind her whom she loved, never perhaps to meet them on this earth again. The thought was a gloomy one! the more so when she began to take in the peculiarities of her position.

The road before her lay through what was generally called and regarded as the "neutral ground"—which in other words means a licensed place for the *desperadoes* of both armies to roam. Gangs of the most fearful men paroled it daily, men who would murder just for the sake, as it seemed, of committing fresh crime, and "keeping their hand in."

It was not a pleasant situation for a woman, truly. The exhilaration, however, induced by the spirited bounds of her noble steed soon dispelled all gloomy misgivings. There is something in being mounted upon a fine charger which stirs the blood, and makes the heart ready to respond to the most daring promptings. What enthusiasm like that of the cavalryman as he feels himself borne rapidly down upon the charging masses of the enemy! The whirl, the rapid motion inspire him with an almost supernatural courage, and his heart beats high and his pulse fevers with the thought of glory!

There is an inspiration in being mounted upon a fine horse, and our heroine gave herself up to the feeling, implicitly. The eleven miles which separated her from her destination, then, were almost passed before she could realise that half that distance had been traversed; and as she approached the banks of the Big Harpeth River, and beheld the last rays of the setting sun crimsoning its waves, first comprehended the extent of her day's journey. The road here began to be thickly overshadowed—the great trees arching over the road and producing a gloom that even the approaching evening did not warrant.

The country began too, to become broken and wild and, to add to our heroine's embarrassment, the turn pike bridge, which here crossed the Big Harpeth, was found to be so injured by the rebels that it afforded scarce accommodation enough for a foot passenger, let alone a horse and rider to cross. A few planks only, carelessly and insecurely laid across the charred and blackened rafters, were the only footholds whereby to cross the bridge; while the dark flood beneath, rolling gloomily on, bespoke the fate of any one who should be so unfortunate as to lose his footing whilst crossing it.

To the right, however, our heroine noticed a small pathway, which seemed to run along the bank of the river, indicating probably the vicinity of a ford further down. Following it a short distance she remarked a nice-looking dwelling-house, which she approached, determining to ask whither the road led—to a ford or not.

On nearing the house, a tall, "*secesh*" looking woman came out and asked in the usual drawl what the stranger wanted.

"I am a hapless refugee," responded our heroine, sadly. "I have just been driven out of Nashville as sympathiser with the South. All I have in the world I carry on my back—for they stripped me of everything—my wardrobe, my jewels—everything!"

"What, the Federals?" asked the woman, at once enlisted in our heroine's behalf. "The Federals have driven you out of Nashville? Is that yere what you said, stranger?"

"Even so. They have sent me across the 'lines' because I dared to

71

say what I thought, and to tell them what tyrants they were; and my only hope is to find my brother, who is an officer in the Confederate Army. If therefore you will help me, and guide me to the ford below, I will be truly grateful to you."

"As for helpin' you, I'd do that right smart," answered the woman, "especially since you're of the right stripe, and ain't one of them darned 'Yanks'; but I must tell you aforehand that that yere ford is rather dangerous jist now, and I reckon you had best put up yere for the night, and I'll get my old man to guide you over in the morning."

"You see," she continued, as our heroine, in obedience to the invitation so pressingly given, prepared to dismount, "you see, Mr. Milam—that's my old man—he's gone to Nashville to get goods."

"To get goods?" queried Miss Cushman, wonderingly.

"Yes, to send over the river, you see," replied the woman, who no longer had any reserve before the "hapless refugee," as she believed our heroine to be.

"But how does he manage to get into Nashville without taking the 'oath?'" she asked again.

"Oh, Lor' bless you, he thinks no more of takin that yere Federal 'oath' than you would of drinking a glass of water!" and laughing sardonically over what she considered a good joke, the woman led Miss Cushman into the house. Here she was made as comfortable as circumstances would allow, and was entertained by the traitorous talk of the old woman who never tired of sneering at the "Federals," as she called the officers of the legitimate government. In all this abuse, Miss Cushman, of course, joined, and was for all appearances the very last person in the world to entertain any feeling but that of hate for the "darned Yanks!"

To use her own expression, though, her blood often "boiled" at these covert sneers and open slanders of the government and people she loved, delivered by this wretched specimen of womanhood; and she felt very much like presenting the good pistol which Colonel Truesdail had given her at Mrs Milam's head, and marching her back a prisoner to Nashville; but it was incompatible with her duties and her oath, so she could but listen, and bite her lips to conceal her chagrin.

During the evening Milam himself appeared. He drove up to the house in a small buggy, filled with articles of consumption, teas, coffee, etc., which of course were intended for his rebel friends on the other side of the river. As may be supposed, Miss Cushman did not find this much out until sometime after.

Milam himself was a tall, hollow-breasted man, with a black eye that looked as though it might shine in the dark, so full was it of fire. His eye too, was of a peculiar shape, being perfectly round instead of oval, and sunken in his head. It may be understood then that his first impression upon our heroine was not a very favourable one, and, as he advanced towards her, to greet her, in answer to his wife's introductory remark, of "a refugee from Yankee-land," the closely-compressed lips and wicked look of his mouth impressed her still more unfavourably.

Miss Cushman, her hostess and son, a boy about sixteen or seventeen, were at tea when Milam entered, and her host immediately took his place at the table, though not before he *had asked grace* in the hypocritical manner so characteristic of him. This grace was like his taking the oath, and intended, no doubt, with the hope of deceiving God, as he had already deceived the officers of his government—at least it is but natural to suppose so, for the next moment, almost, a brutal curse crossed his lips. Before Miss Cushman he had no reserve after the very flattering introductory remarks of his wife, He did not hesitate, therefore, to speak out his indignation against the d——d Yankees who had run off the slaves about the neighbourhood.

To enter into conversation with such a wretch was, at no time, a very pleasant duty; but it was one absolutely necessary, though unspeakably repugnant to our fair heroine. When he re-entered the house, therefore, she sought the first opportunity to speak with him.

"So, you want to find your brother in the Confederate Army, do ye?" he asked, in response to our heroine's statement of the causes of her journey.

"Well, we can help you to do that, I reckon! It's very few over there," pointing across the river, "that don't know Milam or his partner, 'Old Baker,'" he continued, with a coarse laugh. "I've run too many things across—hardware, muslins, sugar, tea, and coffee, aye, even muskets and ammunition—for them not to know me."

"But are you not afraid of getting caught?" asked Miss Cushman, quietly, and in the most innocent manner, as though just asking out of mere curiosity.

"Caught? Not much! Ye see, up at Nashville, the d——d Yanks believe I'm a Union man because I've took the *oath*. As though a *babe*, even, would stop for such a thing as that. Why, I'd take an oath every day in the year, if it would sell me a pound of coffee so, I'll be able to help you. Ye see, old Baker, that's my partner, takes the goods through and disposes of 'em; so, he can drive you in my buggy as far as General

Bragg's headquarters, provided you pay for it."

"I am willing to pay liberally," responded Miss Cushman; "so I can only get to my brother, who, I understand, is with General Bragg, and escape the persecution of the Federal officers of Nashville." It was therefore arranged that our heroine should start early the next morning; Milam first buying her horse and equipments, and lending her his buggy to proceed to General Bragg's headquarters; she paying the man Baker for the use of the same; also, for his services as driver. In pursuance of this plan, then, our heroine started out in the early morn as proposed, towards the land of Dixie, while Milam set out in the direction of Nashville, in quest of some runaway negroes, who had eloped from a neighbouring farm.

Chapter 15: Columbia and the Refugees

Through the woods and over most terrible roads our heroine had now to plod. The horse that pulled their little buggy was a good one, or Miss Cushman and her driver would never have reached their destination; which, by-the-by, was Columbia. For some time before it had rained, and almost incessantly did it storm and pour down rain in torrents, during her ten days journey. Now all who know anything at all about Southern roads can imagine the state and appearance of those which our heroine traversed. Sometimes the mud was literally up to the hubs of the wheels, and, indeed, she had not unfrequently to alight, that the man Baker might extricate the horse and buggy from what threatened to be their tomb. Through long, long, dreary woods, too, and through ruts and swollen streams, down which the clay-coloured water poured, as though ready to sweep everything before it, our heroine, undaunted, took her way.

Talleyrand, we believe, knowing the unnerving effect of rain upon the human system, once made the following remark upon it:

A tumult had broken out in Paris. The king and queen were very much alarmed. Every hour it increased, until at last it threatened to grow into a fearful revolution. Rumour, too, with her thousand tongues, added to the terrors of the royal house. It was said that an immense rabble was marching towards the palace, armed with the weapons they had already taken from the arsenal.

Many of the royal attendants counselled flight: Talleyrand alone said nothing. He had been watching the sky. The dark clouds hung heavy and threatening. A smile of satisfaction, mingled with a strange

74

contempt, dwelt upon his features. A drop of rain had fallen upon his outstretched hand. With his other hand he made a motion to the royal party to stop. "There will be no revolution today," he said, in his voice of scorn. "It rains!"

His prediction was verified to the letter. The populace, maddened into action by their wrongs, had indeed arisen in their might to avenge them. They were marching on the palace; for once rumour was right. All at once a drop of rain fell. Then it came down in torrents. Each revolutionist made for some shelter. They could face death in defence of their rights, but they could not get wet by the rain.

But the rain did not damp the enthusiasm of our heroine. It was an enthusiasm that could be subdued only with life. She therefore bore up beneath the subduing effects of the rain, without a regret or a thought but of her duty to her country.

On arriving at Columbia, however, she was enabled to be a little more comfortable. The hotel at which she stopped, kept by a man by the name of Franklin, was as good as one had any right to expect, though the fare, of course, was fearfully high. Miss Cushman had been paid one hundred dollars in Confederate notes, for her horse and equipments, by the man Milam; she, therefore, had the rebel money ready. But she needed it all at the "Franklin House;" so called from its proprietor. Butter was not to be had, except at an extra charge; which, too, was most exorbitant. The fare was miserable. Sidelings of bacon, fat and filthy, dirty, with rye coffee, composed the meals. At breakfast they had coarse hoe-cakes, to relieve the monotony of the usual fare. For this, eight dollars ($8), Confederate money, was asked per day.

While there, Miss Cushman took it into her head that she would like some variation of this wretched sameness of fare—which, without intending a joke, we may say was but fair. Sidelings of fat, miserable bacon, was not as dainty food as a gourmand might desire. As for our heroine, she rebelled against it. She determined, therefore, to procure a nice little chicken—a delicacy which she had longed for a good while. Calling, therefore, a servant—a slave, of course—she opened negotiations for the same; for so great a tit-bit was not to be had for the asking. Diplomat, then, she said to the sable gentleman who had answered her summons:

"Boy, I am going to give you a dollar."

"Yes, Missis," responded the "dark," his mouth distending and his eyes glistening at the anticipated present.

"But I want you to do something for me."

75

"Oh, yes, Missis. I'se gwine du dat, sure."

"I want you to get me a real nice chicken—a little, *little* chicken," added our heroine, noting the blank expression of dismay at even the mention of such an impossibility, expressed on the face of her sable confident.

"A chicken!"

"Certainly; a chicken," retorted our heroine, beginning to be annoyed at the "boy's" apparent stupidity. "Is there anything wonderful in that?"

"I 'spect you'd tink so, Missis. Why dey hasn't seen a chicken in dis house for an age," responded the darkey.

"Well, look here" returned the fair Pauline; "as I said, I have a dollar for you; but I must have a chicken. If you don't get it, you can't have the dollar."

"'Spect I'll have to do without de dollar, den, Missis; but dis negro'll try," was the contraband's reply.

In due time the much-longed-for delicacy arrived; and what does the reader imagine it cost? One dollar for going for it; two dollars for the chicken itself. One dollar again for cooking it, and fifty cents for the butter used in preparing it. In all, *four* dollars and a half for a chicken that, our heroine declares, was, when cooked, no larger than her hand; which, we beg here to state, is not a large one.

Sometime before Miss Cushman's arrival at Columbia, the railroad track to Shelbyville had been torn up by our troops, and as the new railroad was not yet complete, she was compelled to remain until it was formally opened, which was not for some three days after. This, however, was a grateful rest after her long journey through the woods and in the rain and she improved it as much to recruit her health as to gain such information of the rebel movements as might prove of service. Among those whom she met here were several refugees from "Yankee tyranny," as they called themselves, and these, of course, immediately claimed our heroine as a sister in suffering. She, on the other hand, was not slow to avail herself of this feeling, but used it to obtain much valuable information.

As for herself, when any curious body asked her questions, she was always looking for her brother—like "Japheth in search of his father," she could talk of nothing but that dear brother who was a colonel in the "Confederate service," and who was to redress all her wrongs, varying it by unmeasured abuse of the "wretches" of Federal officers who had driven her out of Nashville. This, as may readily be understood, was music to the ears of her fellow-refugees, who knew no bounds in their praise of her heroism in behalf of "the cause."

They must have felt rather strange, if by any means the truth could have appeared, and our heroine been known in her true character. She played her part too well, however, and although questioned and cross-questioned by the idle or curious, ever kept to the one story, which thereby escaped suspicion.

Soon now her acting was to be tested by more experienced judges—her apparently innocent questions after information met, and her seeming childish waywardness and simplicity sifted. Yet she bore the test, and in turn made the suspicious one her most useful tool. This person was a certain Major Boone, who was introduced to our heroine by the old man Baker, and proved a very valuable friend to our heroine ever afterwards, never suspecting that she was other than a much-injured rebel sympathiser, driven out of Nashville by the unjust persecution of the Federal officers.

The most interesting personage that she met, though, was a man by the name of Kennedy, who had escaped lately from the Nashville jail, and who was celebrated through the country for the "cute" trick by which he had deceived the guard and effected his escape.

As it may interest our readers, we will relate the trick as told to our heroine by the hero himself.

From among the rebel sympathisers who visited the prison he had managed to secure a file. This would have been of but little use if it had not been for the shrewdness which guided his actions.

With the file, however, he succeeded in severing the heavy chain and ball which clogged his feet, taking care to do so near the iron staple which was driven into the band about his leg. This he did at night, and succeeded without discovery. He then tied the two pieces of iron chain together strongly, and strolled around the cell, in which he, in common with many others, was confined.

At the door of the large room, which served as a cell, was a German guard, a round-faced, good-natured, unsuspecting fellow, whom Kennedy hailed as the very one upon whom to practice his *ruse*. Approaching him, he entered into conversation with him, and gradually got him to accede to his (Kennedy) taking a mouthful of fresh air outside of the door. To this he agreed, only on condition that the ball which was attached to the chain around Kennedy's leg should remain in his grasp while he stood outside, so as to prevent all possibility of escape. This was of course what Kennedy had bargained on, and which he was prepared for.

"I can't get off, you know, as long as you have hold of the ball," he said.

"Ya, ya, I knows dat. Dat is true!" responded the good-natured Dutchman. "You no get off when I have de ball in my hands. You no be able to play off any tricks on me."

So, taking the ball and placing it between his feet, the worthy but unsuspecting Teuton sat watching it attentively; while Kennedy, the moment he got outside, had taken his knife and severed the string which still held the chain attached to the ball and made off.

Soon, however, an inspection officer came around to visit the prisoners, and upon calling the roll no Kennedy responded in answer to his oft-repeated name. "Where was Kennedy? Where could he be?" was asked by the startled officer, while a burst of merriment went up from the prisoners, who were acquainted with the facts.

At last, the German sentinel was consulted.

"Oh, ya, I'sh just got him here," was his satisfied response. "Just as snug ash a pug-hin-a rugg."

"Got him safe!" cried the officer, white with rage at the simplicity, not to say stupidity, of the man. "Got him safe! Why, man, don't you see that he has escaped?"

"How he 'scape, Mister Officer, when I got de ball in my hands?" asked the Dutchman, in a tone to which there was no reply.

"D——n you and the ball!" was the heated retort of the inspection officer.

But Mr. Dutchman's head was thick; it took some time for an idea to get into it. Confidently putting his head out of the door then, he looked in the direction of the spot where the supposed prisoner *should* have stood. Lo and behold it was tenantless!—there was nothing but the heavy chain, which was still attached to the ball, but which had been neatly severed from the leg of the escaped convict.

"*Mine Got* what is in *Himmel!*" exclaimed the poor guard, overwhelmed by the discovery. "*Mine Got!* de debbil himself must have took him away."

"The d——l take *you* away, stupid jackass " cried the officer in a perfect rage, pushing past him and raising the alarm. But it was too late. Kennedy had a suit of citizen's clothes near at hand, which his rebel friends had furnished, and donning them without delay was thus enabled to pass the guard at the main entrance without question. He was then far away, and in safety, before his good-natured jailor had finished wondering "how de debbil de man get off, when he have de ball right in his own hands all de time!"

Chapter 16: The Rebel Engineer

As far as our heroine's new profession as a Union scout was concerned, Columbia had proved a rich field. It was with a feeling of having "sucked the orange" pretty dry, that she prepared to leave it. Among the acquaintances whom she had met there, the most useful promised to be her new friends, Major Boone and Captain P. A. Blackman, both of the Confederate service. The first, who was a great lady's man, soon became quite interested in the charming Pauline, a fact which she was not slow to take advantage of.

The latter gentleman, also, was quite as much smitten with the rare beauty and bewitching ways of our heroine, and being a rebel quartermaster just from the vicinity of Vicksburgh, was enabled, unconsciously, to be of infinite value to our cause. Both were very kind. But Miss Cushman had to leave these new friends to proceed to Shelbyville, from whence it was understood she was to return to Columbia, should she not succeed in finding her brother. The man, Baker, was, consequently, to await her, in case she should make up her mind to return.

On our heroine's adventures at Shelbyville, we will not dwell. The place was made immemorial to her afterwards, by being the scene of trials and hardships such as seldom fall to the lot of woman. It was also to be engraved upon her heart of hearts, as the place from which she was delivered by the noble sons of battle—the brave soldiers of the Army of the Southwest. But we are anticipating. To return, then, to our heroine and Shelbyville, where she arrived safely and without having excited any suspicion as to her actions or purposes.

To her great disappointment, she found that General Bragg, whose movements she had received orders to watch more closely than those of any one else, had left. *Where*, no one could tell her. The object of her trip to Shelbyville was thus frustrated in a manner; but, ever alive to the opportunity, providing the slightest glimpse of one offered, Miss Cushman still succeeded in making her trip most valuable to her employers and her country, though, as it afterwards turned out, by doing so she imperilled even life itself.

It chanced thus: At the *table d'hôte* at which she dined, sat a young officer of engineers, who had been occupied drawing important plans for the rebel government. The instant our heroine heard this, she determined in her own mind to break through her instructions, and, at whatever risk, obtain them. She would then return immediately to Milam's, she thought, from whence she could reach the Federal lines with ease, and in time to be of the utmost service to her country.

A very good excuse for returning to Nashville presented itself, also, in the fact that she had been compelled (so she represented) by the Federal officers, to leave all her theatrical wardrobe in that city, not daring to take a thing with her. Of course, her wardrobe was safely locked up, under the care of the chief of police; but she represented to the rebels that it had been ruthlessly torn from her. To recover it, therefore, was, she declared, her principal desire, inasmuch as she might then accept some engagement at some one of the theatres throughout the country, and earn enough money to allow her to pursue her journey in search of her brother.

As though to further this plan, just about this time Miss Cushman received a letter from Mr. W. H. Crisp, then manager of the Richmond Theatre, offering an engagement in that city. This, of course, quite tallied with her plans and gave new impetus to them.

To set about the execution of this plan, she had only to ingratiate herself in the good graces of the young engineer officer no very difficult task with a pretty woman.

A letter of safeguard from Miss Cushman's friend at Shelbyville, Major Boone, answered as an introduction, and soon she had won her way to his entire confidence; and, not satisfied with showing her all the attention possible, actually gave her letters of introduction to General Bragg. After dinner, then, the busy officer was aroused by a gentle "tapping" at his door. As Poe says, in his *Raven*. . .

This it was, and nothing more.

But it turned out rather more serious, for both parties, than was thought for, at the time. Hastening to answer it, the officer found our heroine outside, who had come to request him to write the letters of introduction at once.

"So, you think of leaving us, and so soon?" he exclaimed, his eyes resting admiringly on her beautiful figure.

"For but a short time, I trust," was the response. "As soon as I succeed in getting my wardrobe, I shall return to accept an engagement at one of the theatres; so, I hope soon to see you again."

"You will not, then, forget us all?" sighed the young engineer officer, whom, we strongly suspect, was much more used to battering forts than ladies' hearts. "You will not, then, forget us?"

"Oh, no indeed!" exclaimed Pauline, warmly, her eyes fixed upon the mass of plans and drawings of important fortifications which lumbered up the table. "No, I will not forget you;" and she added to herself, smiling, "Nor do I think you will forget me; especially if I succeed in making way with those papers there." But the engineer officer was all unsuspicious, and, kindly inviting our heroine to walk in and be seated, begged to be excused for a few moments.

"My writing-desk is, I find Miss Cushman, in a room beneath this; so, if you will excuse me for a few minutes, I will prepare my letter to General Bragg, and bring it to you."

The required permission being given, the officer retired, when our heroine proceeded to work.

First of all, she must see that the coast was entirely clear. No one was about—her hand rested upon the papers. What a rich harvest was there! But hark, there is a noise; can it be the officer returning? No, it is but the wind. The next instant the plans are concealed in her breast; but not a moment too soon, for the next, her new friend stands beside her, the letter of introduction in his hand. We doubt if his manner would have been so kind, could he have seen all that was concealed in that fair bosom, whose voluptuous rise and fall he, no doubt, attributed to tenderer emotions than the facts warranted. But all was unsuspected, and when she did leave Shelbyville at last, in pursuance of her plan, the engineer was still as pleasant and unsuspecting as ever.

Chapter 17: A Midnight Adventure

During this period in our heroine's search for the rebel General Bragg, an episode occurred which, from its peculiar character, cannot be passed over. It was one which called forth all her powers, and which, but for her quickness of wit and daring conception, might have ended most disastrously to herself and her cause. Woman wit is proverbial, so that when we have occasion to speak of some rough but honest son of the Emerald Isle, whose quick, ready answer is as prompt as his heart to noble actions, we say that he has "*mother* wit." It is never *father* wit; for wit is a woman, and for the most part is true to her sex.

To this quality in our heroine—that is, a quick perception and readiness for any emergency that might arise—do we owe thanks for the fact that we are now writing with her sanction, a true history of her adventures; for without it her career would doubtless have been cut short with her return to Columbia.

Ever on the lookout, however, for some opportunity to serve her country by acquiring information of the enemy—their numbers, whereabouts, and strength, or any other useful details—Miss Cushman took advantage of a short halt at a place called Wartrace, while on the way to Shelbyville, to display her extraordinary qualities as a scout. As it happened, numerous skirmishes had lately taken place just about this neighbourhood between our troops and the rebel cavalry. Indeed, scouting parties of both armies made this their battlefield, and Wartrace, well named, probably from some old Indian battle fought there, sustained its reputation.

The day before our heroine arrived there had been a skirmish between the hostile cavalry, causing many a bloody head on both sides, and compelling patriot and traitor alike to bite the earth. The country, too, was still overrun with wandering bands of Union soldiers. Could she but reach one of these bands she would be able to transmit information which, given thus promptly, would prove invaluable. She determined therefore to resume her old habits as a scout, and scour the country through in the hope of falling in with some one of these parties of Union Cavalry.

The first requisite was, of course, a man's suit of clothes, and as she had not here, as at Louisville, to which vicinity these ventures had been confined heretofore, a complete wardrobe of disguises, dresses, etc. the only resource was a return to first principles.

Lawyers and writers upon political and social economy tell us that all objects of property were originally got by acquisition: in other words, if Richard Roe had anything that John Doe wanted, Richard Roe was forthwith dispossessed, and his friend John Doe walked off with the coveted object. This was coming into property by acquisition. A harder name is now given to it, or rather a series of names, such as "stealing," "filching," "freezing on to," etc.; all of which are, if not quite so elegant, far more expressive.

Our heroine, then, having no suit at her command legitimately, determined to appropriate unto herself the first one that came in her way, for necessity has no law.

In the same house there happened to be a young boy of some seventeen years of age, whose clothes, it struck her, would just answer. These then became the object of her thoughts, but how to get possession of them she knew not. That the boy slept in the upper storey of the house she knew, but where or in what room she had not the slightest idea. Nothing remained then but to "scout" around, and, hit or miss, make a desperate attempt. Attired, therefore, in a fitting costume for either a ghost or a somnambulist—for it might be that she would have to enact both parts—she took her way to the upper storey.

Now anyone who has ever had the misfortune of missing his own door in a long corridor lined with portals, and that too, in the dark, will understand the position of our heroine. With no other guide than her instincts, she determined to listen and see what she could detect by the breathing of the sleeper within. At the first door, a short, wheezy sniff, such as a respectable old tabby cat would give forth, met her ear.

"That's an old maid, sure—who, if I was to wake up, would scream until she had every man in the house in her room," soliloquised our heroine, beating a hasty retreat.

At the next door, a loud groan; interspersed with most ferocious snorts, saluted her.

"That's a snore over forty years old at least," she continued: "some old bachelor, a match for that old maid over yonder."

The sound that issued from the keyhole of the next door there was no mistaking: it was man and wife, snoring away to their hearts' content in connubial bliss. First the high treble of the good woman; then the deep, rumbling bass of the husband, coming in like a full church organ.

A smile flitted over the face of the young girl; all unconscious as she was of such matrimonial concerts, she understood that the object of her anxious search slept not there.

From the next room, however, came the sound of a good, honest snore, such as might reasonably be indulged in by a strong, hearty boy of seventeen summers. She tried the latch: it was unfastened; but the next minute she was startled by a voice, crying "Who's thar?"

Retreating at a "double quick" she was still enabled to bear the conversation that ensued; for, as it happened, the room had two occupants, one of whom, as ill luck would have it, chanced to be awake.

"What's the matter, Jake?" demanded the snoring companion, who had been awakened by the cry of his room-mate.

"Why, somebody's trying to git in," was the answer.

"Git in? Where's my revolver? I reckon *I'll* make 'em jump," responded the other, now fully aroused.

"What's the matter? Can't you let a man sleep when he's paid for his bed and all?" interposed a crusty voice from the room in which the old bachelor lay.

"Oh, gentlemen! oh, gentlemen! is there anything the matter?" cries here the old maid next door, making her appearance, with a modest simper, in a costume improvised for the occasion, and which resembled the retreat of an ostrich, inasmuch as it concealed perfectly her head while it exposed two long spindle-shanks that were scarcely objects of beauty. "Robbers, did you say?" she continued, with an hysterical scream. "Oh, I shall faint! *Will* no gentleman catch me? The villain may be in my very room. Oh, I shall be murdered! *Will* no gentleman search my chamber? Must I be left to the tender mercies of a villain—of a base, designing villain? Help! Help!"

"Let me go, Sairy Jane!" exclaimed a voice at this crisis. "Don't you hear the cries of murder? Let me go, I say."

"Never, John! No, not while I have got strength to hold you!" was the hysterical reply, delivered in a high, feminine tone, which developed some strength of *temper*, whatever might be wanting in other respects. "Let you go and get murdered with the rest? No, never, while my name's Sairy Jane!"

In fact, heads began now to obtrude from almost every room, and our heroine was about to make a dash at the stairs when a lumbering darkey made his appearance coming up the stairway, guiding some newly-arrived passenger, thus cutting off her retreat most completely.

In a fit of desperation our heroine turned the handle of a small door near which she stood, the room appearing tenantless. To her great joy it yielded, and slipping hastily in she found herself in a low, poorly-furnished chamber. The moonlight which streamed through the window revealed to her, near at hand, complete suit of men's clothes, while spread out on the bed lay the very youth to obtain whose costume she had risked so much. Fortune had favoured her, and, what was better, still continued to do so; for, in spite of the hub-bub prevailing, the young man slept through it all. As soon, therefore, as the excitement subsided, our heroine glided out of the room as noiselessly as she had entered it, carrying with her the much-coveted prize a man's suit of clothes.

Chapter 18: The Scout and the Guerillas

The next thing was to saddle her horse. Equipped then in the suit which she had so opportunely acquired, Miss Cushman stole softly down stairs. In the hall sat a negro "boy," as they call them down South;

but his deep breathing and distended mouth showed him to be fast asleep—unconscious, fortunately, of all surroundings. Who shall tell what dreams may not have floated in misty but heaven born form through the brain of that poor slave? Perhaps he saw himself as of yore, picking cotton in the vast field, the burning sun pouring down upon him, the slave-driver, whip in hand, standing over him. To him no reward came he dare not profit the full sum of his labour—he was a *slave*!

Perhaps he heard lowly mutterings—the portentous sound of the coming struggle, the sharp ring of the rifle, the deafening roar of cannon, those, the battle-cries of Freedom; and standing amid the sulphurous smoke hanging heavily over the regenerated land, beheld humanity and justice break his chains forever!

But our heroine had no time to think of this, for gliding past the slumbering negro she hastily gained the stable, from whence she took one of the swiftest horses she could find. Then springing on his back, she dashed off. Of the country thereabouts she of course knew nothing, but to a mind constituted like her own, uncertainty and peril gave but new vigour to her determination. Should she be arrested by rebel scouts her position might prove a dangerous one. She would be regarded more closely than was advisable, and questioned in a manner far from pleasant; and it would be difficult for her to account for the midnight ride through the country, in men's clothing, of a lady who was supposed by all the world to be safely resting in her bed. These were matters that had to be weighed, but when Miss Cushman thought of the great advantages that might accrue to her loved country by this sacrifice, she knew no longer a doubt.

Deep then in the forests that surrounded the town of Wartrace did she plunge, treading the dry leaves beneath her horse's hoofs and thrusting aside the low branches of the trees that would otherwise have swept her off the saddle. It was a bright moonlight night, as we have already said, and what with the flitting shadows and ghostly lights, it was a wild, fantastic ride; enough to please the imagination of the most romantically inclined.

It was destined, however, to have a new interest attached to it. Our heroine had rode some three miles, probably, out of Wartrace, when she saw a light glimmering through the trees ahead. As she approached it turned out to be a large watch-fire, about which a body of men were gathered. That these were armed men she could tell, for now and then the gleam of a weapon, as the fire lights rose or fell, would meet her eye, but whether they were friend or foe she knew not. Dismounting, therefore, from her horse, she tied him to a small tree nearby and creeping softly towards the camp-fire proceeded to reconnoitre.

The party, whatever they wero, seemed to feel secure in their present position, for no pickets were sent out, or any guard even stationed, except in front of a small stack of arms; and the gleam, it was, from his musket which had first caught our heroine's eye. She was enabled, then, to stealthily approach until she got within earshot of the party, when their character very soon became known.

As she soon learned through their conversation they were a band of rebel partisan cavalry, composed of refuse of guerillas and the Southern Army; and their fearful oaths and bloodthirsty and wicked language would have struck terror in the heart of a less valiant heroine.

As she approached, they had just finished singing a mongrel song, of which the chorus, half-negro dialect and half-plain English, ran something this way:

The Yankees run, ha! ha!
The negros stay, ho! ho!
It must be now the rebs are going
To have a jubalow!

"That's a bully song!" exclaimed one who had taken no part in the singing, and who appeared to be the leader of the band. "That's a bully song! but I am afear'd that those d——d Yanks will spoil our chorus if they keep on killing our men off the way they have been doing of late."

"There's Mike Custorer, he was the best singer amongst us. He's dead and gone, and many another too."

"Yes," continued another, "the d——d Yanks finished poor Mike, but I reckon they didn't get much the better of us, for we hung the rascally negro-sneak the same night, with due honours.'"

"Yes, and I stuck this knife through his gizzard too!" cried a third, triumphantly, "and I'm blamed if I believe it has got the taste of Yankee blood off it yet. I'm precious sure I never tried to clean it, though I *do* eat with it and everything."

"Ha! ha! ha!" laughed another, "I reckon I'd just as leaf eat a fat piece of 'Yank' as I would a beefsteak. I ain't squeamish—*I* ain't. So there's nothin' in that."

Creeping away as hastily as she dare, our scout had nearly reached the spot at which she had tied her horse, when, treading incautiously upon a branch of a tree, it snapped with a loud report.

"What's that?" cried one of the rebel gang, jumping up and seizing his gun.

"Oh, lay down! You're a brave fellow to get frightened at an old stray cow or sheep," growled a comrade.

"That was no cow," replied the other with an oath,

"What is the matter?" asked the captain, jumping up.

"Somebody is prowlin' about our camp, captain," answered one. "Some of them d——d Yankee cavalry men, maybe, that we had a fight with this evening."

"Let every man take his musket, then, and scour the woods," cried the captain. "If there's any about yet we will send them back to old 'Rosy' with bloody heads for our compliments."

By this time our heroine had gained her horse, and slinging herself upon him was fast leaving the glimmering camp-fire of the guerillas behind. Many of the rebels, though, had taken "to horse" at the first alarm, and the forest now rung with their pursuing cries, while the flash of a carbine in the bright moonlight, ever and *anon*, told our heroine that the whole body was astir and in chase of her.

Chapter 19: The Flight and the Pursuit

The scene was one that a Salvator Rosa would have delighted—in what with the wild forest, the broken, uneven ground, the dash of the noble steed, as, urged on by his daring rider, he made desperate efforts to distance the pursuers, and above, the bright moonlight and shifting clouds. The romance was heightened, too, by the accompanying sounds and circumstances; for, beside the wild cries of the rebels in chase, the jingling of their accoutrements and the snort of the horses, urged on to extraordinary efforts, every once in a while, a rifle ball would whiz past our heroine, fired by the dastardly crew in the hope to maim either herself or her horse, and thus secure their prize. But on galloped our heroine—faster and faster, with the rebel band following like shadows of the evil one, which, in truth, they were. Our heroine's horse, however, was the best of the party, and gradually, one by one, her pursuers fell off—sending, on such occasions, a rifle ball after her as a parting salute, and a token of their disappointment.

A few only, those possessing the better horses, were now still engaged in the chase, and these seemed determined in keeping up the pursuit, lead where it might. So close had they approached, that she expected every minute to feel their clutch, when a new obstacle op-

The Scout and the Guerillas.

posed itself, in the shape of a precipitous rack, at the bottom of which a small stream meandered. As her speed had been terrific, this apparently insurmountable obstacle seemed to seal the fate of the unfortunate girl. She did not despair, however, but with a courage that appalled all observers, struck the spurs deep into her steed, and plunged down the mountain side.

Like Putnam, in his daring dash, under somewhat similar circumstances. Her pursuers did not dare to follow, but were satisfied to stand upon the top of the bluff and wing their pistol balls after her; and when she had eventually secured a place free from their shot, and could draw in her horse to allow him to breathe for a short spell, the loud curses and mingled expressions of disappointment of her late pursuers reached her ear.

"Drat the boy!" exclaimed one; "he is plucky, whoever he is, or he would never have tried that leap."

"I'm not sorry he escaped," said another, who seemed of a more gentle nature than the rest. "His bravery deserved to save him."

"Darn his bravery!" interrupted another. "All of them d———d Yanks are brave for that matter. However, he's gone sure, so there's no use in grieving arter him."

This philosophic determination being arrived at, very much to the relief of our heroine, she was sorry to hear it upset, the next minute, by a discovery announced by another of the party.

"Give the chase up? Not much!" he exclaimed. "Here's a bridle-path leading down to the creek, and it will be our own fault now if the boy escapes us. Who knows," he continued; "it may be one of them d———d Yanks that have been prowling around and given us so much trouble. So, here's to lead, boys. I'm off and them that's not afeared of a mere boy will follow!"

So, saying, the speaker took the initiative, and the chase recommenced, inasmuch as the bridlepath discovered overcame the only obstacle which had heretofore separated our heroine from the rebel horde. There was not a moment to be lost then. From seeming security, she was again aroused, and as the numbers of her pursuers augmented every moment—those who had been left behind, coming in, one by one—the chase threatened to be renewed with redoubled vigour. Pushing hastily into the woods, then, which lined the banks of the little stream, she endeavoured to regain, as much as possible, the road to the town of Wartrace; for daylight would demand her presence there, in order to prevent a most untimely discovery, *viz.*: that the charming Miss Cushman had stolen off, in the middle of the night, on horseback, and attired in male garments, and must, necessarily, be a spy.

If captured by the rebel scouts, a like fate probably awaited her; for Wartrace would be the first place to which they would conduct her. She may be said, therefore, to have been literally between two fires, the escape from which was not so easy. On, on she plunged, however, nothing daunted; for her brave steed was still unwearied, in spite of his almost supernatural exertions, and the brave girl's heart misgave her not for a moment. Beside, her pursuers were evidently off the track. Each moment their voices and the tramp of their steeds became more and more indistinct. Joy began to take the place of anxiety and suspense in her heart, when, all of a sudden, she beheld, standing before her, a cavalryman, fully equipped and armed. Not doubting, for a moment, but that this newcomer was some member of the other rebel cavalry known to be in that neighbourhood, she determined to sell her life as dearly as might be.

"Stand aside," she cried, vehemently, to the stranger. "Stand aside, or, by heaven, I will send a pistol ball through you!"

"All right, comrade," answered the cavalryman, faintly. "The Lord knows that *I* don't want to stop you, for it is as much as I can do to keep myself steady on my horse; for I am sorely wounded, and even now I feel the warm blood trickling through my clothes."

"Wounded? What are you doing here, then—why are you away from your comrades?" asked our heroine, thinking him still an enemy.

"You see, we had a skirmish with you 'rebs' near here, not more than five or six hours ago, while we were out scouting, and I was wounded and got left behind, in the scrimmage. So that's how I got here."

"Then you are a Federal soldier?" she joyfully exclaimed.

"I am one of Colonel —— corps."

"Thank heaven for that, anyhow!" cried Pauline again, for, with the rapidity of lightning, a plan of escape had flashed through her brain

"You can aid me," she continued. "Aid me and our country."

"Our country?" queried the soldier, wonderingly. "Why, ain't you a rebel?"

"No, indeed!" was the decided answer. "I will tell you who I am. You have heard of a woman who acts sometimes as a spy, and has done some service to her country, have you not?"

"Yes, indeed."

"You have?"

"I have. I have heard stories of that woman a daring and bravery that would fill books and books. The 'boys' talk of her often."

"Well?" interrupted Pauline, slightly blushing at this unsuspected praise.

"Well, I have taken an oath that if ever I can see that woman, I will ask her to share whatever I have got; for such a woman is fit to be a soldier's bride."

Our heroine laughed, then said:

"Well, then, you have met the woman-scout, and he refuses your kind offer; but she asks you, nevertheless, to save her from the rebel crew who are pursuing her."

"What? Are you a woman?" asked the honest soldier still doubtingly.

"I am. Pauline, the 'Scout of the Cumberland!'" answered our heroine. "*Now* will you help me?"

"With my life!" was the impetuous answer.

"Nay, I hope, through your means, to save both our lives," she continued, at the same moment firing her pistol, which she still held in her hand, into the air.

"What's that for?" demanded the soldier, amazed at this proceeding. "That will guide your pursuers to you."

"Even so," was the response. "Now listen. I have fired that shot to make believe that I fired at you. You must, therefore, swear that I shot you. Whether you do this or not, you would soon have to give yourself up as a prisoner; for your wounds would make it impossible for you to keep on horseback long enough to reach your comrades. Tomorrow, then, at furthest, you would have to surrender yourself to save your life. Do this now, therefore, and you will save me as well, and do a service to our loved land; for I have information that will prove invaluable to our generals, and which must be lost to them if I am captured."

"Fear not. I will do everything—*anything* to save you. And what is more, there is not a soldier in the Army of the Cumberland but would do as much."

"Thanks," returned Pauline, warmly, grasping the honest fellow's hand. "Thanks; Pauline will not forget you. Now to our parts. Another minute will bring the rebel horde upon us; we must, therefore, be prepared. Dismount, then, and stir yourself, so that your wound may bleed afresh. Remember, I shot you because you were a Yankee. You must swear this, if necessary."

"I will," replied the soldier, letting himself fall off his horse, so as to start the wound afresh, according to our heroine's instructions.

The next moment, therefore, when the rebels made their appearance, as had been expected, the tableau was ready, and could not but deceive the wisest among them.

At the foot of a tree lay the disabled soldier, his wound bleeding freely, and in a state of unconsciousness; for so severe had been the fall that a sudden faintness had followed. Over him bent our heroine, the murderous pistol still in her grasp, while the bounds of the affrighted steed of the wounded man resounded through the forest; for, to complete the truth of the picture, our heroine had administered a sharp blow to the poor animal, and sent him flying through the dried leaves and brushwood. On the arrival of the rebel band, then, as we have said, the picture presented had every semblance of truth.

The quick-witted girl had foreseen and prepared for everything, and she was ready with an answer then, when the leader of the rebels advanced, and demanded who she was.

"I am a farmer's son, over near Wartrace," was her reply, "and I surrender to you; but I have shot your best fellow, here, and I only wish I had shot more of ye."

"What does the boy mean?" asked one of the party, at a loss to understand the meaning of these words.

"I mean just what I say," returned our heroine, in a bitter tone. "I am only sorry that I didn't kill more of you darn'd Yankees, that comes adown yhere and runs all our negros off."

"Yankees? Why I'm blessed if the boy don't think we're 'Yanks!'" exclaimed three or four at once, completely misled by her skilful acting.

"I don't know about that," interposed one more incredulous than the others. "We must see about this soldier that the boy says he shot, and then we can tell more about it. Look up here," he continued, shaking the wounded and still fainting soldier. "Look up here!" But the poor soldier did not stir, "I'm blessed if I don't believe he is dead!" said the doubter, finding that no answer came

After a while the soldier revived somewhat, when the doubter again approached him. "I say, 'Yank,'" he exclaimed, "who was it that shot you?"

Raising himself slightly, the true fellow looked around him, when his eyes suddenly fell upon our heroine. With his finger he designated her as the person.

"There!" cried one of the party, who had seemed better disposed towards the "farmer's boy." "There! he says the boy shot him. What do you want better than that?"

"What made the boy run away from us, then?" persisted the doubter.

"Why, don't you see? he thought we was 'Yanks,' and we thought that *he* was a 'Yank;' so, you see, that's jist the way it was, I reckon. Wasn't it so, boy?" turning toward our heroine, who, of course, assented warmly to this version.

"Why should I run away from my friends?" she asked. "If I had only known yer were Confederates, I'd not had all this ride; but yer see, I thought yer was some of them d——d 'Yanks' what's been about yhere for some time," she continued, imitating the Southern "slang" in talking, and affecting the manners and habits of a country lad. This she did to such perfection that soon all doubts were dispelled, the more so from the fact that one of the party now came forward and declared that he had heard the shot fired just about the time designated by our heroine.

"It's true as gospel," he said, "that I heard that yhere shot; but I reckon it's jist as safe to keep a sharp look-out upon the lad till we're Sartain!"

So, saying, and placing the poor, wounded soldier upon a horse, and commanding Pauline to follow, the rebel crew prepared to take their departure to Wartrace.

Chapter 20: The Capture and Escape

This was more than Pauline had bargained for and threatened to place her in a most awkward predicament. First of all, if she was taken to Wartrace she would be immediately recognised by her fellow-boarders. Even, however, should she escape recognition, the disappearance of the clothes from the room of the young man would create an outcry that would lend to detection at last. As we have seen however, she was full of expedients, and though the faithful soldier looked at her once in a while, as though despairing that she could possible escape detection, she was ever ready to give him a reassuring smile, that would for the moment calm his fears in reference to her.

This poor, wounded man had spoken words to our heroine that had thrilled her soul, for, beside his personal interest in her, he had proved to her that her name and fame had found a record at least in the hearts of those for whom she had risked all even life. It is sweet to meet with gratitude. There is nothing, perhaps, so refreshing and pu-rifying to the heart as to meet with this most rare but certainly most desirable virtue. Gratitude is the wealth of sweet perfume, that the flower has given out in the day, and which comes back to it, refreshing and re-beautifying it, as a dew in the night.

How warming, how cheering was it to her then to hear the words of commendation from the lips even of the kind but stranger soldier! It assured her that her efforts had not been spent in vain—that there was some gratitude in the heart of the soldier, if not in anyone else. The tears had welled up to her beauteous eyes, then, when the soldier, in his true knightly phrase, had said that he would "die for her, if necessary;" and at each anxious glance that he turned toward her, the grateful girl could not sufficiently thank him in her heart, though of course her *lips* were sealed. For himself, the brave fellow evidently cared nothing; his whole thought was of the fair and daring girl for whom he had suf-fered himself to be captured, and who, in spite of the sacrifice, he had the mortification to see was destined not to profit by it.

To carry out her part properly, Pauline had to play the rebel to the life, and of course she dare not show any outward signs of sympathy with her brave friend; nevertheless, once in a while she managed to steal to his side and bestow a grateful pressure on his fevered hand. Her mind was bent on escape, however, and to it she lent all her powers. Oft she would lag behind under pretence of her horse being weary, but the leader of the band would immediately hurry her up, adminis-tering blows and kicks to her faithful steed, and showering oaths upon herself for lagging.

In the meantime, the cooler air, and that peculiar darkness which passes over the earth just before the sun rises, told that daybreak was fast approaching. By the length of their ride, too, our heroine came to the conclusion that their place of destination must be near at hand. We have said that it was dark, and in the peculiar gloom of the forest and the hour, objects looked indistinct and undefined. This fact often led to slight scares on the part of her conductors, for they seemed par-ticularly fearful of encountering one of the bands of Federal cavalry which they declared were still roving about those parts.

Cowardly in their dispositions, for they were, in one word, *des-peradoes*—men too base even for the rebel army—they had no desire to meet the "Yanks," whom they knew would show them but little mercy, probably hanging them on the first tree as a lot of "bushwhackers." Having observed this, Pauline determined to take advantage of it, to effect her escape. They were passing through a narrow gorge of the road, which was thickly overshadowed by tall forest trees, when our heroine determined to try her plan.

The spot was just such a one as an enemy would select for an ambush, and of this fact the rebel horde seemed aware, for they urged on their horses, and peered anxiously on either side. Pauline had strayed behind the rest, and was hidden by a bend in the road. Now was the moment to act. Taking out her revolver, which still contained five loads, she fired them rapidly in succession. Imagining that their fears were indeed realised, the whole rebel party took to flight, promiscuously; urging on their horses in true Johnny Gilpin style, nor daring once to look wound them, for fear a halter would suddenly slip upon their necks.

Fear lent a thousand terrifying doubts to their minds, while their imaginations gave even the echo of the pistol shots a new sound. They were surrounded, they thought. A powerful number of Federal cavalry had been laying in ambush, and flight alone could save them. These were their thoughts, flashing swift as lightning through their brains, and away they went pell-mell.

Laughing until the tears streamed down her cheeks our heroine set about taking advantage of this new turn in affairs, for she could not doubt but that, finding they were not pursued, they would soon recover from their flight and return for her. She first, though, looked about her for her brave friend, the soldier, but the rebels had taken him along with them, evidently believing him to be too good a prize to allow to escape them. He was probably the first Federal soldier that the scoundrels had ever captured, for their trade was plundering and burning, rather than fighting. Finding that the brave fellow was indeed carried off by the rebels, our heroine now turned her attention to her own escape.

Striking into a by-road, therefore, she fairly flew over the rough ground, and without further obstacle reached her hotel. Here her first duty was of course to her horse, for a good soldier, and such Miss Cushman was, never forgets his noble steed. Afterwards she stole softly into the house past the still sleeping porter, and, regaining her room, hastily divested herself of her borrowed attire, and slipping on her own garments again, prepared to enact the part of the ghost.

This time, however, she met with no accident; the young man whose clothes she had borrowed was all unconscious of the fact, and was still sleeping as when she left: so placing them carefully on the chair from which she had taken them, she once more proceeded to her own room, from which she issued soon after in answer to the summons to breakfast, as rosy and fresh as though she had enjoyed an excellent night's rest, instead of the hairbreadth adventures which had in reality filled it.

As for the rebel gang, she afterwards saw them about Wartrace, bragging of their wonderful fight with the "Yanks," and how they were lying in ambush "some half a hundred strong;" how pistol and rifle shots resounded on every side; and how, "*not one bit intimidated*, they set upon the d——d 'Yanks' and put them to flight." She burned often to expose the rascals, and tell them that they had fled like cowards from the modestly-dressed lady that stood before them; but she did not dare to do this, but had to take her satisfaction in laughing in secret at these boasters, while they never once suspected that the beautiful and fascinating Miss Cushman and the rude peasant boy were one and the same person.

Chapter 21: Love and the Fair Spy

After several stirring adventures at Tullahoma, where our heroine also made a short stay, she returned to Columbia, where she found the old man, Baker, awaiting her, as *per promise*. Great as was her desire to proceed at once to recross the "lines," and convey the valuable information which she had gathered, as soon as possible, to the commander of the Army of the Southwest, Miss Cushman found too rich a field in Columbia, to think of leaving it until every grain of information was safely garnered.

We have already said that the lady had made several acquaintances daring her short delay at this place. The most important of these were Major Boone and Captain P. A. Blackman, rebel quartermaster just from Vicksburgh. Now the reader may readily imagine that these were prizes to the spread net of our heroine, who did not fail to avail herself of their friendship to get all the information she could, as well as to probe, as far as possible, the secrets of the rebel intentions or movements. What will not a soldier do when "lovely woman" leads him blindfold?

Venus, alone, conquered Mars—so our histories of the gods tell us; and these poor, misguided gentlemen were so weak as to believe in the touching story of our fair heroine, and to believe still more, we fear, in the rare beauty of her eyes. At least, they loved to bask in their sunlight.

Indeed, there was, perhaps, no woman better suited to lead captive a soldier's heart. Full of all the dash and daring of a headlong, headstrong boy; full of grace and animation; loving adventure with an intensity that bore down every other feeling—our heroine was surely intended for a "pirate's bride."

She could converse, too, upon all manly sports and habits, with the ease and polish of a high-born gentleman; and yet, withal, was so much a whole-souled, loving, clinging woman, that a strange fascination seized those who approached her. They not only loved her, but many madly, hopelessly adored her.

This is no exaggeration. Pauline Cushman would have filled well a place in the page of history, as "the Enchantress," with a chorus, in real stage style, to. . .

Ever be happy! bride of the sea!
Pride of the pirate's home!

But it was not as a *woman* that these fascinations were exercised: they were used only as a part of the stock in trade of the *spy*—of one who had vowed to serve her country at whatever cost. She was, as we know, a consummate actress; and this was part of her role. That there were many dangers attending it, aside from those of physical suffering, we know, also; but as we have seen her withstand the temptations and peculiar allurements of the "green room," we find her now encountering, with casings of steel, the temptations of the camp. Pauline had that within her heart "which passeth show." She had an all-consuming love of country, which led her to dedicate herself to it alone. It is, then, as a *scout* that we must think of her, and not as the quiet, the propriety-loving Miss Cushman.

Pauline, "the scout," then, led her two rebel lovers a pretty dance; but alas! though the Confederate States have abrogated everything not peculiar to their soil, disowned our Constitution, uprooted the glorious name of our nation from their hearts, and even thrown Yankee Doodle overboard, Shakespeare seems to have maintained his ground; for the old saying of his, that "true love never yet run smooth," was as applicable, in their cases, as it would have been north of Mason and Dixon's, or even in the "tight little island" itself. The warm affection felt by the gallant rebel officers was, as will be seen hereafter, to be dealt with no less unkindly than is the fate of lovers generally. Indeed, they got many "*nasen*," as the Germans say, and which means tweaks of the nose, from their superiors, on their mistakes in this line. Yet who should blame a man for falling in love, when—

It is his nature to?

As for Captain Blackman, the rebel quartermaster, so high an opinion did he conceive of our heroine's ability as a soldier, that he urged her to adopt man's apparel, and join the Confederate Army—promising her to make her *aide-de-camp*, with the rank of lieutenant.

This flattering distinction Pauline acceded to, though with some reluctance, and promised to don the unmentionables, and actually accompany him as his *aide*, as soon as she should return from Milam's. With this understanding, a full and in every way complete rebel officer's uniform was forthwith ordered by the enamoured captain for his fair *aide-de-camp*. As a more complete knowledge of camps, fortifications, and warlike preparations would be highly useful to the new officer, our heroine took advantage of the captain's whim to ride with him all over the neighbouring country; thus gaining every information of the plans and projects of the rebel leaders.

On such occasions, the remarks of the gallant officer were most amusing, and often our heroine would find it difficult to keep from laughing outright at the overweening confidence entertained by the rebel soldier.

"What would not the Yankees give to know what you know?" he asked one day.

"What, indeed?" was the non-committing answer of our heroine.

Another matter, too, which bordered strongly upon the ludicrous, was the rebel captain's sympathy for our bewitching heroine, in her mock anger against Colonel Truesdail, the Federal provost-marshal of Nashville. The gallant Captain Blackman was particularly moved at Pauline's recital of the suffering which she had experienced in consequence of this officer's inhuman treatment.

"Never mind!" he would say. "You only wait here a few days, and I'll take you through to Nashville. Then you shall have all the satisfaction you like out of Truesdail, and I'll see that you get back safely!"

★★★★★★★★★★★★★★★★

One point must be noted in this chapter, and that is, the fact that our heroine here distinctly departed from her instructions. She had been told, advisedly, not to make drawings of the fortifications, etc., of the enemy; for it was well known what additional dangers she might thereby incur; yet the opportunities were so unusual and tempting that the ambitious and patriotic girl refused to obey these teachings of prudence and caution. At Shelbyville and Tullahoma, she made careful drawings of the rebel works; and not a gun but had its proper position, or a man that was out of place. Indeed, the rare excellence of these drawings, necessarily rude, was their truth, and they were generally acknowledged to be so by those who afterwards had an opportunity of judging.

These forbidden sketches she concealed, like Major Andre, the ill-fated, in her boot, between the inner and outer sole. We shall see what came of this departure from orders—though with the best intentions—those "paving stones," it is said, "to the infernal regions." In this case, they served to pave the way to horrors and sufferings such as a woman is seldom called upon to endure, or history to record. But let us not anticipate.

Chapter 22: Betrayed

The weather being remarkably fine, and our heroine having gained all the information she needed, it seemed a most suitable moment wherein to return to Nashville. As we have already seen, she had impressed upon her rebel lovers, admirers, and sympathisers that she was returning to Nashville in order to secure her theatrical wardrobe, so that she would be in a position to accept the engagement proffered her at the Richmond Theatre.

The truth of the matter, we know, was that she was desirous of conveying the information, which she had so arduously collected, to our generals, knowing it to be of the highest importance to their success. It was therefore determined that she should, in company with the old man Baker, start at once for Milam's house, to proceed from there to Nashville. This plan was accordingly carried out, in the first part at least, and the roads being good, and the season most favourable, our heroine arrived at the Big Harpeth Bridge, on the "*secesh*" side of Milam's house, without adventure or stay.

Here the villainy of the old man Baker first appeared. This old hypocrite had been seven years in the Nashville penitentiary, and had only escaped it, we fear, to merit, and perhaps secure, a more ignominious end. Believing that Pauline was off for Nashville, and that she would be unable to harm him he now exhibited his rascality in a striking manner.

On approaching the bridge across the Big Harpeth River, he had requested Pauline to descend from the buggy which had conveyed them thus far, and cross the bridge on foot; at the same time representing that the ford was impassable, owing to late rains. He then suddenly disappeared, leaving our heroine with but a small moiety of her baggage, some distance from her destination, and night rapidly closing in. Indeed, it was quite dark when, at last, Pauline reached Milam's house. Nearing the door, she saw her old "*secesh*" sympathiser, Mrs. Milam, who was, to say the least, surprised at again beholding her.

"What? you back again?" she cried, amazed Then, almost in the same breath, she muttered, "I *do* hope nothing has happened to the old man," meaning her husband.

Our heroine saw at once that her sudden return had awakened suspicion in the mind of her hostess and sought by every means to allay it, but in vain. Milam's continued absence contributed to this feeling, and when, at last, it was found that there was still no sign of his coming, all parties retired to bed brooding secretly over the unfavourable turn events had taken.

Never before had our heroine felt the dread sense of coming danger so strongly as she did that night. It weighed upon her, yet with her natural heroism she cast it off. A cool brain and a mind full of expedients will, she said to herself, yet save me. But she was wrong. There are moments when the utmost prescience of man fails. Nature, at such times, takes upon herself the kind office of a watchful mother, and warns us of the coming danger. This warning came to the brave girl as she lay beneath the roof-tree of that arch-traitor and bad man, Milam, but she disregarded it. Had she yielded to this feeling, indescribable and inexplicable as it is, she might have been saved.

She should have started for Nashville that very night, even though she walked every step of the way; instead of which she lingered, calling to her aid her own courageous nature to combat the kind promptings whispered by her more watchful soul, for these warnings of coming evil have their origin there.

The next morning our heroine met Milam. He had not returned home until late at night, but had evidently been duly warned of her arrival.

After some conversation, he said:

"You know Captain Blackman, I believe?"

"I do. What of him?" asked the fair girl.

"Oh, nothing! Only he sent a letter through me, the other day, to see about your trunks. So, I stopped at the City Hotel and inquired for them, though it is ticklish work, I tell you."

"Well?" interrupted our heroine, impatiently.

"Well, I heard that they had been taken to the provost-marshal's office. Colonel Truesdail had seized and still held them," was the answer.

"Colonel Truesdail has my baggage?" demanded our heroine, still incredulously and pretending to be very angry.

"He has your baggage under lock and key, and swears that no one shall have it."

"Well, *I'll* have it!" cried Pauline, bursting forth in a torrent of indignation, all of course assumed. "*I'll have it* if I have to walk all the way back to Nashville to get it. Will you sell me a horse to go on?" she continued. "I will give you ninety dollars for my old horse back again. Here they are, all in Confederate notes."

"Well, I don't know!" returned he, still doubtingly, but taking care to pocket the proffered money. "Well, I don't know! But I'll see about it."

With these words came the full consequences of our heroine's misplaced confidence. Like an earthquake on some quiet village, forever before free from such rude convulsions, she found this dread danger ready to burst upon her. When she had been at Milam's house before, the bold and bad man had revealed his secrets to the young girl, who seemed about to go South to remain permanently. His smuggling tricks, his false Unionism, were all known to her. It may be believed then that he was ready to meet with suspicion any desire of our heroine to reach the Federal authorities.

At the expression that she would have her trunks "even if she went herself to Nashville for them," Milam's face had suddenly changed. From that moment Pauline felt that she was at the mercy of this base and wicked man.

Disdaining, however, to show her fears, our heroine sought every possible means to attain by stratagem what her address had failed to obtain her.

Milam's boy, a young lad of some seventeen summers, had been cleaning his rifle, preparatory to a hunting expedition, and approaching him Pauline set to work at her plans.

"What a nice little rifle, Johnny!" began she taking the piece from the boy's hands and examining it with the eye of a connoisseur.

"Why, what do *you* know about rifles?" demanded the boy, scoffingly.

"What do I know about rifles? You shall see," and, loading the gun

101

as well as a regular soldier could do, she looked about for a mark. At last, one was found. A little squirrel had come out upon the branch of a tree, some distance off, and was unsuspectingly perched upon his haunches nibbling away at a nut.

Raising the rifle quickly our heroine fired at the little fellow, and the next moment the animal fell, pierced through the heart. A cry of admiration went up from the astonished boy.

"Why, you *do* know something about a rifle, after all!" he cried, admiringly.

"I know enough to be able to beat you shooting, anyhow," retorted our heroine, hoping to spur the boy on to aid her plans. "And I'll bet ten dollars, I can go out, if you'll borrow your father's horse for me, and kill more squirrels than you."

Falling readily into the trap, the boy responded:

"I'll take that bet. Just wait here till I go and get the horse."

Once on horseback, Pauline determined she would attempt to escape and reach Nashville at once, but fate had determined otherwise. When Milam had finished talking with our heroine, he had left the house, saying that he was going up to the Union lines "to see the old man Shute," one of his partners in guilt, "and not over yonder," jerking his finger towards the rebel side of the river. That he was not sincere in this, our heroine had every reason to suspect, but suspicion was now made certainty.

Milam had, it was evident, become secretly alarmed at her determination to return to Nashville, seeing that she knew his secrets, and had laid his plans to defeat it. He was gone, therefore, just long enough to reach the man Shute, and allow the latter time to cross the river, with word to the nearest rebel-scout station and return. Our heroine had not long to await the result of his treachery, for as Milam, accompanied by his colleague, entered the front door, a man of rough exterior made his appearance at the back entrance of the house.

"Your name is Cushman?" demanded the latter, abruptly, approaching our heroine, and fixing his eyes keenly upon her.

"It is Pauline Cushman!" she answered.

"Have you a pass from Tullahoma, to get beyond our lines?" he continued.

"By what authority do you ask?" was our heroine's response.

"You will soon see," retorted the man, laughing roughly. "My name is Fall, and I am a Confederate scout."

The name was one well known to Pauline, for she had heard of the man before. She was therefore compelled to answer when he continued his catechising.

"Have you the necessary pass to enable you to cross our lines?"

"No. I didn't know that one was needed."

"Well, then," added the rebel scout, more kindly, for, though rough in appearance, he was as polite as one could reasonably expect "well, then, I am afraid you will have to go with me to our station at Anderson's Mills. General Bragg's last order is to arrest everyone going out of the lines without a pass."

In vain did Pauline plead: the rebel scout was immovable.

"How can I go?" she cried at last, "when I have no horse? My horse is not here."

"But your side-saddle is," said the scout, "and we can put it on Shute's horse, and so take you along."

By this mention of the side-saddle, Pauline knew at once to whom she was indebted for this arrest. Had she doubted it even for a moment before, this circumstance indelibly fixed it upon her host, for who else could have so completely revealed her past movements?

Milam, however, though ready to do any mean action, was most desirous to make our heroine believe in his innocence, and approaching the scout, demanded noisily what this meant.

Burning with indignation, Pauline held up her hand warningly, as he approached.

"What does this, mean?" she cried, scoffingly, repeating his words. "It means that you have violated your duty as a host. It means that you have betrayed me?"

"*I?*" demanded Milam, confused and growing red in the face. "*I?*"

"Aye, *you!*" returned our heroine, her eyes flashing and her whole figure dilating with scorn. "And mark you: as sure as my name is Pauline Cushman, I will be even with you yet!" Then turning to the scout, Fall, she said: "Go on. I am your prisoner!"

Chapter 23: The Temptation

For some hours after our heroine set out with the scout, Fall, mounted, as had been proposed, upon Shute's horse, all went quietly. Her vexation made her taciturn, and although her companion tried, even kindly, to enter into conversation, so as to relieve the tedium of the ride, his attempts were always repulsed. Her guide and captor, as she soon found, though of rough exterior and manner, was really, at heart, a good-natured fellow, and as he rode on, carelessly, in front of her, he would turn, every once in a while, and make some friendly remark. But Pauline had no ear for anything. Before her arose the one fact that she was under arrest. Where that might lead to, heaven alone could tell. It might be to life-long captivity—it might be even to the gallows!

With these thoughts racing madly through her brain, the wildest projects of escape suggested themselves. She would tempt the scout with drugged liquor some of which she always carried with her. A thousand plans flitted through her brain; but were rejected, one after the other, as either impracticable, or attended with too much risk. At this instant her hand fell upon her pistol. Why had she not thought of this before? she asked of herself. Here was the means of deliverance!

In the meantime, all unconscious of his danger, the rebel scout rode carelessly before. One shot and she was free. Yet, was this not too much like murder? she asked herself. Would she be justified in thus taking a human life? But was it not to save her own life? she queried. And what will one not do to save one's self? She would try it, therefore!

Before her rode carelessly her captor, little dreaming of the short path to eternity that lay open before him. Pauline's hand was on the pistol; another moment and a human heart would have been stilled forever. It was a fearful temptation. Life, liberty, and one enemy less for her country! The pistol was raised, when, just at this moment, the unsuspecting man spoke. His words were full of kindness, and with a beating heart, the pistol fell again to her side She was proof against everything but kindness. That unnerved her. The man's life was saved!

She began to think, too, on reflecting, that the sound of the pistol would probably be heard by some of the numerous bushwhackers who were always lurking about that country, and, as she entered into conversation, the feeling of attempting some desperate remedy for her ills gradually passed away, and she thanked heaven that she had not listened to the terrible temptation of the moment.

At length, captor and prisoner reached Anderson's Mills, where Pauline was examined by Lieutenant Johnson, the officer in command of the post, and made to surrender her pistol.

The officer, finding that she had no pass, informed her that he would be compelled to hold her as a prisoner of war, until her case was reported to General Bragg, and acted upon by that personage.

Moreover, our heroine had the mortification to hear that she would not be allowed to return to Milam's, even for a moment, though she had left at the smuggler's a large satchel, containing her rebel uniform, given her by Captain Blackman, and several other articles of pressing use and value.

Under any other circumstances, it is probable that she would have enjoyed this little excursion to Anderson's Mills. The place itself was of singular beauty—presenting a fine rolling vista that charmed the eye of the beholder. Under any other circumstances, we say. However, as it was, she consoled herself as best she could, during her compulsory stay, by taking note of such characters as she met there.

Mention has already been made, in these pages, of numerous rebel sympathisers of Nashville, whom, it was thought, had communication with their Confederate brethren. These men Pauline now met in force Among them was R. C. McNairy, a well-known merchant of Nashville, and uncle to the celebrated rebel scout, Duval McNairy. Old Alexander Fall and his son, being father and brother to the young man who had arrested our heroine, were also among the number of these degraded beings, who, having less courage than their "*secesh*" brothers, strive still to consummate the ruin of their country by baser means.

When Miss Cushman met them, the whole party, including some rebel officers, were stretched on the green sward, with their fishing-rods by their sides, and no very modest-sized bottles of whiskey in their hands; and our heroine could not but wish that some heaven-sent thunderbolt, or whizzing Yankee bomb, would descend to annihilate these rascals, great and small.

Principal among them sat the famed rebel-scout Duval McNairy. This man was in every way remarkable. Of about twenty-nine years of age, with light hair, smooth, youthful face, blue eyes, and healthy-looking, clear complexion, Duval McNairy was one whom some of our sensation novelists might fittingly choose for a hero. Added to this, he had a frame that an Adonis might have envied, and a courage and daring that had made his name famous throughout the country. It was with sincere regret that Pauline saw so splendid a specimen of the scout arrayed against her country. Classed, as he will be, with its attempted destroyers, his fame will go down with the ruin of the accursed fabric of treason. How differently would it have been had he been found on the side of the right! Then his name would have lived forever to become a household word with the loyal hearts throughout all time.

Yet, as we have said, this man was in every way remarkable, and of course he had his peculiarities. One of these was never to wear a coat. He was, therefore, seen at all seasons, winter and summer, the same, attired only in a close-fitting, flesh-coloured flannel shirt, with a white or striped one over it. A large black silk neck-tie and blue overalls, with one leg invariably tucked in one boot.

This young man hailed our heroine in great glee, informing her that the whole party went and returned, to and from Nashville, whenever they pleased—bringing goods and intelligence from the former place, and fooled the 'Yanks' completely.

Making a mental note of this fact to serve as a check upon them in the future, our heroine accepted an invitation from the jolly conclave to dine with them *al fresco*.

This dinner afforded many opportunities for our heroine to gain much valuable information in relation to the way these gentlemen managed to deceive the Federal authorities; for they drank freely, and while doing so, spoke still more freely. That they were all regarded as strong *Union* men by the authorities at Nashville was their boast, and were, in consequence, permitted to pass the lines whenever they choose, on the pretext of a day's fishing.

"A Southern man can get the better of a 'Yank' any day, I reckon. Ain't that so, Miss Cushman?" asked Duval McNairy.

"I reckon," was our heroine's reply, with a twinkle in her eye that she could not altogether suppress. "Just take, for instance, the fact of you gentlemen being here. Why, the Yankees will never suspect it."

"Certainly not," chimed in the others. "Why, it's just as easy to fool them as can be. All you have to do is to take the oath, and you are never bothered anymore."

Soon after this merry dinner—and in spite of the picnic character of it, or perhaps from this very reason, our heroine enjoyed it hugely—Miss Cushman was placed in charge of the famed scout, Duval McNairy to be conveyed, still as a prisoner to Spring Hill, where it was supposed General Forrest had his headquarters.

Fortunately, she had come across her horse on the road to Anderson's Mills, at the house of one De Moss, and claiming him at once, had taken possession of him. With her noble steed, then, and excellent saddle, Pauline felt comparatively comfortable, the assurance that she was being led to a Southern prison, perhaps to a fearful death, notwithstanding. But it may be that she did not realise fully the dread prospect of despair and anguish that lay before her. Heaven, in its mercy, hides even from ourselves, sometimes, the fearful ordeals through which we are to pass.

Must it not have been so with Pauline? We know well her courage; we have seen tested her wonderful presence of mind, and reliance upon that Power which alone can rescue our souls from despair. At this very instant these powers were to be called into requisition. On every side did adventure and peril, such as is seldom encountered, save in romances, await her; yet she was as calm and unmoved as though taking a pleasure ride, instead of nearing, at every step, a dishonoured grave.

That this *was* no pleasure ride, the next chapter will reveal; for, even at the outset, did the terrible romance of her being crowd upon her.

Chapter 24: M'Nairy and the Bushwhacker

As the night closed in, our heroine found herself again on the road, still a prisoner; and she looked at the fading rays of the sun as a prisoner only can look at them, wondering if those joyous harbingers of heaven shall greet her long. Across the dark vales, tinting the mountain tops, lighting the brooks in their sportive haste, the last rays of the departing monarch lay dying. Deep in the forest the gloom of night had already fallen, and it was only on arriving at some clearing that the last struggling gleam of day could be perceived. At last, even this vanished, and bold and beautiful in the vault of heaven stood forth the evening star. One by one, then, did the little "gimlet holes of glory," as a child has poetically called them, appear, as though a joyous band of angels come to dance together

Beneath, and in striking contrast to this heavenly beauty, clustered the dark trees together like guilty things, moaning their agonies of mind, and casting up their giant arms to the little stars, as if in supplication. Still lower down grew the thick underbrush and ranker grass, wet by the tears of mercy shed from the heavens above.

As the two moved farther into the forest, the shadows grew thicker and thicker, sometimes taking the most monstrous forms, so as even to deceive her guide. But there were dangers there, even surpassing the real or fancied claims to terror which nature showed. Bad men patrolled these woods: deserters from the rebel ranks—men made desperate by hunger and privation.

These men saw their hearths desolated, their children carried off, themselves even torn from their homes, to bolster up the rotting fabric which a few had reared upon the ruin of their country, and called it freedom! They had found the leaders, who had prated so much of State rights, subvert all State and private rights even, in the fearful despotism which they built on their destruction. And these men, finding that the privileges which once belonged to their *slaves* no longer belonged to themselves—that the sacred rights of property, liberty, aye, of life itself, was theirs but in name these men, unwilling to throw their bodies beneath the chariot wheels of their rulers—unwilling or unable to witness unmoved the ruin of their homes fled from the rebel ranks into which they had been impressed, and, taking up their abodes in the mountains, became savages.

These men had been despoiled of everything, and that, too, by the ones who had dragged them into rebellion against the land they once loved, on the pretence of giving them liberty. These men were being eaten by the boast they had worshipped. Around them they saw nothing but ruin: before them lay naught but despair. On every hilltop was a home desolated and deserted like their own. From men they became fiends, killing and plundering alike the defenceless woman or the strong man.

How many such are there throughout the South having their refuge among the mountains, and living upon the proceeds of their bloody traffic!

This fact Duval McNairy was fully alive to, and a certain watchfulness was evinced that could be elicited by no common danger; for these bandits, or bushwhackers as they called themselves, respected a rebel but little more than they did the Yankees. At any unusual noise, then, our heroine could perceive her guide lay his hand quickly upon his pistol, prepared to act; and, as it happened, just at this moment some sound attracted his attention. Bidding Pauline wait where she was until he returned, he rode in the direction of the noise to investigate its cause.

The same instant a wild, terrible-looking wretch dashed out at our heroine from the dense undergrowth that lined the gloomy forest-road, and, grasping her horse's bridle, fiercely endeavoured to drag her from her saddle. But half clothed, with a famished look, and a wild, terrifying glare from his hollow eyes, the fiend tore at our heroine. There was not a moment to lose. She had not time, even, to summon the aid of her guide, for the wretch grasped her light form with the clutch of a satyr. With the quickness of thought, Pauline seized a dagger which had fortunately been overlooked by her captors, and which she had concealed in a side-pocket, and drove it with frantic force into her assailant's shoulder. With a fearful oath he staggered back, as, giving her horse the whip, she dashed past him and regained the side of her guide, who was returning to see what had become of her.

The whole occurrence occupied probably but; a moment, yet it was one that often returned to haunt the dreams of the daring girl.

The almost frenzied gleam of the wretch's eyes, the terrible scowl, the powerful, maddened grasp, as he sought to tear her from her steed—all came back again with the same freshness, when, long after, she had learned to talk calmly about it as among the things that were.

At the next post our heroine was enabled to give a description of this would-be assassin, for there are moments when an object or a face becomes *photographed*, as it were, upon the memory. In one brief instant the victim recognizes his murderer. In one minute part of time, too small even to be computed, the form and features of the guilty one are stamped indelibly upon the mind. So, it was with our heroine. The glaring eyeballs and emaciated visage were ever present to her, and, as she gave an accurate description to the scouts at the next post as we have said, she was afterwards informed that the ruffian had been captured the day following.

It may be believed that our heroine will remember the perpetrator of this attempted outrage as long as life lasts; while it is just as possible that the wretch, if alive, still recalls his brief acquaintance with the Union spy, Miss Cushman.

Chapter 15: General John Morgan

A lonely farmhouse served as a shelter for our heroine and her guide that night, and by daylight the next morning they were again in the saddle.

The day was a glorious one, and Pauline, while backing in the warm and cheering sunlight, soon dispelled the gloomy passages of the night before, though they ever dwelt with her as a terrible and unreal dream.

What had been hidden in the darkness now stood forth revealed in the bright rays of day. The trees, which had seemed to moan their despairing praying in supplication to the night wringing their hands in the agony of their woe, now stood gently swaying to the breeze, the beatitude of the repentant sinner stamped on every leaf.

As the sun neared the zenith, Pauline's guide proposed to stop at the house of a well-known physician for the purpose of refreshment. Alighting, therefore, our heroine was shown into a comfortable dining-room, where a plentiful lunch was soon spread for their acceptance. While engaged in the pleasant duty of refreshing themselves, after their long ride, the noise of tramping horses attracted their attention. With the almost insane hope that it might possibly be a body of Federal troops come to her rescue she rushed to the window, but was soon undeceived, for the hated grey of the Confederate uniforms met her eye. However, chained by the sight, our heroine continued to watch the new arrivals.

One who seemed the chief was attired in an elegant Confederate uniform, bearing a general's insignia of rank. He was a man of apparently some thirty-six years of age, of medium height, and noble, gentle manly figure. When he smiled it was with an expression that won confidence at once, while his fair, light brown hair and blue eyes gave an expression of amiability to his countenance seldom exceeded. He was mounted upon a magnificent charger, and surrounded by his staff, and with his splendid uniform of grey, braided on shoulders and cuffs with broad gold cord, presented as handsome a picture as one need care to look upon. This man was the celebrated partisan chief, John Morgan, whose daring and whose renown, good and evil, has spread over the civilized world.

In the South it is probable that this man's name, degraded as we know it to be, will live secretly honoured after this cursed rebellion shall have been crushed out. Few but will remember John Morgan, for, with all his crimes, he combined much that was calculated to win the affection of the many, and restrain the censure of the few.

Approaching him, McNairy, our heroine's guide, made some communication in low tones. Listening with seeming surprise, the general then approached the spot where our heroine was standing, and, introducing himself with courtly politeness, at once engaged her in conversation.

"Your guide has informed me, Miss Cushman, of the peculiar circumstances to which I owe the pleasure of this meeting, and I have a proposal to make, which I trust will prove acceptable," he said.

Our heroine bowed, while the general continued:

"As I have work for McNairy in an opposite direction, I therefore take it upon myself to beg that you will allow me, henceforth, to be your guide in his place."

"Say rather, in place of my *guide*, to be my jailor," said Pauline, bitterly; "for I am a prisoner."

"However," she added, with a smile, "I have no objection to my new jailor: understand me in that, general."

"In truth, I don't think you will find me a very severe guardian," returned Morgan, smiling in his turn. "For to tell you the truth, I am very susceptible, and if there are to be any prisoners here, it will be

I who am the prisoner, and your bright eyes the jailor," and offering Pauline his hand he led her courteously back to the table, where the conversation ran pleasantly and freely, until the hour arrived for our heroine to again set out, this time with her new "guide."

This change Miss Cushman found considerably for the better, for the general was gallant and even elegant in his demeanour, and though dealing once in a while in a little sentiment, was as charming a companion as one could wish. It was difficult to recognise the rude fame which had clung to him, and made his name almost infamous. Nor, as far as our heroine could judge, did this gentleness of manner seem assumed; on the contrary, its naturalness and readiness constituted its chief charm. It was with sincere pleasure, therefore, that Pauline found herself under such guardianship, and it was with regret that, arriving at Hillsboro', she took her leave of the famed guerilla chief.

"We shall soon meet again," he said, pressing her hand warmly. "But man proposes and God disposes," says the old proverb, and it was some time before our heroine again saw her volunteer guide; though she reverted with pleasure, in after times, to the many pleasant rides and picturesque scenes which this trip afforded.

If this flattering notice of one who had nothing but his courtliness to recommend him, should grate upon the ears of any of our readers, we have only to say that truth warrants it. Whatever he may have been to others, he was always the gentleman to our heroine, and it is not our own impressions that we are giving, but hers.

It is a little strange that men, engaged in a project as base and despicable as the destruction of one's country, should assume a cavalier manner and fascinating gentleness, altogether in contrast to their actions; yet so it is. Few of the leaders of this rebellion but affect these traits. Can it be that they hope, by these means, to deceive the world as to the baseness of their designs? or is it that, ashamed of themselves, they would seek to covet their guilt even from their own eyesight? Who shall read their hearts? Who fathom the doubt and despair, the guilty fears, the damning ambition, which in turn consumes them, and which is sought to be hidden by the cloak of chivalry?

Although this was not the last time that our heroine met the famed John Morgan, we may be forgiven, perhaps, if we leave the burden of our truthful recital for a moment, and revert to a subsequent interview which she had with this celebrated and venturesome man, under circumstances slightly different.

This meeting took place in the prison at Columbus, Ohio, where

111

Morgan was in confinement after his famous raid and capture.

As our light-hearted heroine approached, she sang in a low, bantering voice, a verse of the ballad, "Trust to Luck." It had been one of his favourite songs, when she, herself, was his prisoner, "away down South in Dixie." Then, reaching out her hand, as she entered his dungeon, she exclaimed, heartily, and with a smile, half of fun and half of pity:

"How are you, Johnnie?"

"Pauline!" cried the general, in surprise and joy yet, withal, a little confused. "We've met again at last."

"Yes, indeed; but the boot is on the other foot *now*," responded Pauline.

"That's a fact!" he rejoined, with a hearty laugh. "And it's not difficult to tell, *now*, where *you* belong."

"No. I am true Union; but you must own up that you were deceived nicely," said Pauline.

"I do own up; though I must say, that you are the first and only one that could boast of getting the better of John Morgan. And, even then, I don't know whether I am to blame myself for it," he continued, with some return to his old gallantry, "for those eyes would deceive the devil himself!"

Morgan was, to use the high praise of our heroine, "ever gallant and chivalrous to those in his power, and cheerful and manly when in the power of others;" but he could well afford to be so at this juncture, for already were the plans of escape of himself and his companions, from their Northern prison, in progress of consummation.

We all remember with what joy the capture of this daring raider was announced throughout the loyal sections of our country, and remember equally well the rage and disappointment that filled the hearts of our people, when it was understood that he had escaped. It may, therefore, be of interest to note the causes of this.

On arriving at the prison, the general and his companions had been taken entirely under the charge of the military, who compelled the prisoners to clean out and regulate their own cells. This task, humiliating as it was, was cheerfully undertaken by the prisoners, for it enabled them to concoct and carry into execution the plan by which they subsequently effected their escape. The manner of this escape was, at the time, a nine days' wonder. How men could dig a long tunnel, and manage to conceal the dirt taken out of it, without being discovered, was a question asked by many. There must have been some connivance on the part of the guards, exclaimed emphatically some few; while others, who knew that such was not the case, could but wonder at the success of the rebel chiefs daring plan.

The whole fact is, that, had the ordinary warden of the jail been in charge, the thing would have been impossible; for, under his jurisdiction, the cells of prisoners were examined thoroughly, twice a day. "With the military authorities, however, this was not the case, and it was comparatively an easy thing to dig an excavation beneath the walls, as was done. Indeed, when our heroine visited him, he, no doubt, had more than half his preparations to get away effected; for, as she was going away, after expressing a hope that he would be comfortable in his rude prison, he said, saucily:

"Oh! I'm just resting here a few days, and shall go down South again shortly."

A week or two later the bird had flown.

Chapter 26: The Dying Rebel

To return to our heroine. General Morgan having been compelled to leave her, other duties calling him, he had given his precious charge into the hands of another scout, who was to convey her to General Forrest's headquarters. Morgan had been the tenderest of captors; and as though to herald in this change for the worse, the sky now became over-clouded, and soon torrents of rain deluged the earth. Loud and fearful crashed the thunder overhead, while ever and *anon* a flash of lightning would come that would fairly blind one. In vain the poor trees bent and bent their branches: the ruthless wind and raging storm snapped them off like pipe-stems. The roads, which were none of the best at any time, became now almost impassable so flooded were they with water, converting them into masses of clay and mud.

Under such auspices it was impossible to proceed, and towards night Pauline and her new guides, for there were several, were compelled to halt at a small hut by the wayside, and ask for shelter.

This turned out to be the home of a wounded rebel soldier, who had lost both his limbs in a skirmish which had taken place but a short time before, and who was suffering all the torments of the damned.

It was a fearful scene, and one that, in spite of our heroine's situation, could not but enlist her sympathies. She had little cause to like the rebels, as we well know; but she was still a woman, with a woman's true heart, ready to sympathise with friend or foe.

Indeed, the most inveterate enemy of secession must have been touched to pity at the miserable spectacle which here presented itself. Stretched upon a wretched pallet lay the dying man, groaning and uttering loud curses in his agony of mind and body. At his side hovered his poor wife, the tears streaming down her worn face. At each sound she would start in dismay, for the Yankees were reported to be in the neighbourhood, and might make their appearance any moment. In vain our heroine tried to reassure her on this point.

"Oh no!" she would cry: "they will murder my poor husband in his bed, and burn the house over the heads of my little ones. Oh, I know they will! I know they will!"

Reasoning was useless, and the only thing that Pauline could do was to endeavour to alleviate the sufferings of the poor wretch, who lay cursing the fate that had made him a rebel soldier. What a contrast to the noble Union boys whom she had seen die! Not once had she heard them breathe a regret that they had sacrificed their lives in behalf of their country. If they died, it was blessing the glorious cause which had immortalised them as its champions. If they suffered, whether in the hospital or on the field the martyrdom was borne as a joyful recognisance of their love for the Union.

No regrets, no despairings, were there. *Their* patriotism oozed not out with their wounds. What *they* were fighting for had its home in their hearts, and was not to be banished so long as life lasted. How different was it with this poor, suffering wretch! The cause for which he had offered up his life was a bad one: to it no blessing could attach. He had battled to destroy his country, and no bright vision of glorious fame dare gild the dread future which spread before him. It is ever so. Those who die even in a bad cause respect it not, and if secession were dead tomorrow, there would be none, even among its leaders, to weep upon its tomb.

Like all Southern women, the wife of the wounded man was the greater rebel of the two, and was constantly in trepidation lest the Yankees should suddenly pay her a visit. In vain did Pauline endeavour to make her comprehend that the Yankees were not fiends—that her life, the life of her husband, and their home and little children would be safer in their hands even than they were at present. The woman's senseless fears could not be stilled, and every moment almost would she gaze out into the stormy night, or even venture out into the drenching rain, terrified lest the dreaded Yankees should be near; for, as she said "They always come in the backway." Pauline could not, under any other circumstances, help being amused at the woman's obstinate and groundless fears; as it was, the wretchedness of the surroundings and the sincere sorrow of the woman filled her heart with other feelings.

Around the bed of the wounded man had clustered his little children—mute and tearless, for what do children know of sorrow? A sight more touching, a home more wretched, it would be difficult to imagine,

With her heart full to the brim, our heroine took her way to the small room which had been allotted to her use; and here, as she sat alone, with the groans and cursings of the suffering wretch striking like sledgehammers on her sympathetic heart, her memory turned over one after one the leaves of the past. Were there not hearts in the far North who would sorrow at her tarrying hearts—that would die with her, that had done more—had *lived* for her? But she was not one to give up to gloomy thoughts. *Action* was her motto; and, springing up with all her old elasticity of spirits, she said, almost speaking her thoughts: "Here I am sitting, *thinking*, when I should be at work! If I keep on this way I will indeed never return."

A plan for escape had been revolving through our heroine's head for some time past. This had been founded on the evident fear in which she had found her hostess, and which she had before noticed in her companions, that the Yankees were about. This fact had given her hope, and upon it she determined to act.

During the ride she had noticed that her captors had listened attentively to every noise. The rustle of a leaf, the breaking of a bough, had been sufficient to make them grasp their pistols and loosen their swords in their scabbards. That the Yankees were about was evident; or even if they were not, she determined to make believe that they were.

Where and when "old Rosy," as the rebels as well as our own men called General Rosecrans, would strike was a momentous question at that time in every rebel's heart. No one did they fear more, for none struck so swift and sure. It had occurred to Pauline, then, to raise the cry that "old Rosy" was coming; when she knew that a general "skedaddle" would ensue, *instanter*. Another hope which she had was, that the scouts in whose hands she had been placed were unconscious of the political and military importance of their prisoner. They had seen such courtesy shown to her by their officers, and heard General Morgan, especially, express his perfect confidence in her being able to clear up any charges that might have been brought against her, that she was sure that should the cry be raised that the "Yanks" were coming, that her guides would drop her immediately, so as to effect their own escape.

Her horse, too, as she had noticed, stood, still saddled, in a small out-house, ready for her at any moment. The time, it was true, was but illy suited for such a venture, for, outside the rude house which had given her and her companions shelter, the storm still raged as fearfully as ever. But what was the storm or the terrors of the night in comparison with the unknown but half suspected dangers to which her guides and captors were taking her? Once imprisoned in a Southern jail, there was no telling how long she might lay there, enduring worse than death. Should she not try?

Chapter 27: A General Skedaddle

Crouched close to the fire in one of the little outhouses, attached to the main building that shielded our heroine and her jailors, Pauline had noticed an old negro man, whose sympathetic gaze had followed her every action. There was that expressed in his sable features which showed that his poor untutored heart was capable, at least, of compassion and sympathy for the griefs of others. Believing that she could trust him, Pauline determined to make him the instrument by which to carry out her plan of escape.

Watching her opportunity, therefore, she determined to accost him and induce him to aid her. In the room in which she was, the rebel guards were sitting, smoking and talking of their adventures in a low tone so as not to disturb the wounded man in the adjoining room. She had, therefore, to wait some time for the desired opportunity, while she listened languidly to their rude conversation.

"Well," said one, "as for me, d——d if I be'nt tired of this yhere war. I reckon we've jist fit long 'nough. The 'Yanks' have got too many for us. One man can't fight half-a-dozen of 'em. Another thing, they're so full of their darned mean tricks. Why yer never know whar to find 'em. They may be on yer any minute!"

"On yer! I reckon so," acquiesced the woman of the house, who had not yet recovered from her fear of the Union Army, and who had left her suffering husband for a moment, only to inquire if any news had been heard yet in reference to the fancied approach of the dreaded foe.

"On yer, indeed! Yer may well say that. Why there's poor Miss C——, what's got a sick brother what's got the consumption, lives jist down yhere," pointing with her finger in the supposed direction. "Well, the 'Yanks,' they've been to her house often. One day, our own boys will be there, and the next, the confounded 'Yanks' will make their appearance; and all the Confederates don't take the Yankees do," continued the woman.

"What! You don't mean to say that the Confederates rob their own people?" asked our heroine, in seeming surprise.

"I jist reckon they do," was the answer, given with a certainty that there was no controverting.

"Well, if Miss C—— ain't had it hard since this yhere war's commenced, I don't know who has!" continued the woman. "There's her poor brother what's got exemption papers from our officers, and yet, whenever the 'Yanks' come, they threaten to carry him off to jail up North, and whenever the Confederates come, they make him get up out of bed and show them his papers, and worry Miss C—— so, that the poor thing don't know a bit of peace."

"Well, that is a shame!" exclaimed several; while one, a sergeant, demanded:

"Got his exemption papers, has he?"

"Yes, in black and white!" answered the woman.

"Whew!" whistled the sergeant. "Well, if Jeff's give him his exemption papers, he must be a pretty miserable cuss," while a general laugh showed that this hit at the policy of the rebel government to "rob the cradle and the grave" was well understood by the men who composed its army.

At last, the woman returned to the sick couch of her husband, and "order reigned in Warsaw" once more. One by one, the little group gathered about the miserable, smouldering fire, fell into a sound slumber, and soon the room was resonant with the deep breathings of the worn-out and harassed rebel scouts. What they were dreaming of our heroine did not wait to find out, though there was one who talked in his sleep and who startled our heroine just as she was stealing softly out of the door, by exclaiming:—"The papers! The papers! Are they safe?"

Her heart beat loudly as she thought that she was discovered; but the next moment assured her that it was but the talk emanating from the dreaming head of the tired soldier. She remembered that, during the day; he had been particularly anxious about some important papers, with which he seemed to be entrusted. At each noise he had started, like a murderer at the sound of the detective's voice, believing the "Yankees" to be upon him, and the papers, whatever they were,

were immediately the source of much solicitude.

With his companions it had been the same, and that they were despatches of the utmost importance our heroine could not doubt, and it was upon their desire to save these mysterious "papers," as much as anything, that our heroine had depended for her success in her attempted flight. They would drop her to secure the papers she knew well. Stealing to an outbuilding or kitchen, where sat the old "dark," whose sympathetic gaze our heroine had noticed as he passed to and fro through the room in which she was seated, she said to him, while the old fellow jumped up in surprise stood scratching his head and twirling an old weather-beaten hat,

"Uncle, will you do something for me? You know where I come from, don't you?"

"Bress de Lord, yes, little Missis," the good old fellow promptly responded, below his breath, his eyes roiling cautiously on all sides as he did so. "I'd do an thing for de lady; dat I would!"

By the true-hearted manliness of the answer, Pauline knew, in a moment, that she could trust him. In all her intercourse with this wretched and downtrodden race, she had never had one to deceive her yet. She trusted him, and continued:

"Now, Uncle Bill, here's a ten-dollar greenback that I will give you, all for yourself, if you'll go up the road a piece, and then run down again this way, shouting as loud as you can that the Yankees are coming. You know, you can get double that for it in Confederate notes, and then you'll have twenty dollars all to yourself."

"Yes, yes, Missis; dat's so!" acquiesced the old "dark," grinning, his eyes, too, fairly dancing with delight. "Yes, yes, Missis; dat's so! One dollar greenback better dan two sich notes as yer git down yhere."

"But mind you," added Pauline, "if you fail, the rebs' will hang me, and I'll take good care that they swing you too."

"Oh, I'll do it all right, sure. Jist nebber you fear," answered the old negro, pleased beyond expression at the big prize, all his own.

"Be sure that you do; for my *life*, perhaps, depends upon it. So be careful; and whatever they say, or threaten, or swear, all that you have got to do is to stick to it, and declare, by everything sacred; that the 'Yanks' are really coming. Do you understand?"

A low "yah! yah!" from old "uncle," showed that he did, while he said, mysteriously: "Lord bress you, Missis; I'se jist as glad to see dem run (with a point over his shoulder in the supposed locality of the sleeping rebels) as you are, yourself!"

Leaving him, then, Pauline slipped back quietly again to the room in which were the rebel scouts, whom, to her great joy, she found yet sleeping. Taking her seat by the fire, she waited patiently and calmly for the denouement of her plan. As it happened, her captors soon began to wake up, and, indulging in their principal characteristic, to boast, began to tell their wonderful adventures. To have believed them, they alone had, at various times, contended against the whole Union Army. To them had belonged the whole praise of many a victorious field, and to them should the gratitude of a rescued country be due Making allowance for the difference in the manner of expression, the country and the age, one listening with his eyes shut had certainly thought that he had fallen in with a party of Falstaffs.

Our heroine had heard of guns that "shoot around the corner," and deeds heroic, ordinary and extraordinary; but she heard more hair-breadth 'scapes and adventures that night than would fill ten reasona-bly-sized volumes of Baron Munchausen, or have given material for a dozen yellow-covered novels.

She could console herself with one thing, however, that, whatever their fighting qualities heretofore, she would have the satisfaction of seeing all their courage wilt and their loud boasting be turned to scorn, as soon as it was even reported that the "Yanks" were coming.

Time, however, elapsed, and the plan as projected by our heroine seemed about to fail. Had the old negro deceived her? She could not, she *would* not believe it.

Time dragged on slowly, and about a half hour had passed, in, to our heroine, the most acute suspense The noisy boasting of the rebel scouts had again quieted down, at the particular request of the wife of the wounded man, who had reappeared for a moment for that purpose, and naught now was to be heard but the beating rain and howling wind outside. But suddenly a terrific uproar arose.

"The Yanks! the Yanks!" screamed a dozen voices; and soon as many women and children, headed by the old negro man, to whom our heroine had confided her plan, came running pell-mell into the yard. Such an uproar was seldom heard, and what increased it was, that those hearing it joined in the cry quite as loudly as those that had first started it.

Nearer and nearer came the alarming cry, until bursting into the room where the rebel scouts sat with Pauline in their midst, the crowd of terrified darkies and whites shouted:

"Run! run! You haven't got a minute!" While the old negro, who was at the head of all this commotion, and with his eyes fairly starting from their sockets, cried still more loudly than the rest:

"Run! run! mas'r! de Yanks am a-coming! blessed sakes, de Yanks am a-coming!"

Such a hurly-burly as there then was! No one waited to inquire into the truth of this story. Each was for saving himself, and although our heroine really felt sincere sorrow at the terror and worriment into which the poor wife of the wounded man must necessarily be thrown at this *ruse*, she could not help laughing at the good time these brag-garts made in their haste to escape the dreaded "Yanks."

Soon the coast was quite clear, and springing upon her trusty steed our heroine started off in a direction and at a pace calculated to put each instant a greater distance between her and her rebel friends.

Chapter 28: The Midnight Flight

Away through the mud and the mire; through the gloomy forests and flooded roads away dashed our heroine, on the road to Franklin. The storm, as though leagued with the rebel hordes, now burst forth again with even redoubled fury. Above the fearful thunder crashed, as though it would split the heavens, while the flashing lightning and blinding rain was enough to strike terror to the most fearless soul. It was with the greatest difficulty, too, that Pauline kept her saddle, for often, in the dark woods, so dark that she could not see her horse's head, the bending limbs of the trees, the broken branches, and other obstacles, would almost pull her from her horse.

Sometimes these sudden checks would send a thrill of horror through her, so human did they feel in their clutch, until she would seize hold of them to throw them off, when she would find that it was nothing but the winding branches of some storm-beaten tree, or some hanging plant or vine. At other times they would wrap about her neck like slimy snakes, and clutch at her like demons imbued with life. Most young women, under such surroundings, to say nothing of the hour or circumstances, would have died from horror and dread, but Pauline was composed of sterner stuff. But one thought occupied her mind—*escape!*—escape from the horrors of a Southern prison, from the jaws of death!

Ah, ye that sit at home by your snug firesides, ye know nothing of what a Southern prison is. True, you have heard of them in the papers. You have read books describing them, written by unfortunate

The fearful midnight flight.

inmates. You have read in them of the privations and bodily sufferings which our brave soldiers have to undergo there, placed, as they invariably are, under the custody of human fiends. You have heard of them being shot down, like beasts of prey, by thoughtless and inhuman boys, because they approached too near the barred window of their prison, to get a mouthful of fresh air and a ray of God's light.

You have heard of them huddled up together, like the slaves on a slave-ship; eaten up with vermin and dying in their own filth. You have heard how they have been fiendishly murdered to gratify the spleen or devilish promptings of their captors. But all these are merely the acts done to the *body*—the sufferings of the human frame. Who shall describe the agony of mind, the terrible tortures of heart and soul that these poor wretches have undergone? Who shall tell this, the worst part of all their sufferings? Who can relate the burning memories of home, the longings for the distant loved ones, the thousand tortures that tear the heart-strings worse than the rack; and agonise more than a thousand deaths?

Oh, no! these things have not been described, for there is no *human* language that can give them utterance. God only and his weeping angels understand fully their extent. Happy for us that we are incapable of realising them.

This much of existence—we cannot call it *life*—in a Southern prison, then, you can but guess at. You are more accustomed to regard the withered limbs, the skeleton form, the starved, eager eyes, as the type of this chivalric confinement; but you do not see the hair grown grey, the eyes grown lustreless, the hearts seared, the minds blasted by it; nor imagine the mental horror which these young yet old forms must have suffered to cause this sad, heart-broken expression, which neither time nor companionship can change.

Besides, you read of prison life, with your feet snugly encased in your warm, embroidered slippers. You sit by your cheery, glowing fire, the tea-kettle singing, perhaps, on the hob; the bright gaslight flooding the page of your book. And you say as you read, "Poor fellows! What they have suffered!"

Poor fellows! Ye know nothing of it! Whatever your sympathies, whatever your perception, your refinement of sensibilities, you cannot tell what these hearts have suffered, without you have yourself undergone the same agonies. God, and those who have suffered, alone know!

Our heroine had, in her adventures, her dangers, and her investigations, learned something of all this, and could *guess*, at least, at most of it: beside she had death staring her in the face.

With the gallows ever present in her mind, then, as a probable fate, should she be overtaken by her rebel friends, and a gloomy prison in prospective as a *milder* alternative, it is not to be wondered at that all other feelings were submerged in the frantic effort to escape. On, on, then, she plunged, galloping for life through the forest bridle-paths, and through the swift currents of the swollen streams; regardless of self and everything, save escape from the hated rebel hordes.

The blinding rain, which poured down literally in broad sheets, as though it had ceased merely to *rain*, and had become a second deluge—the terrific claps of thunder, the soul-harrowing glare of the lightning, together with the dark woods and ghostly midnight hour, would have been enough; but in the tangled underwood, the rain washing their faces, and the lightning giving them a fearful appearance of life, lay the dead bodies of two rebel scouts, murdered, by whom we know not, but lying weltering in their gore.

Happily, our heroine knew not this, at the time, though her brave steed stopped suddenly at the unhallowed spot, and, sniffing the mur-der-tainted-air, refused, for a moment, to proceed. A sharp cut from his rider's whip, however, made him bound forward again, and once more they were flying like the wind, with the storm and gloom pursuing them like fiends.

Pauline had been observant enough, during her ride of the day, to know where to expect the appearance of the rebel scouts upon the road. She had also caught the challenge and passwords of her rebel companions; and these now stood her in good stead, for, on approaching the Franklin pike, she was here and there confronted, at a few rods distance, by a rebel picket.

Fortunately, she had no use for her firearms. She had prepared herself, however, in this particular; having taken the pistol of the wounded rebel soldier, at the little house at which she had sought refuge, and which, in the hurly-burly of alarm, had been secured without detection. As we have said, however, she had no occasion to use this, but smoothed the military difficulties that barred her way by the judicious use of a certain "pocket pistol" she had contrived to hide in her apparel from her captors. This, the rebel scout Duval McNairy had given her, and she here acknowledges its usefulness, as well as excellent quality of its contents.

When, therefore, she was confronted by the rebel scouts, with

"Who goes there?" she would answer by saying, "A friend!"

"Dismount, friend. Advance and give the countersign!" the rebel scout would then add.

Alighting, Pauline would then approach the challenger, leading her horse by the bridle, and when halted, would answer, "Jeff Davis and the Southern Confederacy!"

Questions then followed as to how an unprotected woman happened to be out on such a night, and at such an hour? But, whimpering and crying, a nice little story was soon concocted about her father living somewhere across the country and of being "caught out too late away from home," "being detained by the storm," etc., etc.; which, when taken together with the persuasive powers of the "pocket pistol" aforesaid—a good canteen, full of "the real stuff""—was generally satisfactory.

She would have to act, too, the complete rebel woman—full of spite and hate for the Yankees; and sometimes she would take a drop or two of the burning liquor, and swallow it down, to the health of the "Confederate Army." This generally satisfied the picket, who would rapidly arrive at the conclusion that anyone who carried such good liquor, and seemed so "true blue," could not be a dangerous subject; so, she was allowed to pass.

Thus, she worked her way beyond no less than five rebel pickets, and liberty seemed once more secured. But alas! for the fallacy of human hopes! When she finally reached the sixth and last one on the Franklin pike, stationed about three miles distance from the town, her good fortune deserted her. The picket here was an old man, free from all small vices, and as incorruptible as a marble statue. She gave the countersign and told her story—she wept—she tore her hair. It was all useless.

"I must have a written pass," he said, decidedly. Our heroine's heart beat heavily. Was she so near liberty to be foiled at last?

But no; the man must have some vices! she would try money. She had a gold piece still. She would try the effect of the unusual sight of gold. She would try the *spiritual* appeal, too. All in vain! he was a nonsuch—he cared not for money, and never drank.

"I am the last picket on this road," said he, "and have to answer for everyone that goes by; so, you must go back and get a pass. You can find a night's lodging at some of the farmhouses up the country, and make it all right tomorrow, no doubt."

Then, marking the distressed and dejected look of the poor girl, he added:

"I am very sorry, Miss; but my orders must be obeyed."

Once more our heroine grasped her revolver, with a determination to remove the only barrier left between her and freedom; but recollecting that her horse was spent by his furious pace through the heavy roads of the forest, and that the report of the pistol would bring the fleet rebel pickets upon her in a twinkling, and render all future chances of escape impossible, she chose the more prudent plan, and turned back through the drenching rain, with aching limbs and a heavy heart.

Chapter 29: The Lonely Farmhouse

On that same night, in a lonely farmhouse situated near the border of the Franklin pike, lights might have been seen moving fitfully from one window to the other, for death was in that house. A few hours before there had been a merry-making there. The firstborn of the worthy owners of the farm had been christened, and a few of the nearest neighbours had been summoned to participate in the festivities consequent upon such occasions. The young girls had come, many, indeed, without *beaux*, for the war had placed men at a premium in that section of country, but still determined to enjoy themselves; and had danced, and hugged, and kissed the baby to their hearts' content. The proud mother had stood looking on, blessing in her heart the little crowing thing, while the father, no less proud, had pressed the hand of his wife in sympathy with her motherly joy at seeing her baby so much admired.

Everyone knows how particularly dear the firstborn is to his or her parents. It is the first bond of unity between man and wife, the first link in the chain of married joys which is destined to bind them together forever—at least as long as this world shall last to them.

Before this bond of union there is always a feeling that something or some untoward circumstance may separate them; but although it is, alas! sometimes different, with the welcome little stranger at her breast, and the husband and father leaning proudly over the back of her chair, the happy young wife and mother feels her tenure of love secure, and the blessed assurance is doubly loved.

We do not mean to say by this that the later offspring are not loved as dearly by their parents as the firstborn, but there is a feeling attached to the first that can never be experienced but once. This is the reason, perhaps, that the first-born is so frequently the "pet." Unfortunately, too, the position in the family circle is not without its disagreeable side, for the firstborn, not unfrequently, has "all the bringing up," and is sometimes "brought up by hand," in a literal sense. Fathers and mothers have to serve an apprenticeship as parents, and the first-comer has to serve them as a practising block, to be "patted" into or cut into any form they may please.

Unfortunately, they sometimes lack the knowledge of what form they desire the young cub should be licked into; so that he is made to take many, ending in his being nothing in particular, and everything in general. One thing certain, the firstborn, as we have said, has all the "bringing up," but he has, too, a love which is peculiar to itself. With what sorrows, then, does a parent resign even to heaven this treasure! Yet in this lone house by the wayside, even in the midst of their merry-making, had this sacrifice been demanded of the young couple that constituted its inmates.

The dance had gone merrily on, the little one fondled and petted, when all at once the cherished babe had been seized with a violent attack of croup, and before medical aid could arrive had expired in its sorrowing mother's arms.

When, therefore, our heroine tapped at the door to ask for permission to enter and rest for the night, she encountered a wailing household, with sorrow fresh among them. She had been guided there by the light streaming from one of its windows, but it was the lamp of Death, who had taken up his abode in the lone house by the wayside.

In the master of the mansion, however, Pauline found a kind-hearted and sympathetic man, all the more so, perhaps, from the calamity which had just befallen him; yet he said, and truly;

"This is no place at present. Our hearts are too full to receive strangers."

"I know it," said our heroine, "and, believe me, I sympathise deeply with your loss," for he had explained the sad occurrence. But I am weak and weary. I am alone and unprotected. You will not cast me forth to die upon the road? In the name of humanity, in the name of your lost treasure, I appeal to you."

The worthy farmer, whose name was Baum, could not resist this appeal; so, bidding our heroine enter the house, he himself took charge of her jaded horse.

Returning soon, he bestirred himself to get her some supper, which she ate in a silence unbroken except by the sobs of the poor mother, as she knelt by the little bedside of her dead child. A melancholy situation enough!

To Mr. Baum our heroine related her story as before. She saw that a doubt dwelt upon his face, but whether he suspected her or not she never knew. However, he was interested in her, and said:

"The pickets will all be called in at four o'clock in the morning, and at that hour I will arouse you."

"The pickets will be called in?" queried Pauling eagerly.

"Oh, yes," answered the farmer. "You know the 'Yanks' are so near that it would be unsafe for a picket to show himself the minute day-breaks. A sharpshooter would pick him off before he could say Jack Robinson, for the lines of the Federals and Confederates are very close here. They therefore call in the pickets on both sides as soon as day begins to break, and the minute it grows dark again push them out to their old places!"

Thanking her new-found friend for his kind and most acceptable information, our heroine betook herself to the room allotted to her, her heart once more buoyant with hope; and, overcome with fatigue and anxiety, fell into a sound slumber.

Chapter 30: Recaptured by Rebel Scouts

Pauline slept, she knew not how long, when a loud, peremptory rap at her room door caused her to spring from her couch. At first, her heart beat wildly, and a thrill of terror seized her. Her sleep had been filled with the most horrible phantoms, if we may so call them. At one time, she was being led to the gallows to be executed as a spy. Overhead, shutting out the sight of the sun with its ignominious shadow was the rude gibbet; around her, she could see the surging sea of uplifted faces, come to witness the execution of the famed Union spy. All was as clear to her as though it was really happening; and it can be readily imagined that the sensation was anything but agreeable.

Then the scene would rapidly shift; she would again be drinking the rebel toast on the stage of the Louisville theatre. The crowds upon crowds of people before her, the bright lights, the musicians, all could be seen with vivid truthfulness; when, all of a sudden, the dark woods would envelop her, the boughs of the trees clutching at her, and the wet vines twining, like slimy serpents, about her throat. These visions were flying, in rapid succession, about her over-fatigued brain, when the loud knocking at her chamber-door again recalled her to her situ–

ation and its dangers—not visions merely, but dread realities.

With her faculties collected in an instant, however she opened the door cautiously, as she was still partially undressed, and beheld the stalwart figures of four rebel scouts, who, it seems, had been on her track all the way from Hillsboro'.

Feigning the utmost delight at seeing them Pauline said, cheerfully, as though quite acquiescing in their views:

"I'm glad to see you once more, gentlemen, and we will continue our journey tomorrow all fresh again. The cry that the 'Yanks' were coming so terrified me that I cut away as fast as my horse would carry me; for I have heard too much of their brutality to weak, defenceless women, and suffered too much, already, of their overhearing and insulting manners, to wish a closer acquaintance. But I am really glad to see you, and as soon as breakfast is over in the morning, we will start out together again."

"Hum!" grunted one of the party, the spokesman. "Hum! I reckon you may as well come at once. Your horse is all ready, and waiting for you; so, dress at once, and come right along with us."

The tone proved to our heroine that her story was scarcely credited; so, she hastened to reply:

"Oh, certainly, certainly; all right, gentlemen!" while she bit her lips with baffled longing for the free road, and no favour, once more.

Miss Cushman was soon dressed, and, thanking her kind host, who had begged of the party to remain all night, and allow our heroine and her jaded steed to obtain the rest they so much needed, set out on her journey.

The rebel scouts had resisted every persuasion to adopt another course, even going so far as to say to the kind farmer: "If we didn't know you to be a good Confederate, Mr. Baum, we would a-thought you was a d——d Yankee dog."

Sulkily enough, then, our heroine turned her horse's head once more towards Spring Hill. All night did they journey, stopping, at long intervals, to rest for a few moments, and then immediately pushing on. The scouts evidently thought, and rightly, that they had secured a large prize in the brave girl, and that their reward would be commensurate. They, therefore, took care not to allow their eyes to wander, for an instant, from our heroine; and although she watched every possible opportunity to escape, they were ever on the alert to prevent her carrying her plans into operation.

At one of the places at which they stopped, for a mouthful of coffee and a cracker, a little incident occurred which we may here relate, as evidence that Union feeling, to a greater or less extent, exists everywhere in the South. It occurred this way: Our heroine being completely worn out by her fearful ride of the earlier part of the night, her guides saw that she must have refreshment. As day was breaking then, it was determined to stop at a farmhouse by the wayside, and obtain a cup of coffee, or, rather, "rye;" for coffee was unknown in that part of the country. The light smoke curling up from the chimney telling them that the inmates of the house were already astir, the scouts, together with their prisoner, rode right up to the door at once, and, after dismounting, walked into the house without further ceremony; Pauline, of course, being with them.

A woman of middle age was engaged making the fire in the little kitchen, and, merely turning her head for an instant, regarded the intruders with looks of anything but welcome. As soon as she understood the facts of the case, however, her manner changed, and she hastened to spread before our heroine the best that she possessed—seeking to tempt her appetite in every manner.

Pauline was at a loss to understand this sudden change in the woman's manner; but it was soon explained, in a way quite as unexpected as it was touching,

A little child, a boy, who had entered the room during our heroine's stay, had been much petted by her. She is passionately fond of children, and leaving the rebel scouts to satisfy their grosser degree of hunger, she took the little child aside, and taking a seat in a recess some distance from the breakfast-table, sat him in her lap. It was a strange feeling to her, to have the little fellow caressing her with his infant hands, and laying his head confidingly upon her breast; and she thought of the peaceful life which she might have led, had her romantic disposition and love of country been less; for, although unsexed, as it were, by the terrible ordeals which she had to incur, Pauline had a good, true woman's heart, capable of all a mother's love and devotion. The child seemed to feel this, for, putting its little arms about her neck, it whispered: "Me love you."

"You do?" queried our heroine, the tears almost starting to her eyes, at these, the first kind words she had heard for a long time. "Why do you love me, little pet?" she continued.

"'Cause my mamma says you're a good lady, and that they are bad men," answered the child, pointing its little finger stealthily towards the place where the rebel scouts sat.

"But why does your mamma think I am good and they are bad?" asked our heroine, curious to know the reason of this distinction.

"'Cause they are—'cause —'cause—" the child hesitated, then laid its little head close to her ear, and whispered: "'Cause they fight the good people and kill them."

As our heroine afterwards discovered, the mother was as good and true a Union woman as one could find, and was in the habit of wearing a small Union flag next to her heart. At the same time her eldest boy and her husband were the rankest kind of "*secesh,*" and were as loud in their denunciations of the Union as she was earnest in its defence illustrating well the fearful dissensions this fatal war has made, even in the feelings of the same family. Verily, father is arrayed against son, and brother against brother!

With a remarkable intuition, the woman had quickly discerned the true position in which Miss Cushman stood. She saw, at a glance, what might have escaped a thousand other eyes, *viz*; that the scouts were jailors, and their female companion a prisoner; and during our heroine's stay, she evidently sought every opportunity to aid her. All efforts at escape, however, were rendered abortive by the lynx-eyed vigilance of her rebel companions, and Pauline was forced at last to take her leave of her kind hostess, still a prisoner.

About ten o'clock that same morning, our heroine again found herself in the kindly presence of the famous rebel-chief, John Morgan. His reception of her was as polite as usual, and sending off the rebel scouts, as before, on various errands, he assumed the care of her once more.

"So, so!" he exclaimed, laughing. "It seems that I am ever destined to be the cruel jailor of as pretty a bird as ever flew!"

"Not the very *cruel* jailor," dissented our heroine smiling

"Say you so? Well, then, no not the jailor, but the knight-errant of as lovely a lady as ever the sun shone upon."

"For which devotion the fair lady feels truly grateful," returned our heroine, in the same light vein; "being assured that her brave knight will fight the coming battle for her, and see that her name is cleared of the foul stain which has been put upon it."

"Of what does the fair lady stand charged now?" asked Morgan, falling into the old courtly phraseology so natural to him.

"Of what do you think, sir knight? Of nothing less than *treason* to our goodly government."

"This is infamous!" exclaimed the general, indignantly; relapsing into common sense the moment he got angry. "But no doubt it will all come right yet; and when you have cleared up all the charges against you, which you can do easily, I presume, you shall be made my *aide-de-camp*. I will present you with this splendid silver-mounted pistol, a splendid gold watch and my diamond ring, which, in the meantime, keep as a token of my promise. We will then show the world what a female soldier can do; for, by heaven you are more of a soldier than half of my men."

Thanking him for his kind offers, and interest shown in her behalf, the "fair lady" told him that she would consider the matter most gravely, when all the "ifs" and "ands" were out of the road, and thus the badinage continued until the hour of dinner, after which they were to go together to the headquarters of her judge—General Forrest.

Chapter 31: Before General Forrest

A brief allusion may with propriety be made to the famous Sue Monday, who was afterwards Morgan's companion, and whose adventures would doubtless prove both amusing and characteristic in their recital. This well-known individual had his origin—for Sue was a man—in the often-expressed regret on the part of the general that our heroine, Miss Cushman, had not acceded to his desire to have her act as his *aide-de-camp*. One of his staff officers having often heard the wish expressed, bethought him of a plan to play a joke off on his general, and also aid the Confederate cause.

Among the young fellows about the camp was one noted for his feminine voice, delicate complexion, and graceful and womanly form. This young gentleman was forthwith dressed as a woman, and introduced to General John Morgan as Miss Sue Monday, a dashing and fearless young lady, anxious to join the Confederate service.

Delighted at finding the great wish of his life about to be realised, and the long-projected plan, first proposed to our heroine, about to be brought to completion, Morgan "bit" at once, and eagerly proffered the "young lady" a place upon his staff.

Of course, the trick soon became apparent, and the general enjoyed the laugh as much as anyone, and seeing the feasibility of the disguise, frequently employed the young man in expeditions in which a female would be more likely to succeed and less liable to danger than a man.

It is seen, then, that Morgan was sincere in his expressed wish to

have our heroine turn Confederate soldier and whilst they were din-
ing, he never ceased to urge it upon her—banteringly, apparently, but
actually and truly in earnest.

At length, however, the time came for our heroine to set out for
the camp at which they were to find General Forrest, her inquisitor;
and the gay jests died away on her lips as she thought what might
result for good or evil from that examination.

Morgan either did, or pretended to feel that her examination
would be but a short one, and end in her instant acquittal, but his gallantry was such that he would have been prompted to hide the dark
side of the picture, even had he seen it himself.

General Forrest received her with a warmth most unexpected and
delightful to behold, had it arisen from any other cause than the one
unveiled in his opening salutation. As it was, it caused the heart of our
heroine to sink in her bosom like lead, for it revealed the dread danger
opening before her.

"Well, Miss Cushman," was his salute, as her name was announced,
"I am glad, indeed, to see you. I've been looking for you for a long
time. You're pretty sharp at turning a card, but I think we've got you
on this last shuffle, and I've made up my mind not to part with you
during the war."

Pauline fixed her eyes keenly upon him. From *that* face she knew
she had nothing to expect. Tall, and as erect as an Indian, with a full,
dark blue eye, replete with expression, General Forrest's was one that
was marked by no sign of good nature. Indeed, our heroine had often
heard of his harshness to his own soldiers, and his bitterness towards
ours. Before the war, so it is said, he had been a professional gambler—
an occupation fitting him well for his present office, and a fact that
may account for the terms used in his opening address to the pale but
determined and undaunted woman that stood before him.

"You've been here before, I find," he continued, referring to a
piece of paper which he held in his hand.

"No, sir!" retorted Pauline, instantly, with all her wonderful ener-
gies aroused, "it is untrue!" Then added she with well-assumed indignation, "I have never been here before, and I'd like to send a bullet
through any man mean enough to say so!"

Forrest gazed at her a moment, with no little surprise depicted
upon his countenance, and Pauline continued:

Yes, sir; and I would put one through you if I could, were you to
repeat the charge."

He continued to measure her with his glance for a moment or so, as much as to say, "Is this merely acting, or is it genuine indignation?" Becoming convinced of the latter, however, he rejoined:

"Well, you're made of good fighting stuff, anyhow, if you *are* a woman. I got my own fighting material from one of the sex—my good, brave mother. But let us come to the point: you have certain documents about you and should their evidence show you to be, as I suspect, a *spy*, nothing under heaven can save you from a hempen collar!"

This was, at best, anything but pleasant news, but not thrown off her guard for a moment, she retorted with a careless gesture:

"Well, sir, suppose that you proceed now, and root up the whole thing; bring it all out. I am ready!"

Taking up a bundle of letters that lay on the table, the general weighed it significantly in his hand.

"Now you see, I have the advantage of your Federal generals, for, without sending a single spy across the enemy's "lines," I know positively *everything* that transpires at the Federal headquarters, a vast deal better even than the clerks that do the writing there."

To this our heroine could but express astonishment, and the subject changing, the general began, as was often his custom, to boast of the wonderful deeds of daring he had performed.

"Yesterday," said he, exultingly, "I killed fifteen Yankees with my own hand, in a skirmish, and," bringing his clenched fist down on the table, so as to make everything shiver, "I'd like to wash my hands in the blood of every one of the infernal crew!"

"The only one whose blood *I* would like to dip my hand," answered our heroine, with emphasis, "is Colonel Truesdail, of Nashville."

"Ha, that's so!" cried Forrest, ferociously. "I'd give the world to capture that man, and I've given strict orders that, if ever taken, he shall be hung on the first tree, and his body brought to me that I may embalm it for a curiosity. D———n him!"

Forrest then took possession of her horse, remarking at the time that Truesdail's money had probably paid for it.

"I have no time now," he said, "to investigate your case. It is a complicated and difficult one. I will, therefore, send you to General Bragg's headquarters, at Shelbyville, and if you should be so fortunate as to prove your loyalty to the South, you may always depend upon General Forrest for protection. But this, I am sorry to say, I do not believe pos-

133

sible, and therefore say, *prepare for the worst*, for hanging is not pleasant!"

With these momentous words still ringing in her ears, our heroine was conducted back to the quarters allotted to her in camp, and placed under a heavy guard, but there was that within her that sustained her—a true reliance upon Him who guides all things, and a feeling of devotion for her country that made her feel that she could even *die* for it, without one word, one thought of regret. But the worst was yet to come.

Chapter 32: A Night in Camp

The quarters to which our heroine had been assigned were little suited to a woman: a canvas covering, a knapsack for a pillow, and two government blankets, stolen from our boys, for a bed, comprising their only luxuries. It was next to impossible to sleep, also; for the noisy carousing of the rebels camped around seemed to last the night through. After midnight, though, when things became a little quieter, Pauline began to reconnoitre, to see if by any possibility she could effect her escape. Lifting a corner of the tent, she peeped anxiously forth. The sentinel to all appearances seemed to be asleep; for he stood silently resting on his gun. To push her body through the small opening in the canvas was but the work of an instant; but the next a sharp sword-point glittered at her breast.

"Hold up, yhere!" cried a voice which startled the sleeping sentinel, for he was really asleep. "Hold up, yhere!" Then the voice continued: "Miss Cushman, you are very sharp; but fortunately I was about, to foil you, this time. You will now please retire to your tent, and remain there, or I shall have to issue orders which will not only be repugnant to my feelings, but ungallant to your sex. As for you, sirrah," he added, shaking the guard as the wind would a willow wand, "you shall suffer for your carelessness. Consider yourself therefore under arrest!"

"General," pleaded the poor man, trembling like a leaf from the rude action and damning words of his chief, "General, I—I—"

"Silence!" roared the general, in a voice of thunder "If your negligence escapes *death*, consider yourself lucky." Then, calling the officer of the guard, he bade him change the sentinel, and confine the one who had been so negligent in a dungeon to await his trial.

At this moment the moon burst through a mass of clouds which had before obscured it. and revealed the erect form and lithe figure of General Forrest. It was the general himself, then, who had been prowling about as was his custom, striving to find out his men in a fault, and then punishing them severely for it. As a natural consequence he was not liked by his troops, though his fighting qualities were admitted and admired; and our heroine heard the remark made more than once by the rebel soldiers, as they groaned beneath some new injustice inflicted upon them by their too strict general, "If General Forrest don't look out, it will happen with him as has happened with many another of our generals since this yhere war."

"What's that?" another would ask.

"Why, *he'll be shot by his own men,*" was the answer followed by a significant chorus of "That's so!" echoed and re-echoed on every side.

While lying in her miserable tent that night, our heroine had also an opportunity of hearing how our poor fellows who were captured fared; and it made her heart ache to hear the terrible ordeals through which they had to pass, and which were referred to with joy and fiendish delight by the rebel soldiery. We have said that she could not sleep; consequently, she was compelled to listen to these dreadful recitals of inhuman barbarity, though each word struck like a sledge-hammer upon her heart.

For greater security General Forrest had ordered a squad of men to move close up to her tent, and build their camp-fire and pass the night watching. Soon, therefore, its ruddy glare bathed all within its circuit with the reflection of its light, and as it arose and fell, or flickered in the air of night—touching here and there the glistening visors of the rebels' caps, or some part of their accoutrements, the scene was one that might have charmed a more fastidious observer.

The most delightful part of a soldier's life is probably passed around the bivouac-fire. There all the cares or dangers of the day are passed, and he relates his deeds of wonderful prowess, or talks over the sprees that he had on his last furlough; and snatches from the dread realities which surround him a few of the pleasures which he had imagined a soldier's life to be wholly composed of.

Some, more given to sentiment, lay looking at the flickering fire, while they dream long and sad dreams of home. They see in their "mind's eye" the blazing fire at home, and the happy household gathered about it. Brothers, sisters, aged father, and tender, hopeful mother—these fill, one after the other, the magic mirror which memory, awakened into life by the flickering fire, calls up, and holds unbidden before them.

Others, again, allow their minds to dwell upon tenderer subjects;

135

and, in *their* dreams, a young girl, with her needlework in her hand, is seated by the far-distant hearth. The whole interior of the little cottage, as each remembers it, is seen—the bright row of tins: the "dresser," with its piles of delicate china; the old dog slumbering by the fire; and the glowing red light streaming over all. Then, at the door, a low knock is heard: the maiden starts as she whispers the soft "Come in." Then follows the betraying blush, the; loving embrace: —and after all the poor fellow comes back to reality, to find that he is only by a camp-fire, amid his fellows, instead of being where his heart would fain take him.

Men of a rough, unwieldy nature are, however, the most common, and such a party was now collected about the fire in front of our heroine's canvas prison-house. These were boasting loudly of their adventures in various ways, and telling about the ——— Yankees at the prison-pen at Macon, Ga., which it seems they had been guarding. Many of the narrators were mere schoolboys, yet their bitter and most heartless language showed them to be adepts in hate for our poor, defenceless fellows who had been under their charge. All of them spoke with a strong Georgia "burr," as it is called, which showed them to belong to that section of country.

"Wall," said one, in reply to something his comrades had remarked, "I'd a-pitied 'em Yankee prisoners a'most, if it hadn't been that I know'd they was 'Yanks.' There was one poor feller used to come to me every mornin', and ask so pitiful, 'Do you think mother'll know me, when I get home?' and then he'd go off a-ravin' about being exchanged and wantin' his mother."

"I reckon he must 'a had the rams!" broke in a heartless wretch, scoffingly.

"No, he had—I forget what the doctor-folks call it—but he was *homesick*, yer see," answered the first; "and it preyed and preyed on his mind till he got kind o' crazy 'bout it. Oh, there was lots o' them just the same way."

"Wanted to see his mammy! —the cowardly skunk!" interrupted the worst wretch of the party again.

"No, nor he warn't a coward, nether," responded one less brutal. "I seed him as well as Ned, here, an' I know he warn't a coward, for I saw him fight; an' I tell you he fit like a wildcat. But then, you know, a feller has to get broke down in his spirits, with nothin' to eat, and the hot sun a-pourin' down on his head all day, and the heavy dews at night. When I seed that feller, that Ned Taylor thar talks of, for the fust time, he was as handsome a boy as anyone dare be. I seed him once chargin', and I shan't forgit that day, nuther, for that very same boy came near takin' *me* prisoner, only some of our fellers came up, and we captured him instead.

"His eyes war as bright as the point of his bayonet, and his cheeks were all aglow just like that fire thar. And he wasn't no coward, nuther, but when we took him he said, 'Well, rebs, I reckon I'll have to give in, though I'd rather die than do it.' Well, when I seed that boy agin, I scarcely know'd him: he hadn't no bright eyes then, or if they was they were bright with hunger. I tell you I felt sorry for him; and when he begun to talk 'bout his mother, I jist thought of my own poor mother, an' I tell you I got melancholy like, an' I thought it wore a thunderen shame to treat 'em quite that hard."

"Well, it ain't no harder nor they treat our fellers when they cotch 'em," broke in another who had thus far remained silent.

"No," acquiesced the one who had sympathised with the Union soldiers: "no, I reckon it ain't; for they do say that our men, when they are taken prisoners by the 'Yanks,' have to eat with the negros, and negros are put to watch 'em."

"That's so!" echoed a host of others. "The colonel says he seen it—that time he was a prisoner up North."

"Well, then, it just sarves 'em right!" remarked one. "For my part I think the sooner thiy are killed off the better!"

"Why, of course it is!" said the most brutal of the party, and who had laughed at his more sympathetic and less heartless comrade. "Of course it is, an' if you fellers will listen, I'll tell you how we used to make short work of the d——d negro stealers, when we caught 'em tryin' to git off."

"Yes, yes, go ahead," cried several, anxious for their companion's story. "Tell it to us," they continued.

"Well, then, listen, and I'll tell you how the hounds got one feller, and how he kicked an' squirmed. By ——, if it warn't as good as a play!" And, drawing about him, the brutal crowd prepared to listen so his story.

Chapter 33: The Bloodhounds on the Track

"Wal, yer see, the 'Yanks' were a-gittin' away pretty smart," he continued. "Fust one mornin' we'd wake up to find twenty or thirty of the devils off, and the next mornin' there'd be more off again. So, our captin he says, says he, 'Boys, something's got to be done, and I'll tell you what I'll do. I'll give any man a thirty days' furlough that'll shoot a Yankee prisoner that's trying to escape."

"So, yer had better believe there was some shootin' done after that. Ha! ha! ha! it was just as good sport as shootin' possum! I remember one day some of the Yanks got crowdin', and they pushed one weak feller off that little bridge that went across the creek down yonder. Well, just as it happened, the feller fell just outside of the 'dead line,' as the boys used to call it, and a feller of our company, named Mike Lotter, shot him and got his thirty days' furlough.

"The Yanks wanted to get him back, and one of 'em had hold of their comrade and was pullin' him across the line on his own side, but Mike he wanted a furlough bad, an' I reckon he just finished him off in double-quick time, though the 'skunk' begged hard for his life all the time.

"But that's got nothing to do with my story, so I'll just begin where I left off.

"Our captin, then, had told us that he would give each feller thirty days' furlough if he shot a prisoner tryin' to escape; but even that didn't help matters, for the Yanks said that they'd *rather* be shot than stay there, and though there war a-plenty killed tryin' to get off, it didn't have no effect at all. Every night a'most, twenty or thirty of 'em would get off, the devil only knows how, and as soon as they got into the woods would spread out into small parties of five or six, and work along that way. Almost every negro they met would help 'em, and bring 'em food; an so workin' their way at night, and layin' covered up in the leaves and bushes by day, some of 'em managed to git across the 'lines,' not many though, for some of 'em was purty weak when they started, and had to lay down in the woods till they died.

"Howsomever the captin said it wouldn't do nohow. The general was a-blowin' him up,' cause so many Yanks got off, and says he, 'The only way we can do now, is to get the hounds and start 'em after 'em the minute we find they're off.' So the very next week we got the hounds, an' as luck would have it, there war work fur 'em right away, for the very day before a young feller, 'bout nineteen, got away. He had a day the start of us, but that wasn't nothin', for we rid an' he had to walk, and that, too, in his bare feet. So, it promised some sport.

"Well, as soon as the hounds were let loose, they got his track at once, an' away we started. It wur as good as a 'coon-hunt, I can tell you; an' as we passed the grand gentlemen's houses, they would holler out: 'Whar yer goin'? Are yer on a Yankee hunt?' and then we'd say, 'Yes, gentlemen, sport's up; so you'd better come along.'

"Then they'd call the boys for to bring their horses, an' they'd jine us; an' of course they all had a flask full of good old brandy to pay their way. I tell you it war sport!"

This time, howsomever, our fun seemed a-goin' to be spiled, for as it happened, all at once the hounds began to throw up their heads and to yelp.

"'Here's somin' wrong,' says the captin. 'Blast me ef I don't believe them hounds has lost the scent,' and sure enough, they kept a-runnin' 'round an' round an' yelpin', an' nobody could get any sense out of 'em.

"'I reckon we're stuck, captin,' said one of the fine gentlemen, 'so you'd better come to my house and get dinner before you ride back to camp.'

"'Dinner? No, by —— I swear I won't eat nor sleep till I catch that infernal Yankee skunk!' roared the captin, an' we all know'd he'd be as good as his word.

"But still the hounds couldn't find the scent, for it seems the boy had dipped his feet in tar so as to throw the dogs off in case they were arter him.

"At last one of 'em got on the trail agin, an' you'd better believe there war some hurrahin'. The captin was a'most wild with delight, and it was fun to see 'em pushin' through the low underbrush like mad, especially when the feller came in sight. It seems that he had heard the hounds a-yelpin' some time afore, an' you ought to a-seen him makin' tracks. But the feller was game, an' I tell you he made fast time, while his eyes stood out of his head like as though he was mad.

"At last, the first dog sprang on him an' took a whole mouthful of flesh out of his arm, but the feller flung him off and rushed on: but now the hull pack came on him, and set at him like wolves. The feller fought hard, but it was no use; the hounds had tasted blood and they tore him piece by piece. We tried to get 'em off, but the tarnal beasts wouldn't mind us a bit, but flew, some at his throat, some at his breast, while two held him by each arm. By—— I never saw anybody tore to pieces the way that boy was!

"Howsomever, he was good grit, though he was a 'Yank,' and he didn't say a word, but just fell back a-fighting to the last minute. Once he did turn his wild eyes toward us, as though 'bout to ask mercy, but then he just turned to the hounds agin, proud-like, as much as to say,

139

'No, I'd rather be eat up by *you*, than to ask one moment's mercy from yer masters!'"

"Did he die?" asked one of the listeners, who had evinced some interest in this terrible story.

"Die?" laughed the narrator, scoffingly. "I just reckon he did. Why his whole witals was tore out of him! But he didn't die right away, and just afore he did, he said faint-like, for he was a-sufferin' awful, 'So near! so near home!' for yer see his only thought war of home, an' then our captin, an' he war a purty cruel man, too, he jist cried like a baby. An' there var a young lady thar, an' she took on like mad, an' everybody, the gentlemen an' all, allowed it war a shame. But it were good sport, I tell yer, better nor a 'coon-hunt!"

Had not our heroine heard it with her own ears she would never have believed that such fearful barbarity could have existed even in a traitor's heart. As phase after phase of the dread tragedy was developed in the rough language of the reciter, she would start up and press her hands upon her head to see if she had lost her senses, while her heart stood still seeming to cease its beatings, in horror at the dreadful tale. "Can such things be, and heaven not fall to crush their fiendish perpetrators?" she asked, in agony of spirit. That they are, the testimony of hundreds of our brave men and officers, who have known the horrors of a Southern prison, will bear us out.

Let those who have suffered in that fearful human beehive of crazy, wild, starving Union prisoners—the pen at Andersonville—answer. What they can narrate will far surpass this in horror. It was the first time, however, that Pauline had heard from the lips of the tends themselves the dreadful extent of their demoniacal cruelties, and she could not forbear, when she thought that but a few years before these men had been our brothers, to kneel, and while she gasped faint with horror, exclaim:

"Father, forgive them. They know not what they do!"

Chapter 34: Before General Bragg

Morning came at last, and whatever destined to bring forth—whether life or death Pauline could not but hail it with joy. Anything were better than to pass through the racking horrors of that night.

It was with a sense of relief, then, that she beheld the grey dawn steal softly up the east, and heard the rebel drums and bugles sound the reveille. One more such night she felt would drive her mad. She dare not even think of it; for the horrors which our poor "boys" had to incur in their fearful prisons, started up, like ghosts, to haunt her, whenever she did so.

Her own dangers and sorrows were unthought o The vision of the bleeding boy and bloodthirsty hounds was all omnipotent. She hailed the freshening air of morn, then, with a feeling of thankfulness which we can scarce understand, for it was to her a liberator—a liberator from pangs worse than she had thought it possible for man to bestow. Thrusting aside, therefore, the fly of the tent, she gazed forth upon the cheering face of nature with a pleasure that she had never experienced before.

About her lay the camp, all astir with preparations for the early breakfast, while the glorious sun poured his first warming beams down upon the whole landscape, like a visible blessing from heaven.

At first, the outlines of the distant hills had been indistinct; but as the sun got higher, the gauzy veil of mist was lifted off them, and they appeared dyed in a thousand tints of melting purple and vivid green.

In the camp, the herds of horses, the moving men, the galloping orderlies—off already on some early mission—together with the picturesque groups gathered about the blazing fires, all contributed to make up a picture that might have distracted the thoughts of any one who loved their country less; but with our heroine it was different— the sad yet true story of the night dwelt with her still.

After breakfast—a meal humble in the extreme, really deserving its original meaning of breakfast, for it was nothing more than that—our heroine prepared again to start upon her journey. Through the kindness of General Forrest, she was allowed to have an ambulance as well as a guard, who received strict orders, from the general himself, to pay her the utmost respect. Pauline was so weak that this kindness had become absolutely necessary. Fatigue, undue excitement, and loss of sleep, had had their effect upon her, and she found herself as prostrated as though she had but arisen from a sick couch. The ambulance, then, was extremely welcome, while the necessity of the guard was soon evinced when the time came to pass through the rebel camp.

In front of the quarters of General Forrest stretched the camp-ground, and though the general stood upon the steps of his house, and watched, so great was the insubordination of his troops, in spite of his severity, that they pressed around the ambulance containing our heroine, as boys do around a show-man in the country.

"Oh, look at the Yankee Spy!" one would exclaim, "Ain't she pretty?"

"D—n her!" another would say. "She might be as beautiful as a Venus; but I be d——d if I wouldn't hang her on the highest tree."

"Oh, jist look yhere at her!" the others would cry, thrusting aside the curtain of the ambulance and peering in at our heroine.

At last, however she was through all this and on the quiet road, where she could collect her thoughts somewhat, for the coming interview with the well-known rebel General Bragg.

This general's quarters were, it seems, at Shelbyville, and after a great deal of jarring and jolting on the journey, lasting two days and a night, our heroine reached her destination. During this journey she had many opportunities of seeing the state of the country, and learning the temper of the people, while the conversation of her guards showed plainly the feeling of the army.

"You wouldn't never have caught me down here, a soldiering," remarked one, "if I hadn't had to come. You can bet high on that!"

"Or me, nuther," chimed in his companion, quite a boy. "But they didn't give me much chance; for one day, jist as we was a-goin' to sit down to dinner, in come a Confederate officer.

"'Ho! ho!' says he. "This is the way you fellows expert to git free of the blasted Yankees, is it? Two good, strong, ablebodied, cowardly curs a-sittin' here, and fellows twice as good as they dare be, a-doin' their work for 'em. Fall in here, blast you! or I'll order out a squad of men to burn the house over the heads of such mean, skulking wretches!'

"So, in spite of all 'dad' could say, Tim, that's my brother, and me was marched off, an' here we are."

"Wal," squeaked another, in the half-boyish, half feminine tone of voice which designates the period of change from boyhood to manhood, "Wal, I was at school, at the Academy at ——, when one day we were walking along the road, two and two, on our way to church. Just then, up rode some officers on horseback one of them we could see was a general.

"'Here, general,' said one of his staff to him, 'here's a batch of recruits.'

"'By ——, that's so,' responded the general and forthwith we were marched off and mustered in; though our professor remonstrated about it, too, saying that boys of fifteen years of age couldn't be of any use; but the general said that we were bound to do as he pleased in the matter, so there was no use in arguing.

"'Won't be of any use?' he answered. 'If you had seen my boys at

Spring Creek, you'd a-said they were some use, and not one of them, rank or file, was over sixteen years of age. But enough said. If these are the men, I take them to be, they will volunteer to go at once; but if they are mean, cowardly cusses, why of course they'll be glad to make some excuse, and stay at home with the gals, and be tied to their mother's apron-strings!' Of course, we all volunteered to go, for it wouldn't have done to make out that we were cowards, for we were not."

"And have you not regretted it?" demanded our heroine

"No. I did feel a little homesick at first, and at my first battle wished I was safe back again at school; but after all, most of the boys were tired of school, and looked upon going into the army as a kind of 'lark,' and actually got to like the life. Another thing, they knew that they would have to go, sooner or later, and the more that went at first, the shorter the war would be."

"That's so," acquiesced the other. "A feller gets, kind o' satisfied at last, and gits attached to his comrades, and soon thinks no more of goin' home."

These facts gave our heroine a pretty clear insight into the feelings of the common soldiery of the rebel Confederacy. Nine-tenths of them had, at first, been driven into it; but being there, with their habitual laziness of thought and feeling they had remained in it, and now knew no other desire, than, perhaps, to have better food than the rebel commissariat afforded.

Many other interesting conversations occurred with her guard, who were all young and well-behaved, as well as good-hearted fellows; but we have neither time nor space to dwell upon them, even though they might prove of interest to our readers; for we must hasten on to that most dramatic portion of our heroine's adventures, when she is brought before the rebel General Bragg, who was, in this case, her inquisitor.

To return, then; on arriving at Shelbyville, she was shown at once to the general's headquarters, which were in the heart of the camp. On entering, she was met by a small-sized man, with small, dark-grey eyes, iron-grey hair and whiskers, and bronzed face, This was General Bragg.

With a stern but still gentlemanly manner, he bowed in acknowledgment of her salute, and the mention of her name by the guard, who, handing over his papers to his superior, now retired.

After glancing over the papers, with an expression cold, but full of meaning, he began his cross-questioning and examination, a matter in which he was celebrated.

"Of what country are you a native, Miss Cushman?" he asked, waving her to a chair with his hand.

"I am an American, sir; but of French and Spanish parentage," answered our heroine.

"And you were born, where?" he asked again,

"In the city of New Orleans."

"Hum!" coughed General Bragg, doubtingly. "How comes it, then, that your pronunciation has the Yankee twang?"

"It comes, probably, from the fact that I am, professionally, an actress," she answered, promptly, "and as I am in the habit of playing Yankee characters very frequently, it may be that I have caught the 'twang' by it, and show it in my ordinary conversation as well as on the stage."

"Hum!" grunted the general again. "But what brought you down South?"

"I was not *brought*, sir; I was *sent*," answered Pauline, proudly.

"By whom, may I ask, Miss Cushman?"

"By the Federal Colonel, Truesdail."

"And *why* were you *sent*?" inquired Bragg, with a sly look of incredulity, as much as to say, "It is a likely story to say you were *sent*!"

"Because I gave warm utterance to my Southern feelings, and refused to take their oath of allegiance," replied our heroine, pretending to shed tears, "and a pretty way I'm paid for it, too!"

"Why wouldn't you take the oath?" persisted Bragg, as unsoftened by her sniffing as he had been by her youth and beauty. "Why wouldn't you take the oath?"

"I had declared that I wouldn't take it and I meant to stick to my word!" returned Pauline stoutly.

The general studied, the expression of her countenance for a moment, and then continued:

"What was the main charge that the Federals, had against you?"

"I had publicly drunk to the success of the South and our Confederacy. It was on the stage of the Louisville theatre, and I did it at the request of two paroled Confederate officers, who, if they were here now, would tell you the same thing," and our heroine went on to relate the whole occurrence of the toast, etc.

"Well, what happened then?" remarked the general.

"I was at once discharged from the theatre, and went to Nashville, where I got a fresh engagement, only to be sent away in turn; for

Colonel Truesdail, the Chief of the Federal Army Police, getting wind of my Southern sentiments, and hearing of my drinking the toast wishing success to the South, immediately ordered me to leave the Federal jurisdiction, and wouldn't even allow me to take my trunk or theatrical wardrobe with me."

The perfect coherence of her story, as well as her calmness and apparent truthfulness in its recital, seemed to produce their effect upon the general, who, after a brief pause, resumed in a more kindly tone:

"Miss Cushman, this statement of yours may be all correct, but still, I should like to have you give some *positive proof* of your loyalty to our cause; for, as it stands, I must say it appears at best very doubtful."

"General," replied our heroine, very firmly and pointedly, "I have been seized and brought hither to meet charges laid against me, I presume, but assuredly not *to investigate and decide my own case*. You cannot be expected to believe *my statement*; therefore, all I can say is, to produce your charges and the evidence, and when the examination is over, I think that my loyalty to the South will shine with as bright and steady a lustre as does your own.

"After that, if you still doubt me, or if one suspicion still lingers in your mind, give me a place near you in battle, and you will see that Pauline Cushman will fight as bravely and faithfully as any man in your army!"

This speech seemed to half amuse and half convince the suspicious old soldier; but it would not have amused him had he known that beneath that hand of velvet grew muscles that were as hard and strong as steel; that those limbs, so delicately and charmingly fashioned would, in spite of fatigue and anxiety of mind, have borne their possessor for miles through the untrodden forest, if necessary.

In short, he would not have laughed at all, had he known that, in mind, spirit, and bodily strength, the fair being standing before him was twice his match. The untamed, early career of our heroine had done this for her.

Her rambles with the bold Indian youths and lasses had given her this unusual strength and quickness, but now it was not her policy to exhibit it; and, as she stood before the rebel general, she was but the gentle, wronged, and unfortunate lady, whose weakness and dependence were her most charming traits. This much for being a consummate actress; but to our story and our heroine's examination, which, we take it, will require another chapter.

Chapter 35: General Bragg and the Fair Spy

"You say that you are devoted to us, yet you come away without a thing. There are many articles which you might have brought us, and which other ladies have seldom failed to bring concealed with them—articles that are scarce in the Confederacy, such as quinine, or other valuable medicines for our poor soldiers," resumed General Bragg, returning once more to the charge.

"I have told you, sir, how that happened," answered our heroine. "I was not forgetful of my duties to the Confederacy, but had large quantities of those very articles stowed away in secret places in my trunk, but, unfortunately, Colonel Truesdail perhaps suspected something of the kind, for he most positively refused to let me bring it with me, and I thus lost everything."

"How do you expect, then, to recover your property?" asked Bragg, his suspicions rapidly being sat at rest.

"I do not know, indeed," was the answer, "without I succeed in finding my brother, Colonel A. A. Cushman, who is somewhere in the Confederate service and procure his aid."

"So, so, you have a brother in the Confederate service, have you? Well, now, should you not discover him, what then will you do?"

"I am at a loss to say," sighed our heroine, drooping her eyes sadly. "But if I can by any conceivable means get my wardrobe again, I shall seek an engagement in Richmond or Atlanta."

"Hum! Is this Colonel Truesdail a married man?" queried the general, curiously.

"I have reason to think so," answered Pauline, with a merry smile, "for he had a son boarding at the City Hotel, in Nashville, where I stayed."

"But where did Colonel Truesdail himself reside?" persisted Bragg, hoping, no doubt, to catch her in some inconsistency of statement by thus questioning and cross-questioning her.

'I don't know positively," was the answer. "At the time of my arrest I was taken to his office, at a house in High Street, near the capitol."

"Can you describe his personal appearance?"

"Yes, indeed. He is of medium stature and slight figure; with grey hair and heavy black whiskers; rather dark complexion and black eyes. I saw him only once and that was when taken before him, after my arrest."

"I should like to get hold of him!" exclaimed the general, thus revealing a plan which he had perhaps half-formed of making a dash upon the city of Nashville and seizing the prominent Union officers that might happen to be there. Therefore, doubtless, all these questions. "Are the Federals well supplied at Nashville?" he continued.

"I believe they are, but I have no certain knowledge on the subject. An actress is but a poor judge in such matters," answered Pauline.

"What seems to be the popular feeling at Nashville?" asked the general.

"Well, it varies every day, just as the tide of battle rises and falls. Sometimes, when the Confederate arms have prospered, everybody almost is strong 'secesh.' Again, when they have been unsuccessful, Union men are plenty. But they are driving almost all the Southern sympathisers across the 'lines.'"

"Have the Confederates many friends at the North?"

"Yes, there seems to be a good many," answered Pauline, with the memory of the many rebel sympathisers of Louisville and Nashville still fresh.

"Do they seem content to remain on that side of the line?"

"Oh, yes, indeed; they are glad to stay anywhere so that they can only keep out of the fight."

"The cowards!" muttered the general, bitterly, rising and walking the room rapidly. "I thought so!" he continued. "I thought so! The only friends we have at the North are those who are too cowardly to fight for us; and yet there are men here who believe in help from the people of the North: *pshaw!*" Then turning once more to our heroine he resumed his questioning, trying, of course, to elicit all the information he could of the movements and intentions of the Federal troops and generals, while our heroine, on the contrary, sought to afford him as unsatisfactory answers as possible in this respect, without creating suspicion.

An untruth she dare not tell, for she knew that that would betray her at once, for General Bragg knew well the correct answer to almost every question he asked, and was testing her, probably, to see if she sought to conceal any tidings or information that would be useful to the Confederacy if so, she must be a spy, and would be dealt with as such.

It was, therefore, a keen contest of wits and subterfuges between the astute old general and the young girl, in which we wager to say the latter got the best of it; He therefore continued his questions, carelessly, apparently, but watching our heroine's face keenly all the time.

"Are there many steamers plying to Nashville?" he asked.

"I think not; I believe the water is too low," answered our heroine.

"Who is in command of the Federals there?"

"General Mitchell was, until lately; but he was superseded, a few days since, by a Brigadier-General Morgan."

"Hum!" grunted the old general again. "Is there a large armed force there?"

"I am under the impression that there is; for I observed many encampments in and around the place."

'Are they fortifying?"

"I think they are, at two or three points," replied our heroine. "But, general, these are curious questions to ask a *woman*," she remarked, lightly.

"They are asked of a woman who knows their proper answers," replied the general, in a voice full of meaning, and which, for the moment, caused the heart of our heroine to sink like lead within her.

"Answer my questions, therefore," he added, gravely, "and tell me if you noticed any fortifications thrown up about the capitol?"

"Yes, it appeared to be heavily fortified."

"That is better!" remarked Bragg. "Now again. Are the Federals arming the negroes?"

"I cannot say; but I noticed the negroes at work on the fortifications."

"They *will* arm them, and then we shall have our own negros shooting at us," muttered the rebel general, bitterly.

"Is Governor Johnson at Nashville?" he continued.

"I fancy not," replied Pauline.

"Where is General Rosecrans, with his army?"

"I do not know; but have heard that his headquarters are at Murfreesboro'."

"I should very much like to fall in with him," said Bragg; "we have been waiting around here for him a long time, and when he comes, I shall give him a warm reception, I can assure you."

Our heroine smiled faintly, for she thought that the boot might be on the other foot, for she knew "Old Rosy" well; but she said nothing—discretion being, in this case, "the better part of valour."

"As for yourself, Miss Cushman," continued the general, "I have to tell you, plainly, that there are very serious charges against you, and I must give you into the custody of our provost-marshal general, Colonel McKinstry, who is, however, a very just and humane man, and who will treat you kindly. Your subsequent fate will depend entirely upon the result of our investigation."

"Colonel McKinstry is, then, precisely the man I desire to see; for through him will the proofs of my guiltlessness of these charges appear," rejoined our heroine, boldly. "And if they *are* proved false, how then, general?"

"You will be acquitted with honour," replied he.

"How, though, if I am found guilty?"

"You know the penalty inflicted upon convicted spies. If found guilty, *you will be hanged*," answered the general, dryly.

Chapter 36: The Faces of the Dead

The fearful words of the rebel chieftain fell like the icy hand of death on Pauline's heart. It was not death, alone, but the ignominious mode of exit from the world it suggested, that was so terrible.

"*If found guilty, you will be hanged!*" The words weighed upon our heroine with fearful import, and it was as much as she could do to keep her hands from clasping her throat, as though the hangman already had his clutches there.

Had she then lived, in honour and worth, to come to this at last? She turned pale at the thought, while the, unmoved features of the rebel general opposite to her showed what little mercy she had to expect there.

True, others, now loved and respected, had died an ignominious death—had suffered even on the gallows. Andre, the ill-fated, the talented, the brilliant, had died thus, and in a bad cause; yet was not his memory cherished and his faults palliated, even by Americans, at this day?

"If I die thus," thought our heroine, "at least it will be said that I died in a holy cause. 'The *Union!*' to rue the talisman of my whole being, shall be my last words ere the drop fall; and, though others may laugh and scoff at the ignominy of my exit, I shall rest satisfied, so that I but feel that I die for my country!"

Thus, our heroine reasoned to herself; but, in spite of it all, the dread feeling of disgust and repugnance at the disgraceful means of death suggested would arise and choke all attempts at reasoning. "No! no! not hanging!" she would then mentally exclaim: "anything, any other death than that!"

It was with a struggle, therefore, that she forced a smile to her lips, while she said lightly, as though devoid of all feeling in the matter, "Come, now, general, I don't think that I would prove a very ornamental object, dangling at the end of a rope!"

A grave, one might almost call it a sardonic, smile played on his stern features.

"If I *must* die," continued Pauline, "you will, I trust, let me choose my own mode of death."

"I cannot answer for anything of that kind, because, if I did, you might prefer the *natural* way of dying," said General Bragg, with a lurking, devilish humour in his eye.

"No," rejoined Pauline, quickly; "no, I would not seek to cheat either death or you. I am not afraid to die. It is the disgraceful means of death that alone annoys me. I would, had I my choice, prefer to be shot."

"Well," said General Bragg, with an ill-disguised sneer, "I have yet to learn that it matters much how a *spy* is disposed of, or how they go out of this world—whether by hanging or shooting."

"It matters everything to one who like myself, general, has nothing but honour to bestow as a heritage upon my friends or relatives."

This remark seemed to have considerable weight with him, and he bowed his head on his hand for a brief moment in deep and anxious thought. At last, he spoke again:

"Let us drop this subject," he said. "There is one more thing that I wish to question you about: where did you get the pistol that was found upon you when you were arrested at Baum's house?"

Wondering within herself that the general should know aught of this pistol, which, it will be remembered she had succeeded in securing while at the house of the wounded and dying rebel, at the time the general "skedaddle" had taken place, she answered, little dreaming how much rested upon her reply:

"That pistol, sir, I got at Hillsboro'. The scouts who attended me had taken refuge from the storm in the house of a wounded Confederate soldier."

"Yes, I know that much," interrupted Bragg, with an impatient wave of his hand to proceed to the point at once.

"Well, sir, while there, there was a cry raised that the Yankees were coming, when your brave fellows instantly took to their heels, leaving me, a weak, defenceless woman, to contend against them and meet them single-handed. It was then that I took the pistol which was afterwards found upon me, determined to shield myself from insult, even though my own people did abandon me."

The general looked steadily at her for some moments, as though in doubt whether to believe this account or not. As for our heroine, she had no idea of the intent of this inquiry as to the pistol; but, during a later interview with the general, while she lay sick, she was informed why he had laid so much stress upon what had seemed of minor importance.

She therefore did not understand him when he said, sternly, while a cold, hard expression settled upon his features, "*Did no dead faces haunt you in your midnight ride that time, Miss Cushman?*"

It seemed that upon the very night of our heroine's dash through the woods, two rebel scouts had been found shot through the head, not far from each other, and near the forks of a road that she must have passed in her daring flight. One of them had been despoiled of his pistol and belt, while the other had not been disturbed in this particular.

From this circumstance suspicion had fallen on our heroine, and Bragg, in spite of himself, was forced to believe that she had been their murderess.

"It was with difficulty," he said afterwards, "that I could be brought to believe that so fair a woman could be guilty of so deep a crime, but the evidence was most strong against you."

The affair being sifted later, our heroine was fully and honourably exonerated of this fearful charge; and her account of the pistol proving correct, the good opinion of the general in this respect, at least, was once more regained.

When General Bragg told her of the circumstance, and the charge that had rested upon her, our heroine, as we have said, was ill, in her chamber. It was at the twilight hour, and the grey light of the waning day fell in indistinct masses through the little room. Sickness had weakened Pauline's nerves as well as her body, and when the general ceased speaking it was not without a peculiar shudder that she thought over the whole occurrence.

Well did she remember the forks of the road alluded to, and once more in memory did she hear the rushing of the storm and the almost human groans of the labouring trees as she swept rapidly past. Again, did the bright and deadly lightning flash upon the scene, but to make it the more terribly dark the next minute; and through it all she saw, with a shudder, the upturned faces, pale and fearful, of the murdered scouts.

151

Chapter 37: The Rebel Provost-Marshal

After leaving General Bragg, Miss Cushman was at once conveyed to the quarters of the provost-marshal general, Colonel McKinstry, to be interrogated by that functionary.

This gentleman, whose duty required him to be stern and implacable, was still gentlemanly and resembled the Federal Colonel Truesdail very strongly.

It may have been that the same profession—at least *branch* of the profession, that is, provost duties had something to do with this resemblance. Like duties and thoughts, it is said, will mould even dissimilar features to a certain resemblance in common. This resemblance Colonel McKinstry and Colonel Truesdail possessed. The same deep lines furrowed the faces of both; the same gloomy, Spanish expression dwelt in each feature; while the hair and eyes were almost facsimiles. Their ages, too, must have been nearly alike—Colonel McKinstry having, perhaps, the precedence in this respect.

The colonel received our heroine most politely; for, as General Bragg had said, he was both kind and just; and proceeded at once to interrogate her. After many questions, which, though important, we need not here repeat, he finally asked her how she became possessed of the Confederate uniform that was found in her satchel when first arrested at Milam's.

Feeling convinced that in this instance the plain truth could not harm her, she frankly stated that, loth as she was to reveal family secrets, she would have to yield to the provost-marshal's persuasions and tell him that Captain P. A. Blackman, Confederate Quartermaster, had professed the warmest regard and affection for her, and had proposed that she should accompany him as his lieutenant.

At this the brow of the provost-marshal contracted.

"A Confederate officer's uniform, Miss Cushman, would have been an excellent disguise for a spy, you will confess. Through its means one might be able to penetrate to the heart of every camp in the Confederate States; to every fortress and even to the councils of our generals."

"It is true, sir," answered Pauline, "but I can assure you that the manner in which I became possessed of that uniform was, as I have stated, entirely in pursuance of my friend, Captain Blackman's, plan."

"Did, then, this Captain Blackman take so great an interest in you that be wished you always to remain near him?" queried the provost-marshal.

"He loved me, to speak plainly," responded our heroine, blushing. "And, if you need any proof of that, I have a number of notes and letters addressed to me by him, which will amply prove the truth of my assertion. Here is one now," she continued, extending to him one that she had received just before her first arrest. "In it, I doubt not, you will find some mention of the position as lieutenant which he designed to honour me with."

"It is indeed so," muttered the colonel, knitting his brow closer and still more sternly. "It is astonishing how a pretty woman will make the best of our officers forget their duty!"

Then, ringing a small bell which stood upon his table, close at hand, he added, as the orderly made his appearance:

"Send Captain —— to me." This was the colonel's *aide*, and while Pauline was lost in amazement at this action, the captain entered.

"Sit down at once," ordered the provost marshal, "and issue an order for the arrest of Captain P. A. Blackman, Confederate Quartermaster."

"Why you would not arrest my poor friend, would you, colonel?" pleaded Pauline, in dismay at her friend's suffering on account of her disclosures. "He was not to blame!"

"Well, as to that—I don't think he was altogether without excuse," answered the colonel, gallantly. "But an officer that would serve his country, Miss Cushman, must learn to resist a pretty face, as well as the charges and onslaughts of the enemy."

Pauline was extremely sorry to see her friend come to grief thus suddenly, and urged her efforts to save him, as far as prudence would allow of; but without avail.

"But would you have gone with the captain in your new uniform?" asked Colonel McKinstry, quizzically.

"Ah! that remains to be found out!" she at once replied, with an air of mock reserve.

The colonel could not repress a faint smile, as he graciously rejoined:

"Your statements, thus far, Miss Cushman, *seem* to be perfectly correct; but I have here proof which, I regret to say, will overwhelm you."

He then proceeded to take from his desk several papers, which our heroine recognised with a start of alarm. At the sight of them a trembling seized her, that she with difficultly kept from being observed; for they were the very papers which she had abstracted from the table of the rebel engineer-officer at Columbia, together with the sketches

153

and memoranda that she had made of the various fortifications at Tullahoma, Shelbyville, Spring Hill, etc. These she had secreted under the cork soles of her gaiters, and the latter, it appears, had been purloined from her satchel, left in the wounded soldier's house at Hillsboro'. How she deplored, then, the fatal whim, which had made her depart from the instructions so impressively conveyed to her by Colonel Truesdail, to make no written statement, or no drawing; but to carry everything in her memory.

These papers were now arisen in judgment against her!

"Do you know these documents?" asked the provost-marshal, gravely.

Assuming a light manner, though, heaven knows, her heart rebelled at it, she admitted that she did.

"Now, what was your object in making these sketches?" he continued.

"With a hearty laugh, Pauline answered: "Oh, they were mere fancy sketches. Nothing but the merest guesswork; gotten up with the idea of stuffing the Yankees when I should find myself among them, so that I might be permitted to recover my wardrobe."

We have said that our heroine was a most consummate actress, and this assertion, made thus boldly, and with such frank carelessness, almost staggered the provost-marshal, in spite of his convictions.

For a moment he eyed her fixedly, then, reverting to General Bragg's great exclamation, he gave a loud "Hum!" and placing her in charge of his assistant, Provost-Marshal Captain S. E. Padden, he said: "That will do, Miss Cushman; you may retire."

As she did so, Pauline heard the old gentleman mutter to himself: "That woman is the very devil, and would almost convince one that black was white!"

Chapter 38: The Negro Kidnapper

Under the charge of her new conductor, Miss Cushman was taken to the house of a Mr. Morgan, near Duck River, where she was put under guard, in a room fitted up with all the appurtenances of a dungeon, such as barred windows and doubly-fastened doors.

Captain Pedden, himself, was a man of feeling and refinement, and it was a blessing that he was so, for the people of the house, rank rebels as they were, never came near our heroine; allowing her, when, at last, she was taken sick and confined to her bed, to lie, day after day, without ever once coming near her. Greater inhumanity could not have been shown her

Captain Pedden, however, was very agreeable in his manners, and not only came himself, but allowed others to call, whose conversation served to beguile the tedium of imprisonment, and through whom she gathered various scraps of information as to the movements of the Army of the Cumberland and the brave Union boys, always welcome subjects with her, as may well be believed. They were profuse in their denunciations of "that old rascal Truesdail," and told many a story of the traps he set to catch the unwary "*secesh*," and which, to speak truth, they frankly and bitterly acknowledged were too often successful.

Through this means our heroine learned much of the mode of operations of the spies, smugglers, and rebel emissaries about Nashville and the Army of the Cumberland—a source of information of which she was not slow to avail herself, and of which she made a mental note for future use. As illustrating the efficiency of the army police, and as a part of the history of the times in which our heroine figured, we give one case; sifted, of course, from the verbiage and spleen of the rebels who told it.

Doctor Hudson was the possessor of an elegant residence, and the proprietor of extensive iron works, a large plantation, many negroes, and other property, at Harpeth Shoals, near Nashville. His wife was a comely and interesting lady, much younger than himself, but not less the embodiment of an untroubled and self-satisfied mind.

One day a Mr. Newcomer called at the doctor's house in Nashville, and presented him a letter of introduction from J. Prior Smith, living twelve miles out on the Hillsborough pike. His business, as stated in the letter, was to obtain assistance in kidnapping negroes, especially negro children, and running them through the lines to Smith, to be sold at the South. The enterprise, if successfully managed, would prove exceedingly profitable, and the doctor entered heartily into the arrangement.

Having unbounded confidence in Smith, he was not at all reserved in his expressions, and ended by promising to procure the requisite number of negroes, and run them through the lines. He was to get a pass for his driver and servants to go out into she country for milk for the hospitals, and in that way, they could get the negroes out and such other articles as Newcomer wished to carry with him—the latter acting as driver. The doctor assured him that he could be relied on in every emergency, and that he would not hesitate to do anything to assist the cause of the South.

The next day Newcomer called again, and paid the doctor two hundred dollars, to be appropriated, as distinctly understood, on this account.

The doctor was now engaged, heart and soul, in the negro business, and for the next two weeks held almost daily consultation with his friend Newcomer as to the best means of procuring and getting them to their destination. In a week or so they had obtained six likely boys, who, Smith was informed, would be delivered at any place he should name outside of the lines, and the doctor had procured the promise of four more. So far everything was progressing favourably; but the operations were more limited than suited the tastes of either, and each was constantly on the watch for some opportunity of materially enlarging them. Meanwhile, the doctor was visited by numbers of persons representing themselves as paroled prisoners and spies, to all of whom he extended a welcoming hand. With one, in particular—introduced by Newcomer as a spy of the rebel General Wheeler—he became very intimate, and revealed to him his real sympathies and feelings quite at length. Said Hudson:

"I am a strong Southern Rights man, and not a day passes over my head that I do not do something to assist the Southern cause. I am watched by the detectives, I know, and have been frequently reported, but have not yet been imprisoned, because I play my cards right. I have in my house frequently, and am friendly with, many Federal officers, and, when reported, I prove by them that the charge is false. I have aided in the escape of many prisoners, but they have always thought me innocent."

Mrs. Hudson, however, did not seem as confident and easy as the doctor. She repeatedly cautioned their new friend to be very careful, as they were watched on all sides, and she had reason to suspect that certain suspicious-looking men, who had been there a few days since, were nothing else than spies, sent there by some of the officers. She was assured by him that he was sharp enough to evade any detectives that could be sent to watch him or them, at which she seemed satisfied, and more at rest and confidential than before.

Some of their friends, she said with great glee, had recently escaped from the penitentiary, and intimated that she and a neighbour lady had assisted them to do so, without, however, saying it in so many words. The doctor made an appointment to meet him in town that day, which he did, and pointed out to him, on the street, a number of friends whom it would do to talk to; gave him the names of others, living in the country, who would be of great assistance, and invited him to visit him at his house often, and to call upon him for anything in his power to give.

At this time, large numbers of negroes were employed upon the fortifications at Nashville and it was here that the doctor hoped to procure all that he wished to run South. Accordingly, he called upon Lieutenant D J. Deardurff, Acting Assistant Adjutant-general of the Engineer Corps, and inquired if he could be spared some negroes long enough to build up and repair his fence, saying that he would be very much obliged if he could be thus accommodated.

The lieutenant replied that he might have them as soon as they could be spared; calculating, however, that this would not be until the works were finished, and not intending to let him have them until then. Soon afterward, he was instructed by higher authority, to confer with Doctor Hudson, and consent to arrangements with him to furnish negroes, and was informed that the doctor would call on him soon—which he did in four or five days.

Being treated with some courtesy, he proposed the trapping of boys from ten to fifteen years old, and said to the lieutenant that if he would engage with him in the business, and turn them over to him, he could get at least one thousand dollars for every boy large enough to plough, and, for able-bodied men, from fifteen hundred to two thousand dollars, and that they would divide the proceeds equally. He further said that he could get any kind of a pass he wished, as he had a farm outside the pickets, and would have no difficulty in getting through and disposing of them as fast as they could be furnished. Deardurff assented to the proposition, and told him he could have as many as he wanted; whereupon the doctor took his leave, promising to call for them on the following Monday.

The next thing, now, was to see Newcomer, report his success, and make arrangements for the future; and for this he was not compelled to wait long, as the latter called upon him that very evening. The doctor reported that he had sounded Lieutenant Deardurff, with whom he had just taken dinner, in regard to the negro-smuggling business, and that the lieutenant had agreed to go into partnership with him. He said, further, that he was going tomorrow to see Doctor Seamore, and try to get three or four little negroes from him to take South, and also would go to Lieutenant Osgood, and ask for a pass for himself and servants through the lines, upon which, if he obtained it, he would take out all the negroes he was to get from Deardurff and Seamore. Newcomer was highly pleased, and congratulated the doctor upon his excellent management. He had just returned from outside the lines, he said, and had taken with him six negroes whom he had sent South.

"And while there," he continued, "I found a letter addressed to me from General Frank Cheatham enclosing five hundred dollars, with which he requested me to purchase quinine for the use of his hospitals, I suppose I can procure it from Doctors Cliff and Ermy, of this city, can't I?"

"I am well acquainted with Ermy," replied the doctor; "and I don't doubt I can get all we want from him."

"But how will we manage to get it through the lines?"

"I think we can get Doctor Ford to carry it. At any rate, Ford, you, and I will meet at Rear's tomorrow, and arrange it all."

Newcomer was at the place appointed in due season, but found neither of the others there. Somewhat disappointed, he sent a note to Hudson, asking the reason of it, and received word that there had been a misunderstanding about the place of meeting, with a request that he would call at his house, as he was anxious to see him. Going at once, he was told by the doctor that he had seen and talked with Doctor Ermy about the quinine, and that they could have one hundred ounces for four hundred and seventy-five dollars. Hudson had offered four hundred and fifty dollars, and Ermy said *he* would not object, "as it was for *suffering humanity*" but his partner, Doctor Cliff, would have four hundred and seventy-five dollars, which he had finally agreed to give, thus closing the bargain.

Newcomer expressed himself fully satisfied, and was about to leave the house, when he was approached by Mrs. Hudson, who said that there was in the penitentiary a Confederate officer by the name of Russell, the son of an old friend of her husband, whom she was very anxious to get out and run through the lines.

"Yes," said the doctor, "I would gladly crawl on my elbows from here to the prison, the stormiest night that ever blew, if by doing so I could release him"

"If you can get him out, I give you my word that I will take *good care of him*" was Newcomer's reply.

"I will see him, then, tomorrow," remarked Mrs. Hudson, "and tell him that one of General Wheeler's spies is in the city, who will take charge of him and see him safely through the lines if he can only get out of prison."

It was now the Monday on which the doctor had promised to call again upon Lieutenant Deardurff and he was prompt to fulfil his appointment. The interview was a pleasant one; and the doctor stated that he had made all the necessary arrangements, and was ready for business at any time, asking finally,

"Do you see any chance of being caught in it?"

"No," returned the lieutenant, "I can manage my part of it without any trouble. So far as I am concerned, I have no fear at all, and am satisfied that if the thing is properly managed there is no danger in it. Besides, didn't you tell me you could get a pass of any kind at any time you wanted it?"

"Yes," he answered, at the same time taking out and showing a pass. "I have one here. You see; it says, for myself *and servants*. I told them I had a farm beyond the pickets, and, as I was just commencing work on it, might want to take out more hands some days than others. They had better make it 'servants,' I said, and then it would pass out any number—which they did; and all I will have to do now will be to say that they are my servants. The pickets are changed every day; so, they'll not suspect anything; and I think it's perfectly safe. At any rate, I'll risk it. If there's nothing risked there'll be nothing won, you know. We can make a good thing out of it, and nobody will be the worse for it; because they are runaway slaves, anyhow, whom their masters will never get again, and so will lose nothing by our operations."

Other features of the plan were discussed for nearly three hours, when the doctor asked Deardurff to order his horse, and go with him to select the best route to get them away, and also to call at his house and talk with his wife about it. He did so, and found Mrs. Hudson considerably more shrewd than her husband but eventually gained her confidence, and was invited to dinner the next day. He accepted the invitation, and was generously entertained by the doctor and his family. During the meal, the former inquired if he could let him have any number of negroes, from four to twelve, that evening or night or the next morning, at any place that would suit.

"Do you know what you can do with them?" queried the lieutenant.

"I'll take them out on the farm, and then see what can be done with them, and how many can be disposed of."

"If I were in your place I would go and see Prior Smith and two or three others of your friends and see what they say about it," continued Deardurff, anxious to convince Hudson that he was very much in earnest about the matter.

"That's a good idea. I'll go tomorrow morning, and report to you immediately on my return."

With this they parted, the one to go to his camp, the other to make ready for his journey. Whether this was ever performed it is not necessary to state; but certainly, it was not the next day, for the doctor had more important business with Newcomer, which he must have forgotten when making this arrangement with Deardurff. The next morning Newcomer came early with the money to buy the quinine which had been engaged of Doctor Ermy.

When told what he had come for, Hudson at once ordered his buggy, and was just ready to start for the medicine, when his wife returned from the city, bringing word from Doctor Ford to have nothing to do with it, as he had reason to know that something was wrong. Mrs. Hudson also said that Doctor Chalmers, of Hospital No. 15, had told her that she and the doctor were watched at headquarters, and that passes were only given them for the purpose of catching both of them—that he had known it some time, and would have told her sooner, only he had been cautioned not to say anything about it; but, notwithstanding that, he would warn them of their danger. He was surprised they were not already arrested; and they must keep a good look-out, or they soon would be.

"I don't believe a word of it," said Newcomer. "At any rate, I'll find out before night whether anything of the kind is in the wind, from one of General Mitchell's clerks, who is in my employment"

At this both were much pleased, and said they felt perfectly safe so long as they had such a shrewd friend to watch over them.

Newcomer called again that evening, and found the doctor as ready as ever to assist in getting the quinine through; but Mrs. Hudson was still much alarmed. Promising to come again in the morning, he left without making any arrangements about the matter. The next day he was informed by the doctor that Deardurff had dined with him a day or two before, and that all arrangements about the negroes had been satisfactorily agreed on between them.

Newcomer now said that he had seen the clerk he had spoken of, and that he had told him there was nothing on file at headquarters against him or his wife, and that all Doctor Chalmers had said was false. This made matters all right again in a moment; and Newcomer handed to Hudson the five hundred dollars.

The doctor said he would get A. W. Hendershot, a druggist of the city, to take the money and buy the quinine from Ermy, and he would send his servant to bring it to the house. From thence he would get his wife and daughter—Mrs. Ward who lived five miles out on the Charlotte pike—to take it beyond the lines to the house of the latter, and there leave it for Newcomer. They would, he said, tie twine around the necks of the bottles, and adjust them around their waists, under their clothes, and thus carry them out of their lines safely.

He then introduced Newcomer to Mrs. Read—wife of General Read of the Confederate Army and gave him several letters, which Mrs. Ford wished sent South. The ladies were very agreeable, showing him marked respect, inviting him to call often, and assuring him that he would always be treated "as a friend indeed." Hudson started at once to make arrangements about the quinine, and Newcomer soon followed him.

The next day, Hudson said that he had bought the quinine, and that fifty ounces were then hidden in his house, and that tomorrow he would have the remainder there. Newcomer thanked him for his promptness, and engaged in conversation upon other matters. There was a Federal commissary store burned in town last night, he said, and he believed it had been done by some friend of the South.

"I have no doubt of it," said the doctor.

"If I knew, who did it, I would make him a present of one thousand dollars."

"If that is all you want, I can find you as many men who will do that kind of work as you wish. I will go and see about it tomorrow and let you know."

"All right. I will pay well for it if it is well done,"

"Well, I don't think it is any worse than to capture a train of wagons loaded with the same kind of goods. I'd make the match to set the buildings on fire myself. It is easy enough to do, too. All that is necessary is to take a piece of punk and wrap around it cotton soaked in turpentine; then set fire to the punk, and it will not blaze for hours after it is put in the building; so that a man will have ample time to get away before the fire breaks out."

This ended the conversation and the acquaintance of the doctor and Newcomer. The latter will at once be recognised as the scout and detective. And here, too, it may be stated—as has probably been already surmised—that Walker, the Ashby cavalryman, and Wheeler's spy, the doctor's three friends, were simply members of the army police.

Before the doctor had time to put into operation any of his plans

161

for smuggling negroes or medicines through the lines, he was arrested, together with his wife and the gunsmith Rear. An examination of his house revealed a large amount and variety of contraband goods among which were nine revolvers, three shotguns two muskets, one rifle, three bags of bullets and buckshot, a large quantity of domestic and woollen goods, three bottles of morphine, and ninety-nine ounces of quinine. This latter, it seems, his daughter had refused to assist in carrying beyond the lines, and therefore it was found just where he had secreted it.

Hudson and his wife were imprisoned—the former in the penitentiary, and the latter at her house—while their case was pending. The decision finally arrived at was to send them South beyond the lines, whither they had aided to send so many others. Rear was released on parole and bond, and is, we believe still at large.

Chapter 39: The Fearful Suspense

Captain Pedden, as we have before said, was very agreeable in his manners, and likewise good looking, which is no small consideration with a lady. His figure was remarkably fine, while his hair and complexion were singularly fair and prepossessing. He was young, too, being only about twenty-seven years of age.

This gentleman soon followed the footsteps of the unfortunate Captain Blackman, in spite of the warning which the fate of the latter should have afforded, and fell desperately in love with our heroine.

This feeling he manifested in a thousand delicate little attentions, which, though by no means repugnant, were still accepted unwillingly by the brave girl.

Once or twice, the idea struck her that, through this interest in her expressed and so visibly shown by the assistant provost-marshal, she might effect her escape; but again, she would recoil from the thought of sacrificing one who had been so kind to her, and she determined to remain where she was, come what might.

Captain Pedden, about this period, introduced to Pauline, his friend Surgeon Powell, who, from that time, manifested all a brother's interest in her. This gentleman was very tall, with black hair and dark-grey eyes, and heavy black moustache and whiskers, the very reverse of his friend, but no less good-hearted and charitable.

It was fortunate, indeed, for our heroine, that these gentlemen interested themselves in her; for anxiety and continued fatigue had at

162

last got the better of her strength of mind and generally robust body.

Each day she felt the symptoms of some terrible sickness creeping through her frame, harassing her with the well-grounded fear that, far away from friends and home, she was about to have this added to her other troubles.

Anyone who has ever experienced it, knows the feeling, and can understand its terrors to one realising the dread fact, yet powerless to prevent it. Heaven, in its mercy, however, raised up friends for her, ever amid her country's enemies; and hateful to her as was the rebellion, its leaders, and its supporters, Pauline could not but feel the utmost gratitude to these two strangers, who were ever ready to help her when even her own sex spurned or neglected her.

During her illness, too, Generals Bragg, Cheatham and Forrest were frequent visitors; dropping in to cheer her by conversation, or to pass a fleeting hour. One day, not long before our brave boys took Shelbyville, General Bragg was extolling our old fighting general, Rosecrans

"I hold him to be the greatest of the Federal generals," said the old gentleman. "He certainly, thus far, has shown the largest amount of military genius, and I esteem it my particular good-fortune to be opposed to so illustrious a chief."

Just at this moment, a messenger entered hastily with a despatch. Tearing it open, the general suddenly started to his feet.

"By heaven!" he exclaimed. "Talk of the devil and he's sure to appear! Excuse me, Miss Cushman," he continued, still much excited; "but it seems that your 'old Rosy' is really at work, for here is a despatch which announces that the Federal troops have already reached the 'gap,' and entered the 'pike;'" and, rushing from the room, our heroine could hear him giving hasty orders to furnish the troops with three days' rations, and hold them in readiness to march at once; while she was left to be consumed by alternate hopes and fears as to the truth of the report. "Oh, that it may be true!" she would exclaim, again and again; and from the sick-bed of that worn and persecuted woman went up a heartfelt prayer for the success of that brave army and its noble members, for whom she had and was prepared to suffer so much.

Long, weary days did our poor heroine lay thus, next to the very gate, we may say, of eternity, so violent was her disease.

But it was not the racking pains, which tortured her body alone, that she had to contend with; nor yet the inconveniences of prison life and insufficient fare: an agony of mind, worse than all these, was what consumed her brain and wasted her fair form for she was beautiful, even in sickness, with her long raven tresses and great, appealing eyes, rendered twice as large as usual by the very pallor of her features.

The idea that she must, perhaps, die upon the scaffold, dwelt constantly with her, and her sensations may be imagined as she lay there upon her bed of pain, far from home and friends, with the most damning proofs against her, and the assurance that, if found guilty, nothing on earth should save her from a fearful, and ignominious death.

The court-martial which had been appointed to investigate her case had not yet been able to decide upon a verdict; and this fact added to the uncertainty of her fate, and. lent additional horrors to her situation.

To tell, or even to attempt to describe, the thousand tortures that our heroine underwent while awaiting the decision of her captors, would require volumes. We all know that certainty, no matter how terrible, is more easily borne than the doubts and fears of uncertainty. As long as the danger is unfixed, the imagination holds its sway, and creates for itself a thousand real and unreal terrors.

The moment, however, that it takes a tangible form, and comes presented in its actual force, the mind is able to grapple with it. Hope, too, battles on our side, whereas, before, she has been but a treacherous ally, and at last, we sometimes find that the danger to which the twilight of imagination lent such magnitude, dwindles down to a mere grievance beneath the broad daylight glare of truth and certainty.

It was not exactly so, however, with our heroine; for, whatever the decision, it could but fall with crushing weight, while the suspense that she had to undergo in the meanwhile was cruel in the extreme.

As we have seen, Pauline had but few visitors either to call through curiosity or through sympathy; now, however, a number of "*secesh*" women, of the most violent class, began to come to the house. These women, not content with loud talking and threats against the "vile Yankee spy," as they termed Miss Cushman, indulged in the most fearful and unusual abuse.

"They ought to hang her!" one would exclaim.

"If *they* don't," another *virago* would chime in, "I know who will, and that's meself. I'll see if the confounded Yankee dogs will dare to send their spies down here to spy out all our actions."

"Spy out! I reckon there's no telling how much mischief this women has done, and, for my part, I think hanging's too good for her; she ought to, at least, be made to dance a pretty long while with the

164

rope around her neck," interrupted one still more violent.

These were the words that actually fell, night and day, upon our heroine's ears. Sometimes, too, even the rebel guard stationed outside her door would weary of this continual abuse, and seeing the poor girl completely prostrated with fatigue and pain, would beg of them to cease their clatter, so that she might snatch a moment's sleep; but in vain. "Let her dies, then," they would answer; "if we kill her, we save the hangman a job!"

One day our heroine had dragged herself to the door of her prison, and had even ventured out into the hall—closely watched by the guard, nevertheless—when she encountered this horde of rebel women.

Not content, this day, with heaping abuse and the vilest language upon her, one actually completed the scandalous scene by spitting in her face. Retiring to her room, Pauline fell upon her couch, and, giving way to her feelings, burst into a flood of tears. Alone, sick, and insulted, her spirits broke down beneath the burden: she could stand it no longer, and for the first time in all her adventures, all her sorrows, all her dangers, she wept.

How long she cried she knew not; but when, at last, she gained command of her feelings, she was surprised to hear a wailing in the corridor outside. Listening, she found that the *secesh* women were actually crying as though their own hearts would break. She had subdued them at last. "One touch of nature makes the whole world kin," says the poet, and in this case it held good. Disgusted, doubtless, in their own hearts, at their abuse of this poor sick woman, they had heard her sobs of anguish, torn, as it were, from her very heart, and had involuntarily been restored to their own natural selves, and wept with her.

As she ceased, then, she could hear them saying: "Well, I don't care; after all she is a woman, and it is hard to die on the gallows!" while others would exclaim, as though excusing themselves, "Well, I don't care; I can't help but cry when I hear that poor creature go on so. It goes right to my heart!"

From that time these creatures became human, and our heroine was troubled no more with them

Chapter 40: Sentenced to be Hung

Ten days passed thus, with the dread of death hanging, like the sword of Damocles, ever above her head. Of her fate she knew positively nothing; for Captain Pedden, her best friend, *dare* not convey any information from the court-martial, being bound to secrecy; while the others with whom she came in contact *would* not, even if they could. True, once in a while she gained a glimpse of her situation in some word dropped by the guard who never left her door; but these words, vague and meaningless, but served to heighten her anxiety and uncertainty.

It was like some traveller, who, in despair of ever reaching his journey's end, had been suddenly lifted to a lofty peak, from which his destination was barely visible and shrouded in the mists that enveloped it. It was Tantalus over again, with the fruits of certainty within the grasp, but which, when clutched at, proved but phantoms. Some few facts, however, she could guess at: among these were, that the documents, drawings, etc., found in her gaiters, would be the principal, if not the only cause of her conviction, *if conviction it was to be*. Another fact which bore with damning effect upon her was the made-up story which she had repeated to the man Baum, and which he had repeated, to exonerate himself doubtlessly, to the scouts who had arrested our heroine at his house.

The impression, too, that was abroad among the inhabitants of Shelbyville, was freely conveyed to her by heartless persons outside, who did not hesitate to state their confirmed opinions that she would be hanged, and justly merit it, too. Among her guards. Miss Cushman was singularly popular, and not one of them but was ready at any hour of the day or night to aid her, except, perhaps, in the matter of escape, for which she was bodily incapacitated, or she might have tried her powers to that effect. As it was, however, she trusted to a merciful God, and the chances of a time and place where a single hour might change the entire scene.

Of the poor wretches of rebel soldiers who composed her guard, our heroine cannot speak in sufficient tones of commiseration. The poor creatures had all been taken like so many cattle from the field and made to fight in a cause of which they knew scarce anything and for men who made use of them merely to accomplish their own bad ends. Some of these were little elevated above the sheep and oxen that had been their usual companions, and by their ignorance and misery would have surprised and startled the poorest of our northern citizens. Few of them knew how to read, and a writer among them was a scholar indeed.

Still, as we have said, the poor fellows were ever ready to do what they could to relieve the "poor, pretty lady," as they called our heroine, and she had but to go to her prison door and express a wish for anything, when half a dozen would spring forward to vie with each other as to which should have the honour of waiting upon her.

Later, too, when she was confined to her bed, one of these poor fellows would come in to fan her, for the heat was most intolerable, owing to the fact that the windows were partially boarded up to keep the light and air out, and render it more prison-like. With the heat of the sun, then, pouring down upon this place, it resembled more one of the "leaden chambers" of Venice, where prisoners were confined until the stifling heat of the close and unventilated space drove them mad.

Captain Pedden and his friend Surgeon Powell were then in the habit of detailing a soldier—picking out the cleanest-looking one for the duty—to fan our heroine whilst she would endeavour to snatch a few hours' sleep; but it not unfrequently happened that the task would be reversed, for the poor soldier, sitting at the side of her bed and fanning her, would become so overwhelmed with the heat and fatigue as to drop asleep himself, and would thus lie until awakened by some newcomer, or perhaps Surgeon Powell. Half fed as they were, and dying, one may say, from filth and inattention, our heroine could not find it in her heart to blame them.

It happened sometimes that she had to contend with worse even than that; for often the dread "grey-backs" would come from off the clothes of the sleeper, and crawl deliberately across her bed, while she would have to lie there powerless to prevent it. Her horror at such moments can be better imagined than described, and we should not think of mentioning so disgusting a detail of her prison-life were it not that truth demands that we should give a correct picture of the many, many trials which this devoted woman passed through for her country's sake. It is but justice to her, and to her fellow-countrymen, who should know *all*, that they may properly appreciate and reward her services, and sympathise with her sufferings.

If there be any, then, who cavil at this detail, we must shield ourselves by remarking that, "to the holy all things are holy;" with those who persist in misunderstanding us, we have nothing more to say.

The suspense which had weighed so heavily upon our poor heroine was at last destined to be removed, and a no less dread certainty was to take its place; for one day Captain Pedden, her friend, entered with a gravity greater than usual upon his features. In an instant Pauline detected it, and demanded in faltering accents to know its cause.

"Tell me the worst," she entreated: "remove this dread uncertainty.

167

I cannot bear it longer. It is preying on me like a vulture on a carcase not yet dead—it is killing me. Speak, I implore you, and let me hear my fate!"

"Prepare yourself, then, Pauline, for the worst!" said her friend, kneeling by her side, and taking her hand in his. "Prepare yourself for the worst!"

"The court-martial have then finished their sitting?" demanded our heroine in a faint tone.

"They have: else my tongue must have still been sealed; but now I am privileged to speak at last. Until now I have hoped—hoped against hope, only at last to find myself deceived. Alas! that it should be *my* dread task to convey the fatal news to you; but, though, at first my spirit recoiled from it, I thought afterwards that upon me had it best devolve.

"I have loved you, Pauline," he continued, "as a man worthy of you alone can love; and it is out of that love that I have undertaken this task, for I feared the effect upon you if told by heartless or indifferent lips. Can you forgive me for being the fatal messenger?"

"Forgive you? I have nothing to forgive, but all to bless you for; for you have been almost my only friend," responded our heroine, returning gratefully the warm pressure of his hand. "But tell me. Let me know the worst at once! The court has found me guilty?"

"It has," was the answer.

"And have condemned me to—" she could not finish.

"To death!" replied her friend, completing the dread sentence, while great tears of agony rolled down his noble features.

Pauline responded not. A sigh, almost of relief, swelled for an instant her stainless bosom; then she said:

"If God has ordained this, it is well. When I started out, I dedicated even life itself to the cause of my country, if it should prove necessary. It *has* been called for, and I am ready. There is one question, however, that I would fain ask, and which I can find no words to express. It is, the *manner* of my death. Am I to be shot, like a soldier, or die the death of a malefactor? Speak! It is of this I have been thinking night and day, for these past ten days I am not afraid to die, mind you! but I would fain go out of the world decently."

"Pauline," he answered, "it cannot be as you wish. Alas! I dread to speak it; but you are condemned *to be hanged as a spy!*"

"Great God of mercy!" almost shrieked the poor girl, sinking back on her pillow, overcome by the terrible emotions which had racked her. "It is as I feared!"

Chapter 41: Love in a Prison

The situation of our heroine, mental and physical was deplorable in the extreme, and every act of kind ness shown to her at this critical period came like a boon from heaven, doubly welcome, doubly blessed. Condemned to death upon the gibbet, surrounded by foes with her fate unknown even to her friends it was a situation to shake the hearts of the strongest and firmest. Yet Pauline had a consolation that sustained her through it all—the consciousness that she had done her duty.

This feeling, it must be, which sustains our poor soldiers, and makes them hail with almost joy the bullet which is to bring them death. *They have done their duty*: can a nobler, better, or more consoling thought be found?

This it is which sustains them through all their hardships, through all their sufferings—which, when on the battlefield consumed with thirst, amid the dead and dying, still keeps them up, still gives them that peace of mind which is better than all the riches of this world.

Pauline, therefore, began now to regard even the ignominious means which had been selected by her captors to end her mortal career as something honourable and noble.

As yet she was too much prostrated by sickness to allow the dread mandate of her enemies to be carried out. The rebels were inhuman enough to do almost anything, but even among them there were none found quite fiendish enough to suggest that she should be carried to the gallows in the state in which she then was. She was then free to this extent, that she need not fear anything immediate; and as the military surroundings were liable to undergo a violent change at any moment, there was still room for hope.

It *might* happen that the brave Union boys would yet triumph, as they had often done before, over the base minions of secession, and save her. That Shelbyville was the point which they were aiming at was well ascertained, and of itself gave a glimpse for the rainbow tints of hope; but our heroine thought of none of this: she had made her peace with the world, and was prepared to die—ignominiously, if need be, as far as outward appearance went, but honourably and high purposed, in truth, as her own heart well knew.

She was resigned, therefore, hailing each effort made to please her or to sympathise with her in her fearful misfortunes with an angelic gratitude that won the love of all observers.

Among those who enacted the holy part of the "Good Samaritan," at this juncture, was a private soldier, named Athan R. Smith, a rebel, but a good, hearted man. This poor fellow waited upon her, and showed her every possible attention—a fact which our heroine attributed to sympathy alone for a wretched and unfortunate woman, but the true cause of which burst forth one day in the most unexpected manner.

He had been working around as usual, striving to make the miserable place look as tidy as possible when all of a sudden he stopped at the foot of our heroine's bed.

"Miss Cushman," he said, not daring to look at the lady, and talking as though he was paid so much per hour to get out the greatest possible number of words—"Miss Cushman, I can't bear to see you here, alone and friendless, without tellin' you how pleased I would be if you could accept my home. I have a nice, snug farm down in Tennessee, and no one but a good, kind old mother to take care of it, and who would be as good and kind to you as she has been to me. If, then, Miss Cushman, you could," here the honest fellow stuttered terribly—"if, therefore, you *could* love me, just a little, and would promise to be my wife if anything *should* turn up to save you, you know, why I would be the happiest man in the whole Confederacy, not excepting Jeff Davis himself. Then we can live there with my good old mother, just as happy as a king and queen. Will you say yes?"

Listening to the poor fellow's voluble explosion, it was some time before our heroine could catch the drift of its meaning, but at last she comprehended it. The poor fellow had fallen in love with her, and this was his way of "popping the question." Thanking her kind admirer, while a smile was forced to her lips, in spite of bodily pain and mental torture, Pauline explained to him gently how impossible it was such a thing could come to pass, but failed to convince the honest fellow, we are sorry to add.

"Stranger things than that have happened," he persisted, "and as for your being hung, you are worth two dead women any day!"

Pauline laughed, and, with many expressions of gratitude for his good intention and goodness of heart, said:

"I am afraid, my friend that your hopes are fallacious. Should I therefore die, you must return to your good mother and live with her. So kind-hearted a man cannot but be an excellent son. Cherish your aged mother, therefore, and instead of fighting beneath the banner of men whose war is against weak women like myself—instead of against the brave defenders of the Union—return to the more honourable and more peaceful duties of husbandry. But wherever you go, or whatever you do, the blessing of a poor unfortunate woman go with you!"

The light was fading fast in the small room, and what little there was the brave fellow seemed desirous of avoiding, for he bowed low his head; but when he raised it, Pauline could see two bright tears standing in his honest eyes.

"You are right," he said; "this *is* a cursed cause, and so sure, as they carry out their fiendish intentions concerning you, I will leave the service forever. They may catch me and shoot me, but I will never fight again for men capable of such brutality. This I promise."

Captain Pedden, too, whose care we have already mentioned, redoubled his devotion as the clouds darkened around her, and the above declaration of love was not the only one that our heroine was destined to hear. But, outside of her prison, events were occurring of infinitely more importance.

The glorious rescuers of the Union had advanced slowly but surely, and it was generally believed that the rebels would evacuate the place. As our heroine was too weak to be moved, they would of course have to leave her behind. What joy thrilled her every vein as this announcement was made to her! yet again, her joy was tinged with a touch of sorrow, for she could not but sympathise with her kind friends Captain Pedden and Surgeon Powell, who were much agitated at the thought of parting from her, especially the first.

"But we will meet again, Pauline!" he cried, vehemently. "This cruel war cannot last forever when it shall cease then, I will claim you for my bride; and until then I shall know no other thought, no other wish."

It was vain to tell her friend that his hopes were worse than useless; so, she merely thanked him for his kindness. The captain had come to tell her that upon consultation it had been decided to remove her to the house of a certain Doctor Blackman.

"The council of war is just over," he said, "and it has been decided to retreat. We must therefore leave Shelbyville with all our forces, and in a day or so at furthest it will be occupied by the Federal troops. It behoves me therefore to see that, in parting with you, I leave you in good hands. At present I cannot think you are where you would be taken care of. Mr. and Mrs. Morgan have never shown you the good feeling even which one might evince towards a dumb brute, suffering and in agony. I have determined, therefore, to remove you to the house of an excellent physician whom it is well known is a Union man at heart. He will be kind to you, I know, and his lovely wife will do everything in her power to shield you from insult, and to recruit your shattered health."

At first Pauline remonstrated against being moved at all, for so weak was she that she could scarce raise her head from the pillow; but at last, she yielded to his importunities, being persuaded that he was everything for the best.

"I *cannot* leave you here with these wretches," he said; "you must, indeed, go elsewhere; therefore, I beg of you, make no further resistance, for I shall be forced to be peremptory if you do!"

It was agreed, then, that our heroine should be removed, to the habitation of the good physician, and as she was leaving for that purpose—being carried on a litter, as she was of course too weak to walk—Doctor Powell, her kind attendant, and Captain Pedden, her admirer and true friend, begged of her to keep two little articles to remember them by. They were humble mementos enough, being nothing more nor less than a small vial, used to hold her medicine, and a cake of soap; but they are priceless in her sight, for they recall as well the trying hours of her imprisonment and suffering, as the kind treatment and gentlemanly courtesy which their manly donors had ever extended to her.

Yes, more precious far than gems or gaudy trinkets are these unpretending articles to her warm and grateful heart, for they remind her of those who stretched towards her a helping hand when "ready to perish."

Chapter 42: Saved at Last

Soon after her removal, a consultation of rebel physicians was held to determine whether or not she was in a fit state to be carried along with the army, for it was not without regret that some of the rebel leaders saw their vengeance snatched, as it were, out of their hands.

As is usual among these gentry, they were very far from according in their opinions. "Men of a trade seldom agree," says the old proverb, and it was never truer than in this case. However, those that thought she *could* be moved were overruled at last by Surgeon Powell, one of their profession, saying decidedly that she could not, and should not.

"Why, she could not stand it, gentlemen," he remarked. "She would die by the time she had been carried a mile."

Sick as our heroine was, she did not feel quite so far gone as this expression would indicate, and she has always been of the opinion that the doctor who spoke did so only for the purpose of saving her life, and not because he thought her to be really in a dying condition.

However, whatever the motive, the effect was excellent, for the party retired after deciding that she could not be moved.

From that time forth, then, she was treated very kindly, for Doctor Blackman was really a good Unionist, and both he and his amiable lady vied with each other to assist and relieve our heroine.

Indeed, the dark cloud which had so long enshrouded her fate began slowly to pass away, and the golden gleam of hope's bright sun to cast its warming beams upon her. Oh, how grateful was the change to her worn and tortured heart!

At length, one day, it was rumoured that a large body of Federal soldiers was just outside the town, and great was the stir and bustle in consequence. Staunch rebels got to work to make Union flags, so as to protect their property, while the true Union people came forth to drink in eagerly the news of the coming succour. At last, the battle opened by the dread roar of the artillery. Nearer and nearer the conflict came deepening and rolling toward her like the waves upon some ocean shore. On, on they came—one following the other—crashing, clattering, then dying away for an instant only to burst forth again with a more deafening roar. With what anxiety did not our heroine listen to this music, sweeter even, to her ears, than the voice of the siren to the ancient mariner.

Crack! would go the deadly rifle; rattle, rattle would fall the rain of the old muskets; while, loud above the clatter of cavalry and whistle of minie-ball, would sound the dread artillery. On, sweeping like a whirlwind, it came, growing fiercer, until at length the heavy tramp of the retreating rebel columns could be heard and, heaven be praised! the loud shout of victory, as our brave, brave "boys" charged into the heart of the town, their banners flying and their bands playing. Oh! that was a moment worth a lifetime of such suffering as she had passed through; and, attenuated as she was, nay, almost dying, she felt new life surging through every vein, and, springing from her bed, she staggered to the open window.

Aroused into a fictitious strength by the stirring events of the day, she was, for the moment, restored to comparative health and vigour,

SCATTERGOOD.

Gallant rescue of the fair spy at Shelbyville, Tenn.

and, wrapping a blanket about her, she stood upon the balcony of her room window until every noble fellow of the Union Army had passed. And what a glorious sight it was! Down, far down the long street, as far as the eye could reach, pressed eagerly forward the victorious Union columns—their bayonets flashing in the rays of the setting sun, and the glorious flag of freedom, so proudly sustained in their midst, bathed in a golden light that rivalled its own splendour.

At sight of that loved flag, the enthusiasm of our heroine knew no bounds. It is only those who have suffered for it that know how endeared it becomes to one. From the mere emblem of our land, it becomes hallowed as the very embodiment of our principles and hopes, and to our heroine, especially, it was the beauteous ark that seemed to promise to her shattered frame and bleeding heart an immunity, forever more, from grief. As though to cap the climax of her joy, just at this moment, whilst she was, wild with excitement, and in a perfect delirium of pleasure, trying to essay a faint huzza, who should come galloping by but Major Fullerton, followed immediately by Generals Gordon, Granger and Mitchell. Involuntarily she called aloud to the major, but he had barely time to exclaim:

"Not now! I cannot stop; but I'll see you as soon as I come back!"

The good-hearted Mrs. Blackman, in the meantime, fearful lest they would be classed among the rebel population of the town, had come weeping to our heroine, and begged of her to explain to the Union officers that both she and her husband were good Unionists; at the same time placing a box of jewels other valuables under her charge.

The kind lady also sought to persuade our heroine to retire to her bed again, as she was fearful that the excitement would prove too much for her. But strenuously did Pauline resist all efforts to get her to lie down. She *could* not, she said, tear herself from the welcome sight. Each face in those marching columns was dearer to her than her life!

Just at this moment, too, Major Fullerton came dashing past again, and once more did Pauline call him.

"I am looking for the mayor of the place," he responded, "and cannot stop!"

Vehemently did Pauline insist that he must stop, if for a moment only, and as he alighted and ascended the stairs, she could restrain herself no longer; but, with tears of joy in her beauteous eyes, she fell weeping at his feet, exclaiming:

"Can it be that I once again behold a Union soldier? Who—tell me, sir—who commands our troops?"

He answered that Generals Granger and Mitchell were at their head.

"Where are they, sir?" was her next inquiry.

"Close by," he said.

"Thank God, then!" cried Pauline, in a perfect delirium of joy. "I am safe at last! I'm safe!"

To describe the wild delight that seized our heroine, as she became conscious that she was once more beneath the protecting folds of the loved banner of her country, would require more power than this poor pen possesses. It must be remembered that both body and mind had been weakened by the fearful trials and privations which she had passed through so lately, and it required some time for her enfeebled mind to comprehend the joyous, life-giving fact, that she was saved.

The mind, once so ready at a conclusion, so quick to conceive, so rapid in its calculations, had been broken down; and although kind care and attention soon restored it to its accustomed vigour, for the moment it almost refused to realise the blessed and welcome fact. The grand columns, then, of victorious Union troops, had passed, like some glorious pageant of a dream, across her brain; and though her heart had welcomed it, and recognised the familiar uniforms and loved banners, her reason had almost refused to indorse it, for fear that the whole beautiful sight would vanish and leave her heart-broken and alone.

Now, however, that it was assured to her, the false strength which excitement had lent, left her as suddenly, and she sank upon the chair, overcome by joy and happiness. She was laid gently upon her couch, and the major told Mrs. Blackman, who watched kindly by the bed-side, that he would send Generals Granger and Mitchell to her at once, and departed to execute the duty on which he had been engaged when our heroine hailed him—promising, however, to return at the first possible opportunity.

The scene thus described took place about half-past five p.m., and by eleven o'clock on the same evening, the generals named did her the honour to call, and at once expressed the liveliest interest in her situation.

"Do you know," said General Granger to her, "that on the very night you were at the house of the wounded rebel-soldier, that no less than ninety Union scouts had been sent out scouring the country in search of you?"

"Indeed!" exclaimed Pauline, in surprise; wondering how this part of her history should have become known. "Why, how did you imagine that I could be there?"

"I will tell you," answered the general. "Your arrest at that villain Milam's, by the rebel scouts, somehow got wind. He had the impudence, I believe, to brag of it, so we thought that possibly we might rescue you on your way to or else, at Hillsboro', where we knew you would be carried. With that object, as I have said, a very strong detachment of scouts was sent out to rescue you; but though beating up all that neighbourhood, by some mischance they failed to find you."

"That accounts, then," said our heroine, "for the two rebel scouts who were found killed near the forks of the road, and of whom I was accused of being the murderess;" and she proceeded to relate all the wonderful and startling adventures which had befallen her, and of which this true book has attempted to convey some idea. It was quite late then, or rather early in the morning, before the gentlemen took their departure, occupied as they all were in either relating or listening to the story.

The next morning, however, our heroine was awake bright and early, with the fixed idea in her mind to start at once for Murfreesboro', and get as far into the Union "lines" as possible. In vain did the doctor tell her that it was impossible for her to be moved, or the kind Union generals expostulate with this sudden fancy. Go she would.

"Are you afraid that we will not take good care of you here?" asked General Mitchell, sportively. "Or is it that you doubt our generalship, and our ability to hold the place?"

"It is neither, dear general," Pauline replied "Your ability as an officer is too well known for me to have any doubts of it, and as for your kindness, I am very sure that no princess royal was ever treated better than I should be here; but I must go. I want to be as far as possible from everything that can recall the cruel past. As long as I am here I dream of gibbets; of horrid hangmen coiling great ropes about my poor neck; of prisons with a rebel guard pacing up and down ceaselessly before my door. In short, I recall, each moment in the day, all the fearful tortures which I have undergone here. I pray you, therefore, let me go. I am strong enough!"

"Impossible!" said the general, kindly. "It might kill you!"

"Nay, then. If you *won't* let me go willingly, I tell you what I'll do!" exclaimed Pauline. "I'll walk every step of the way, at least until I sink on the roadside! You know me, and you know I'll keep my word!"

"Well, then, wilful, naughty little girl," responded the general, see-ing the state of high-wrought nervous excitement in which our hero-ine was, and dreading to heighten it, "I expect I will have to let you go, though by rights I ought to arrest you and put a guard over you, for even wishing to disobey my orders."

"I would rebel against that instantly," laughed Pauline; "to be the prisoner of the blue coats would never do, without the prison was a heart, and the jailor a good-looking soldier."

By the general's orders, then, about eleven a.m. that same day, Gen-eral Granger's own ambulance, well stocked with cushions, pillows, blankets, and a mattress, was driven up to Doctor Blackman's door and she was propped up in a chair, and carried down by Generals Granger and Mitchell, while Major Fullerton held an umbrella over her head, as it was raining.

These gallant gentlemen, too, formed an escort of honour around the ambulance, and remained as long as their public duties would per-mit, when, with a God-speed, they turned their horses' heads, leaving our heroine to continue her journey back to that loved land where rebels, fortunately, dared not lift their hydra heads.

Chapter 43: Nashville and Promotion

It was with the utmost regret that Pauline had taken leave of her brave cavalier, General Mitchell, for she felt towards him the gratitude of a sister for his many kind attentions and more than brotherly care. As for the rest of the gentlemen, they were no less thoughtful and kind; and the contrast between her present happy situation and her past misery was so striking that often it would bring tears of joy and gratitude into her eyes.

After the general left—which was not until they had ridden some eleven miles from town—the rest of the gentlemen, including General Granger and Major Fullerton, accompanied our heroine still, until, about six o'clock in the evening, they halted at the house of a Mr. Fletcher, between the Gap and Murfreesboro', where they remained, owing to her exhausted condition, until the following day. Leaving there, then, about noon, they arrived at five-and-a-half p.m. at Mur-freesboro'.

Here our heroine obtained a much-coveted rest, assured as she was that the proud flag of her country floated securely above her. Her mind too, began to resume its accustomed strength, and her thoughts to have a more healthful channel. Not so frequently, at least, did she dream of the dread hangman, nor see the jeering populace, and the rebel soldiers drawn up in line to guard her to the scaffold.

It was, therefore, with some degree of restored animation, that Pauline received her kind friends upon the ensuing morning. They were to accompany her to the Nashville railroad depot, and then take their final farewell, and as the short figure, piercing black eye, and heavy whiskers and moustache of her friend, General Granger, made their appearance, accompanied of course by the gentleman himself, our heroine was almost sorry to see him, for she knew that the hour of parting was fast approaching.

However, these are some of the necessities of our daily life; so, thanking them again for their devoted care, she accepted the new guardianship of Captain Sedgwick, of the general's staff, and took her seat in the cars for Nashville.

It was not without a peculiar thrill that Pauline found herself being rapidly whirled towards that city, which had been, we may say, the turning-point in her destiny. From that place she had started out upon her perilous expedition. Here she had received the warm-hearted grasp of the brave servant-boy and his hearty "God-speed." Well, God had sped her, and brought her back, as by a miracle, safe and sound.

Taking up her abode at her old residence, the City Hotel, an account of her arrival was immediately despatched to headquarters, and she was promptly visited by Captains Fyffe and Temple Clark, who left nothing undone to render her secure and comfortable.

Judging from these gentlemen's account, it was almost impossible to realise that this apparently feeble but beautiful woman had gone through the terrible adventures that she had, and survived them. A man must have succumbed to them, but a woman has greater endurance than one even of the male sex, and never, in spite of the sleepless nights and days of torture, was our heroine more beautiful than at this moment.

Her skin, always pure and handsome, had become as transparent and clear as alabaster, while her great, dark, melting eyes had a softness and languor that they had not possessed even in a state of perfect health. Her dishevelled tresses, too, added to the weird beauty of her face.

In spite, however, of this strange, this almost preternatural loveliness, her health seemed to have received a shock from which it is probable it will never fully recover. Fits of deep depression would seize her, and great tears would steal unconsciously down her marble-like features. Under these circumstances it was deemed best to remove her to a private house, where she could receive more attention than at a crowded hotel. In pursuance of this plan, she was removed to the house of an excellent Union lady, named Mrs. Kirdell, and who resided at the corner of church and High Streets, and there received unremitting attention.

Her visitors here were principally the brave officers of our noble army, including Generals Rosecrans, Granger and Garfield, Major Fullerton, and a host of others no less distinguished. These gentlemen all treated her as though she was a loved sister, and their kindness left no comfort to be desired but the boon of absolute health.

The telegraphic announcement to Colonel Truesdail, who chanced to be at Tullahoma, of our heroine's return from the very jaws of death, had received as an answer the most emphatic injunction from that personage to have "every possible care taken of her."

In consequence of the services the brave girl had rendered the Union cause, and of the unparalleled sufferings she had undergone, Generals Granger and Garfield determined that she should receive some testimonial of appreciation. Accordingly, Pauline was formally proclaimed a Major of Cavalry, and a special permit was furnished her to procure all the necessary equipments befitting her new rank. Thus, she became known to the soldiers as *Major Pauline Cushman*, a title that she is justly proud of; and is determined to honour and maintain as long as life continues.

The loyal ladies of Nashville, hearing of the promotion of the brave and daring spy, and deeply sensible of the honour thus conferred upon one of their own sex, prepared a costly riding-habit, trimmed in military style, with dainty shoulder-straps, and presented the dress to the gallant major with all the customary honours.

While her friends thus vied with each other in their attention to the fair girl, there were others who through sympathy with the traitors from whose inhumanity she had been so mercifully snatched, or through fancied slight, or perhaps jealousy, were not so friendly disposed; and who set their fiendish plans in operation to assail the life of our heroine by more certain means even than the hangman's rope.

We shall now relate an incident which occurred whilst she was lying sick in bed, at the house of the kind lady whose name we have already mentioned.

Chapter 44: The Poisoned Cake

As we have said, among her constant, indeed, almost daily visitors, was General Garfield, now representative from the State of Ohio, and a most excellent and kind-hearted gentleman.

The general being a man who is destined to make his mark in the world, it may not be out of place here to give a short sketch of his singular and highly-honourable career. It at least shows one thing, that a man may be excellent in many parts, and that, though "a rolling stone gathers no moss," as the old proverb has it, there are some so energetic as not to wait until the moss grows, but start out in search of it, and scrape it together from the hillside

If we take the meaning of the old saying to be, success and fame, we may justly say that General Garfield is an exception.

Born, we believe, in Portage County, Ohio, the noble State which he now (1864), so ably represents, he was nothing but a poor farmer's boy.

At an early age, he married and kept a little store. He afterwards run a canal boat near Cleveland, leaving that business, at length, to become the teacher of a school.

Being naturally of a religious turn of mind, and a good and conscientious man, we find him next a minister of the gospel, from which he entered the army to fight in body as well as spirit—with the cannon of the soldier as well as the canon of the church—against the accursed teachings of this dread rebellion. Last of all, we find him sitting, an honoured member, in the halls of Congress, from which his talents, no doubt, will lead him still onward. We see, therefore, that it is possible for a gentleman and a true man to "play many parts," and to fill each with honour to himself and justice to posterity.

In appearance, General Garfield has a German look, with light hair, a mixed blue and grey eye, and a large, manly figure. This kind friend of our heroine was in the habit of dropping in, almost daily, to relieve, by his pleasant conversation and agreeable presence, the tedium of her sick-room.

One evening, whilst he was sitting near her bed-side, talking, as usual, a light rap was heard at the room door, and upon the usual invitation, a lady opened it and entered, bearing in her hands a small parcel, covered neatly with a white napkin. Handing it directly to our heroine, across the foot of the bed, she said, in a graceful tone:

"Although unknown to you, my dear Miss Cushman, your deeds

of patriotism and daring have given you a certain claim upon the sympathies even of strangers. Hearing that you were sick, then, I have taken the liberty of bringing you a nice little poundcake, which I made myself, and which I thought might perhaps prove palatable. When one is sick, you know, little delicacies of this kind are sometimes most acceptable."

They are, indeed," answered our heroine, gratefully, "and I cannot sufficiently thank you for thoughtfulness and kind regard for a stranger."

"Misfortune makes us all akin, you know," answered the lady, sweetly, at the same time moving towards the door.

"They should do so," returned our heroine; "but unfortunately this is not always the case: we do not meet with such good Samaritans as yourself every day."

Bowing in acknowledgment of this compliment, the lady passed through the door, which General Garfield held open for her. As she did so, the general courteously asked to whom Miss Cushman was indebted for this kindness; but declining to answer, as though through diffidence, the lady still passed on.

As it was dusk at the time, and the lady being closely veiled, neither our heroine nor her friend had been able to discover the stranger's features. Her mysterious manner, too, had awakened some curiosity on the part of both, though, as yet, no suspicion.

It was but an echo of our heroine's thoughts, then when the general exclaimed: "That's very odd!"

"Very, indeed!" acquiesced Pauline; then, with t sudden impulse, she added: "General, do me the favour to summon my maid, and bid her see in which direction the lady has gone."

Hastening to do so, it was discovered that the mysterious lady had entered a carriage which stood in waiting, and which had immediately driven away.

No more was thought of the matter, however; the cake, which really looked delicious, was laid on one side, untasted, with some fruit which the general had brought her, for Pauline was too ill to be disposed to eat.

As it chanced, though, a neighbour's little child, coming in upon the day following to visit "the sick lady," and while away some of her tedious hours, a piece of the cake and some of the fruit were given to her to play "tea-party" with.

Fortunately, the child preferred the *fruit*, and ate it alone, while she gave her little dog, which had accompanied her, the cake to eat. Very soon afterwards, the little child came crying to our heroine; exclaiming, in her infantile way, that the "tog" was mad or dying. Sure enough, the poor dumb brute was writhing in convulsions on the floor, and soon afterwards expired in great agony, his body almost immediately swelling to twice its natural size.

Amazed at this incident, when the general called again that evening, as was his wont, our heroine mentioned the circumstance to him. He was greatly alarmed at this incident, and to test their suspicions, gave another piece to a troublesome cat which was in the habit of rendering the night musical with its caterwauling. The result was no less decisive; for in a few moments the poor animal gave up every one of the "nine lives" with which common superstition has invested it, and swelled to an inordinate size.

"The cake is, then, really poisoned!" exclaimed the general, incensed to find his suspicions realised. "And that woman, accursed may she be, would fain have had the sin of murder upon her guilty soul. Oh, heaven, is it possible that there are people so vile!"

That evening, the doctor took a small piece of the cake and, being a skilful chemist, to his horror found it thoroughly filled with arsenic; to such an extent, indeed, that it would have required but a very small piece to have killed anyone so unfortunate as to eat it. It was a most providential escape for our heroine, and most gratefully and humbly did she return thanks to that Almighty Father who had so constantly watched over her.

Who it was that had attempted this fiendish deed neither our heroine nor General Garfield, who left not a stone unturned in the matter, could ever discover. Nor was the motive more clear. Whether it was jealousy, or sympathy with the arch-traitors, Jeff Davis & Co., or any other feeling, Pauline was never able to even imagine; though it was generally thought, by others, that it was some high and proud "*secesh*" lady, who, finding out that our heroine had been so useful as a Union scout and spy, had determined to rid the Confederacy of so dangerous an enemy at any price.

Instant search was, of course, made for the lady who had brought the treacherous gift, but in vain; and until the dead rise to judgment, and stand before the throne of God, face to face—the guilty with the injured—our heroine will never know, probably, the would-be perpetrator of this fearful crime.

Chapter 45: Touching Incidents

Little by little Miss Cushman began to feel some portion of her old strength returning to her, though she will probably never regain fully the pristine health which was her chief wealth, when she set about this expedition, which has since made her name so famous. It was her boast before that she was never sick: alas! it is no longer so.

Indeed, it would be more than a miracle if she could have outlived all the thousand horrors of that fearful stay in rebeldom without bringing away lifelong remembrances, in the way of broken spirits and impaired health. However, our heroine is as ready to meet new adventures in the cause of her country, nor does she regret for one instant that she has thus sacrificed ever thing upon the altar of patriotism. No. There is not one reservation, not one regret, that can attach for a moment to her most perilous but most useful career. Like our noble boys, who die blessing the glorious cause in whose behalf they are engaged, so Pauline Cushman, lovely and delicate woman as she is, blesses the dangers and terrors which have plucked her from the ordinary channels of woman's life, to make her a heroine.

But none can doubt this that have ever seen her, and we hope that all our readers will do so who can, if they have not already had that pleasure; for without seeing her they may be inclined to doubt the assertion, that a woman can depart so far from the original sphere of woman, and still retain all the grace and social elegance of the true lady.

To return: Miss Cushman began to feel the first signs of returning health, and now that visitors were admitted freely to her presence, crowds daily flocked to see and admire the brave "Union Scout" of the Army of the Southwest. Of course, principal among these were the devoted mothers, wives, and sisters of the "boys" of that noble set of soldiers; and to tell how welcome these visits were, would be beyond the power of human tongue, for Pauline felt that she belonged, emphatically, to this glorious army, and to speak of one of its members, was like talking of some loved and absent brother.

It may be believed that she was soon as much beloved by the mothers, and wives, and tender sisters of these brave men, as she had been by themselves, and numerous were the testimonials, some humble, some costly, but all alike dear to her, which she received from these grateful friends. Many, too, were the touching incidents that occurred, bringing oft the briny tears to the eyes of our heroine, sympathetic as she ever is with others' joys or sorrows.

One old lady, almost blind, but of most venerable aspect, and kind, motherly manners, was among her most frequent visitors. This kind old woman had given five noble boys to the cause of her country, and thanked God that they had thus fallen, bravely fighting for the Union, and the preservation of what is dearer than life—our nationality!

Should not such noble women meet with a recompense from a grateful country, greater than the mere bounties or pensions due them on account of their loved and honoured dead? Should there not be a law passed by Congress, allowing parents who have lost more than two sons in this accursed rebellion, a certain annuity, as of right, to be paid them without cavil, and promptly? We hope to see this just scheme jet consummated.

This old lady was very poor, but so happy and so contented that she might have been honoured as a great female philosopher had she lived in ancient times. But *one* thing affected her health, she said.

"Whenever our poor boys get driven back, or don't quite come up to the scratch; oh, then I'm taken down to my bed so bad with the rumatiz (rheumatism) that I can't stir hand or limb. It's very seldom, though, that I have to get sick, especially since Grant's been about. I wasn't sick often when "Old Rosy" was about either!"

God bless the old lady! We hope that she may never be sick again, until she goes peacefully and painlessly to join her five noble sons in heaven!

This old lady brought to our heroine a tidy, which she had knit herself, as a small offering, and although she naturally felt some hesitation about accepting a present from one whom she knew to be very poor, the words of the good soul decided her:

"Do take it," said the old lady, pleadingly. "I want you to have it, and to look at it; for when I give a thing to you, I feel as though I were giving it to my poor boys, for I know you loved them."

One day, soon after the fall of Vicksburg, that glorious triumph for our arms, the old lady was visiting our heroine, who happened to complain that she did not feel well.

"How can you say that?" demanded the old lady with some sharpness. "Why here am I, nigh eighty years old" (she was nearer ninety, but, woman like, she would not admit the fact)—"nigh eighty years old, and I believe I could dance a Vicksburg jig at this very minute if I had a good old-fashioned partner."

"No rheumatism, hey?" asked our heroine, slyly.

"Not a bit! There was a slight attack coming on when we heard of that repulse, the day the boys charged on the rebel works, but the next day's paper cured all that."

Thus, at all ages and in all paths of life, are noble and patriotic hearts found, who are, like our heroine, in heart, body, and soul, in wealth, life, and what is dearer still, the lives of others, devoted to their country's good. Can any other land show as much?

The best proof of Pauline Cushman's worth, too, is found in the fact, that the most patriotic, the most self-sacrificing have ever been the ones to take her by the hand, and hail her as a heroine and a patriot It is not from the "Shoddyites" that she has met with sympathy, though all in exalted stations and of wealthy means have united in doing her honour, but it is from soldiers' wives, soldiers' mothers, daughters and sweethearts that she has been hailed as a sister, and taken by the hand as a friend.

We have told how our heroine was carried from Shelbyville to Murfreesboro' after the capture of the former place by our forces. On the roadside the saw a poor, wounded soldier, apparently in the last agonies of death. Forgetting her own sufferings, she requested her attendants to stop while she pressed her canteen to the lips of the dying boy; for, notwithstanding the dust and blood upon his face, his slender form showed him to be a youth of only eighteen or nineteen summers.

Eagerly quaffing the cooling beverage, and gazing for a moment upon the pallid features of the beautiful being before him, he muttered. "Blessings—mother—sisters," and fell back apparently into the arms of death. They laid him gently down until those detailed to pick up the dead and wounded should come, when, with a fervent prayer for the soul of the youthful soldier, the sympathetic girl and her cortege passed on.

Some months afterwards Miss Cushman was on her way to Sandusky, Ohio, when the train on which she was travelling was detained for a half-hour at a small place called Fredericktown. Someone recognised our heroine, and in a few moments, it was noised all over the village that the famous "spy and scout" of the Army of the Cumberland was on the train, and Miss Cushman, to her utter astonishment, soon became the "observed of all observers."

Among others who called upon her was a young man with blushing cheeks and anxious looks, who timidly asked her if she remembered the incident mentioned above. Reflecting for a moment, she told him she did, when he added, "That young man stands before you, and calls on God to bless you for having saved his life." And then, while tears of joy rolled down his honest cheeks, he called to his mother and sisters, who came forward and embraced our heroine. The scene was indeed an affecting one, and they prayed heaven to shower down its choicest blessings on her who had saved their life, their hope, their pride—the darling son and brother who stood before her.

Hardly a dry eye was to be seen in the car, and when the train moved off, cheer after cheer rent the air, amid the waving of handker-chiefs and cries of live the Union," and "Long live Pauline Cushman."

One more slight incident we must relate, even at the risk of de-taining our reader beyond our proposed length of time, were it only to show the universal homage which our heroine inspired in all who came within the magic circle of her fascinations. Pauline had returned from her usual drive one day, after she had got able to go out, when her maid, while undressing her, said:

"That man has been here again, Miss."

"That man! What man?" demanded our heroine, in surprise.

"Why the man that calls regularly every day, but who has never succeeded in finding you at home but once."

"The man who calls every day, and who has never found me at home but *once*? Why, Annette, what do you mean?"

"Why, did I never tell you, Miss? I thought that I had done so; but the reason that I neglected it was, probably, that the man acted so queer that I began to suspect that he must be crazy."

"Crazy?"

"Yes, Miss. Why, do you know," continued the voluble maid, while she assisted our heroine to a lounge, on which to rest from the fatigue induced by even the short ride which she had taken—"why, do you know he calls here every morning, just after you have started out for your drive. One morning, however, you did not go out—you felt too weak, I believe, and when he called that morning, I told him you were in and would see him, for he looked like a soldier, and I know you always see *them*. So, after debating a long time, at last he made up his mind to come in. All of a sudden, though, as he was following me upstairs, he stopped, and laying his hand on his heart, exclaimed with a sigh, 'I can't do it today. I feel my courage all leaving me!' With that, do you know, Miss, that he took to his heels and ran straight out the door, leaving me standing there, and wondering if the man wasn't crazy."

Our heroine laughed heartily at this, and when she had finished, her sprightly companion continued her tale.

"Well, I didn't know what to think of this; but at last came to the conclusion that he was some secessionist who had come to murder you, inasmuch as he said he hadn't the 'courage to do it that day.'"

"A soldier, was he, do you say, Annette?" asked Pauline, thoughtfully.

"Yes, Miss, he looked like one."

"Oh! well, you need never fear that a soldier would assassinate me," exclaimed our heroine, with some pride.

"Oh! no, Miss, and now I think of it, he was an Irishman, and they are generally, you know, on the right side."

"And more apt to break a woman's heart than her head!" laughed Pauline, merrily. "But, how about this man?"

"Well, Miss, he never was seen from that day until this morning, when he stopped at the door and left this little package, and said he would call this evening for an answer. With that, he was off like a flash."

Taking the little package referred to, our heroine proceeded to open it. It was quite small, and enveloped carefully with clean white paper, and sealed with a wafer. Breaking the seal, a small scrap of faded ribbon fell out. This was all it contained, yet our heroine snatched it up quickly and scanned it closely.

"The very same," she muttered. "How came it here?"

The object of this interest was, as we have said, nothing more than a little knot of old, faded ribbon, which had once been red, but which had long since lost its colour. But to it some memories attached.

While in her prison at Shelbyville, we have already noticed the alacrity with which her guards waited upon her, and, indeed, almost anticipated every wish. Among them, and possessed of all the gallantry of his race, was a young Irishman who had been most devoted to her. One day, after some trifling favour done for our heroine, she had given him, half in jest, a little knot of ribbon, which had once bound her hair, with the words,

"When you get to be a great man, Jimmy, and become good, and stop fighting against the Union, you can send me this; and then, if I ain't married or dead, which is pretty much the same thing, I may be induced to have you." She had said this sportively never dreaming that the ribbon would ever turn up again, but here it was; and curious to know how this had come about, she ordered Annette to admit the "crazy man," as that worthy persisted in calling him, at once.

When evening came, therefore, it brought with it the "crazy man;"

but our heroine scarce recognised in the noble, sturdy figure before her, the half-starved, abject rebel soldier. Instead of the dirty grey clothes of the rebel service, he now wore the true blue of the Union, and was, altogether, as fine a looking soldier as one would wish to gaze upon.

But if our heroine was surprised to behold the improved appearance of her old friend, he was no less so, at seeing, instead of the pale and emaciated form of the interesting, yet miserable condemned, a woman whose beauty partook of the marvellous. Advancing then, with timid steps, he seemed, for a moment, to meditate a second flight. He was soon at ease, however for the warm welcome that he received served to reassure him.

"How comes it," asked our heroine, after some preliminary conversation, "that I see you in the Federal uniform? That is a change for the better."

"Faith it is, Marm," answered the poor fellow "Sure, as ye well know, me heart was never in the cause, down yonder; but as I was conscripted, I had to go. I tould thim I was an alien, but the divil a bit (sparin' your presence) did they mind that at all, at all; but jist clapped me into the army. So faith, sez I, the fust chance will see me off—an' here I am!"

"Well done!" exclaimed Pauline, highly amused at the description. "But what made you enlist in our service?"

"Well, faith, Harm, I'll jist tell yer. Whin I saw your fair self a-sufferin' an' a-dyin' for the Union, without so much as a murmur "out of ye, says I, any cause for which a *woman* can die in that way for, *must* be the right one. So, I determined to 'list right away in the self-same cause, an,' God willin', make up, by me devotion to it, for havin' once been a miserable rebel soldier; though, as heaven is me hope, never a rebel in heart."

"Bravely done!" exclaimed our heroine again. "And as a reward you may wear this ribbon next your heart; believing that its former owner's prayers and blessings will ever accompany you."

"Faith, Marm, it came but off me heart whin I gave it to yer sarvent: but I will put it there again, and whin next yer see me; it will be with all the dishonour of ever being a rebel washed out in me own heart's blood."

It was literally so; for, after the fearful Battle of Chickamauga, a long time afterwards, our heroine received the little knot of ribbon again; but it was dyed a deeper red this time, and was accompanied by a note from the colonel of the regiment in which the brave fellow had served. Part of it read thus:

> Jimmy, who was one of my best men, though, as I understand, a deserter from the rebel ranks, fell literally covered with glory. He seemed desirous to retrieve, by his present conduct, the crime which he had been guilty of against his country, by joining its enemies.
>
> Three times had the standard bearer of our brave old —— regiment been shot down, and the dear old flag humbled in the dust, when Jimmy sprang forward, and, seizing it, bore it proudly and grandly aloft. Fierce was the contest, and about the brave son of Erin the bullets flew like leaden hail; but he did not waver an instant, until, wounded in three places, he at last sank upon the torn and trampled sod, which proved his deathbed, pressing the colours still to his heart.
>
> Being the nearest to him at the moment, I stooped to raise the old banner again, and to cheer my men; when, handing me the enclosed piece of ribbon, which he took from over his heart, he said: 'Send this to Miss Cushman, the Union Scout—the bravest woman I ever saw; the dearest friend I have. She will understand it.'

That night Pauline offered up a prayer in behalf of him who had fallen; thanking God that she, through his instrumentality, had been able to convert at least one rebel, and begging him to bless the poor but noble fellow, who had died fighting at last for the Right.

Chapter 46: Conclusion

We might continue thus relating the many touching and sometimes amusing incidents which marked our heroine's return to the kindly hearts and sympathetic greetings of her fellow Union people, and we might be held excusable in so doing, inasmuch as they illustrate well the most honourable and most beautiful traits of her character. But we will hasten to the time when that grand ovation to her merits commenced, the parallel to which has not been witnessed since the visit of Lafayette to this country, in the one respect of outpouring of heartfelt goodwill and kindliness.

Others have found their ovations in grand pomp and show, but the compliments paid to Miss Cushman throughout the breadth and length of the loyal portions of our loved country were of that character that emanates from the heart, and are more touching and grateful than the most brilliant displays or most loudly-trumpeted peals of fame. To become notorious or famous is comparatively easy—a bad man or woman may attain to either; but, to secure a place in the hearts and affections of the people, one must be innately good.

It has been very justly said that a private soldier knows very well when he is well or badly commanded: just so with the public: they know very well whether the applicants for their notice are worthy of it or not.

Our people have made a pet of Miss Cushman, not only for her private worth and public usefulness, but also for the sake of the grand principles at issue, and in which she has played so prominent a part. They should now learn to regard her in a higher light than that of a heroine, for we might say the she has become the apostle of womanhood in these degenerate days, when women are too much of the lady and too little of the wife or mother.

We wanted some such type of true womanhood to exhibit to these dolls of fashion, while we teach them that it is neither unladylike nor inelegant to serve one's country, or to overstep the ordinary rules of conventionalism in behalf of our glorious Union and its brave supporters.

Indeed, her noble example has already been imitated by other American women since the commencement of this unhappy war, one instance of which is shown in the following letter, written with a true woman's heart, and a degree of patriotism no less all-absorbing than that even evinced by our heroine herself. The letter is dated New York, June 16th, 1864, and was received while Miss Cushman was stopping at the Astor House, where crowds and crowds of the most distinguished personages flocked to pay their respects, and testify to her devotedness. We give it *verbatim* except, in her own name and address, which for obvious reasons are omitted.

Pauline: Your hand. A sister-soldier's greeting to you, for I too have been, and was, until a few months ago, a soldier. Yes, I am a woman, and am proud of the glory in saying I have fought in the bloody Battles of Antietam, Chancellorsville, Gettysburg, and far above the clouds on Lookout Mountain. Yet here I sit today in my quiet room, sighing and longing again for the field and my brave comrades in battle. Listen, Pauline, and you shall hear my story. The One-hundred-and-Second Regiment N.Y. V. was mine. I have fought side by side with its war-worn veterans. I was always of a roving turn of mind, always restless, fond of adventure and excitement, and I can say without boasting, I was yet never afraid of anything or anybody.

When the war broke out, I cursed the fate that made me a girl. I often laid awake all night dreaming of war and battle, until that subject became with me a regular monomania, and at last I resolved to become a soldier.

When the regiment left Long Island for Washington, I followed with a scant purse and my only suit on my back. My brother Will was a corporal in it, and I sought him out. He was astounded, and tried to change my resolve. I was firm; told him I had come to go as a soldier and *would go*. I would not be satisfied to return, and besides I had no money, and he had not received any pay. He knew my stubbornness, and ceased his entreaties, but predicted that the first gun I heard would find me a refugee from it. He prophesied falsely.

Captain Crommie was an old friend of ours. His company was full, but he got me admitted into Captain Avery's company without examination. So began my soldier-life No one suspected me. My hair was already shingled; my features were more masculine than womanly. As I said before, I fought through all the battles up to Ringgold. After that we were offered a large bounty, and one month's furlough if we reenlisted. Contrary to my expectations, Will allowed me to re-enlist. We came home, and here his object became apparent. He had carefully kept me from spending any of my bounty, making me use his.

When we arrived at the barracks, he handed over my bounty to the captain, and spoke a few words into his ear. Then followed a long conversation, after which the captain came to me, and bowing politely, laughingly said, "Miss K——, allow me to compliment you on your bravery. You are smart enough to fool a whole regiment." My face was scarlet in an instant, and before I had time to reply Will hastened me home, where I was received as one returned from the grave, for in his letters he had never mentioned my name.

So, there was an end to my soldiering, for before two days every man in the regiment knew it. So, when the regiment returned,

I remained, and here I am, tired of everybody and everything. I long for my old life of adventure. If I stay here, I shall die. Oh, Miss Cushman! Pauline—best of patriots!—noblest of women!—will you help me? Take me with you as a slave—as a servant, and I will be faithful and true to you. Pauline, hear me! I am bold. Will you write to me? Nellie A. K——.

All throughout the North, the East, and the West, as well as in every loyal Atlantic seaboard city, was our heroine's progress a complete triumphant tour; and night and day were her apartments at the hotel besieged by the curious or sympathetic, and distinguished people proud to be classed among her friends.

Letters pleading for autographs; for permission to publish the various and most romantic details of her adventurous life; pieces of poetry, some patriotic, some love-sick, littered her table, while cards of invitation to *soirees*, dinners, balls and parties from the most aristocratic of our merchant princes, were no less plentiful.

While deeply sensible of the honours thus unexpectedly bestowed upon her, which she rightly attributes to an appreciation of her humble services in the cause of the Union, the heart of the faithful girl yet turns with intense longing to the time when that Union shall once more be fully restored; when a spirit of concession, forbearance and love for the whole country shall pervade the South as well as the North.

Then, indeed, we may all feel proudly confident that the fond hopes of the most sanguine of the early friends of the Federal Union shall be more than realised; then shall each day's rising sun, while time endures, smile upon a free, enlightened, independent, and united people, and our glory as a nation reach its culmination in the wise exercise of a power none may safely resist; in the cultivation of a genuine rational liberty, which, recognising the dignity of the individual man, shall afford ample room and scope for its development.

Our story would not be complete were we to fail to note that the evil got punished, as well as to congratulate ourselves and the world that the good met with some small portion, at least, of its well-deserved reward. As in a Christmas pantomime, we have endeavoured to gather about our recital of these most curious and interesting adventures, all the incongruous characters that one sometimes meets with in the world at large. Whilst we have strictly adhered to the truth, we have entered into details, where we have deemed that they might be found either amusing or instructive, with a minuteness that might seem to the superficial observer as uncalled for.

But our aim has been to prevent dryness or tediousness; we have tried, by our salted sandwich of fun and sentiment, to create a thirst for more; whether we have succeeded or not, depends upon the reader to say. As in a Christmas pantomime, however, we must lay aside all our fun in the last act, and, assembling our characters about the stage—the good and bad strictly divided—proceed to mete out to them their various rewards or punishments.

First of all, then, let us call up that arch-rascal Benjamin Milam. This man had been arrested twice before Pauline had set out upon her Southern trip, but had been released upon each occasion on account of his having had no fewer than three sons in the Federal service; but at last clemency to such a consummate rebel became a positive wrong to the interests of our land, and after our heroine's return, he was re-arrested by General Garfield's order, and securely lodged in the prison at Nashville, where, we believe, he still (1865), remains.

John Morgan, the gay and dashing cavalier, is dead. He was on a reconnaissance near Greenville, in East Tennessee (September 4th, 1864), and stopped at the house of a Mrs. Williams, whose husband was an officer on General Burnside's staff. In the night Mrs. Williams procured a horse, rode fifteen miles to a Union camp, and returned with a company of Union soldiers, who at once surrounded the house. Morgan awoke, drew his revolver, and attempted to escape, but was fired upon and killed.

Generals Bragg and Forrest are each alive at this writing, and each still holds command in the rebel service. When the great day of reckoning finally comes, it is to be hoped the gallows will not be cheated of its due.

Of the fate of many of the minor characters in the book, we are entirely ignorant. Generals Rosecrans, Granger, Garfield and others, and Colonel Truesdail, and the glorious Union boys generally, are making their mark all around the theatre of the rebellion, and can be heard from any day through the public prints.

Having disposed of the other characters, who shall we now find to bestow the meed of worth and honour upon her who laboured for it, and who has sacrificed health, means and every comfort to deserve it? May we not appoint *you*, the beautiful Genius of Good, loved public, and ask you to award, as you alone can award, the thanks and gratitude, as well as the more tangible help, which has been so justly earned from her loved country by Pauline, the Scout and Spy of the Cumberland!

194

Miss Major Pauline Cushman

By Frank Moore

This brilliant and impulsive being, whose life, if it could be fully written, would sound like some tale of romance, is of French and Spanish descent, and was born in New Orleans, in 1833. As she grew to womanhood, the charms of her person and the impressiveness of her manners drew her irresistibly to the stage, where she has had a brilliant career.

When the war commenced, in 1861, she was playing an engagement in Cleveland, Ohio, and soon after went to Louisville, where her histrionic success continued, and was even greater than ever before. Early in the year 1863, while playing in Wood's Theatre, she received many attentions from paroled rebel officers, who were then in Louisville; and, with the desire of making that foolish and ill-timed parade of secession sentiment, which was so often considered true bravery among them, one of these officers proposed to her to offer, in the midst of one of her parts, a toast to Jeff Davis and the Southern Confederacy.

She consented to do so; and, upon reflection, it occurred to Miss Cushman that here was afforded her an admirable opportunity of serving her country, and at the same time gratifying her own love of romance and wild adventure. She at once sought and obtained an interview with Colonel Moore, the provost marshal, who, after serious consultation, and becoming convinced of her genuine loyalty, received her proposition to enter the secret service of the United States.

She took the formal and solemn oath administered before entering that hazardous branch of the service; and the following night, in the midst of her part, and while the crowded theatre had all eyes riveted upon her graceful acting, proposed this astounding toast:

"Here's to Jeff Davis and the Southern Confederacy. May the South always maintain her honour and her rights."

195

The sentiment fell upon the audience like the explosion of a shell. All the loyal persons present were at once mortified and indignant, while the southern sympathizers were delighted. Very prompt action was taken. Miss Cushman was formally expelled from the theatrical corps, and sent south, in the direction of her "sympathies," to be lionised as a victim of Yankee tyranny. She went to Nashville, and sought an interview with Colonel Truesdale, the chief of army police, who gave her the most minute instructions and details as to the information which she must endeavour to obtain in the rebel lines.

Thus equipped, and with full confidence in luck and her mimetic talent, she started out on the Hardin Pike, as the people there call the road which leads from Nashville in the direction of Shelbyville. Within a few days, and amid a variety of adventures, she was able to collect many important items of information, with which she was about to return to Nashville, when for a time the run of good fortune was changed; and one night, while stopping at the house of a quiet farmer, by the name of Baum, she found herself under arrest, and was ushered into the presence of that renowned guerrilla and marauder, Jack Morgan.

Jack had too much chivalry to be anything but civil to a prisoner so fair, young, and fascinating, and was truly profuse in his generosity as he was conducting her to Forrest's headquarters, offering the beautiful Pauline all his friendship, a magnificent diamond ring, and a silver-mounted revolver, and urging her to accept a position as *aide-de-camp* on his staff, as soon as she should be released.

Forrest, she found a rougher custodian, and much less susceptible, than "Johnnie," as she familiarly called the other freebooter. Her first interview with him was a fine piece of melodrama, and would have excited applause and admiration in any theatre in the country.

"Well," said the hero of the card-table and the bowie-knife, "I'm really glad to see you; I've been looking for you a long time; but I've got this last shuffle, and intend to hold you. You've been here before, I take it—know all the roads—don't you? and all the bridle paths, and even the hog paths—don't you?"

Our heroine, drawing herself to her full height, and flashing indignant scorn from her black eyes, exclaimed:—

"Sir, every word you utter is as false as your own traitorous heart! I've never been here before, and I should like to send a bullet through the man who is mean enough to make the charge."

The ruffian gazed on her a moment, and with the savage gleam of the eye that he afterwards wore at Fort Pillow, replied, "Yes, and I'd send one through you, if I could, if you dared to repeat the assertion." Then his admiration for pluck got the better of his temper, and he added: "Well, you've got good fighting stuff in you, if you are a woman."

In the sharp skirmish of cross-questioning which followed, her woman's wit enabled her to spring a doubt in the mind of the cautious *desperado*, and he turned her over to Provost Marshal General McKinstry, who, he assured her, was a humane and just man, and would investigate the charges made against her, and decide on them with fairness.

After a little more bandying of words, the fair Pauline was dispatched to the headquarters of General Bragg; and as she rode away, Johnnie Morgan bade her *adieu* in the following elegant vernacular:—

"Goodbye; I hope we shall meet again, where we shall have something better than corn bread baked in ashes, and rot-gut whiskey at fifteen dollars a quart."

Some months after, she saw the great marauder under circumstances very different. He had been captured, in his famous raid north of the Ohio, and was confined, like any other felon, in the Penitentiary at Columbus, in prison stripe, and with hair dressed by the prison barber. Advancing to him, she held out her hand, and laughingly exclaimed, "How are you, Johnnie?"

"Ah," replied the jolly rebel, "the boot is on the other foot now."

Bragg, she found a different man from either of the cavalry chieftains; and her talk with him was not so spicy, nor so cheerful in its termination.

She saw before her a bony, angular, sharp-pointed man, without kindness or humanity, or any of the milder parts of human nature in his composition; of blunt address, impatient gestures, and heartless physiognomy.

Her colloquy with this cast-iron rebel ended somewhat as follows:—

Pauline. Suppose I am found guilty; what will you do with me?

Bragg. Why, you'll be hanged; that's all.

Pauline. Come, now, general, I don't think I'll be either useful nor ornamental dangling at the end of a rope. Won't you let me choose my method of dying?

Bragg. Well, really, I couldn't, as you might choose to die in your bed, in the natural way.

Pauline. Come, now, won't shooting do just as well? It wouldn't hurt quite so bad, you know.

This interview had given our light-hearted heroine an idea. She was soon after taken very ill, and seemed in a fair way to cheat the general out of his pleasant little amusement of hanging a female, for she was tried (or was so informed, at least) found guilty, and condemned. The execution was delayed only by her continued sickness. At the eleventh hour her fortune changed.

As our heroine was lying on her cot one fine morning in the last days of June, feeling that she would soon be well enough to be hung, there were signs at the headquarters of the rebel general of sudden commotion; and, before she was informed what it meant, the joyous sound of the Union bugles, playing the national airs, reached her sick room; and soon Rosecrans' advance guard was in town. Bragg had fled for the mountains, and she no longer felt the terrors of her unfortunate position.

General Garfield, in consideration of her long service, and suffering and danger, in the Union cause, and of two severe wounds, received while engaged in the secret service, conferred on the heroine the rank and title of major, by which she was afterwards commonly known.